D1446751

SYMBOLIC BLACKNESS AND ETHNIC DIFFERENCE IN EARLY CHRISTIAN LITERATURE

This pioneering work provides a well-documented examination of some of the main references to Egyptians/Egypt, Ethiopians/Ethiopia, and Blacks/blackness in early Christian writings. Byron explores how perceptions about ethnic and color differences influenced the discursive strategies of ancient Christian authors. In spite of the basic contention that Christianity was to extend to all peoples, this book demonstrates that certain groups of Christians were marginalized and rendered invisible and silent. They were, in effect, 'blackened by their sins'.

The book is organized into two parts. The first part explains the theoretical basis for reading ethno-political rhetorics in early Christian writings and provides a taxonomy of these rhetorics by classifying the various usages of Egyptians/Egypt, Ethiopians/Ethiopia, and Blacks/blackness within Greco-Roman writings (both Christian and non-Christian). The second part of the book isolates Christian sources from the first to the sixth centuries. Here, Byron argues that ancient Christians referred to Egyptians, Ethiopians, and Blacks as a strategy for instructing their followers, maligning their opponents, and warning their communities about sins and vices, sexual temptations, and 'heresies'.

This long-overdue analysis demonstrates the sophisticated ways in which Christian writers attempted to shape the self-understandings of their communities through the use of ethnic and color-symbolic language; it also explores how ethnic and color difference came to symbolize certain theological, ideological, and political intra-Christian controversies and challenges. It will be useful for those studying the New Testament and early Church history, as well as literary theorists and gender critics who will find the book a valuable interdisciplinary resource.

Gay L. Byron is Assistant Professor of New Testament and Black Church Studies at Colgate Rochester Crozer Divinity School, Rochester, New York.

SYMBOLIC BLACKNESS AND ETHNIC DIFFERENCE IN EARLY CHRISTIAN LITERATURE

Gay L. Byron

London and New York

First published 2002
by Routledge
11 New Fetter Lane, London EC4P 4EE

Simultaneously published in the USA and Canada
by Routledge
29 West 35th Street, New York, NY 10001

Routledge is an imprint of the Taylor & Francis Group

© 2002 Gay L. Byron

Typeset in Garamond by
Keystroke, Jacaranda Lodge, Wolverhampton
Printed and bound in Great Britain by
The Cromwell Press, Trowbridge, Wiltshire

British Library Cataloguing in Publication Data
A catalogue record for this book is available from the British Library

Library of Congress Cataloging in Publication Data
A catalog record for this book has been requested

ISBN 0–415–24368–8 (hbk)
ISBN 0–415–24369–6 (pbk)

To the memory of my father and mother

Ganius Lee Byron, Sr.
(January 20, 1917–August 22, 1980)

Betty Green Byron Wilson
(October 26, 1932–)

CONTENTS

ABBREVIATIONS

Abbreviations of biblical, apocryphal, intertestamental, rabbinic, Nag Hammadi, and patristic writings follow those listed in the *The SBL Handbook of Style* (Peabody, Mass.: Hendrickson, 1999). Abbreviations of ancient authors and their works follow the list in the *Oxford Classical Dictionary* (Oxford: Clarendon, 1999), xxix–liv.

ABD	*Anchor Bible Dictionary*, 6 vols. Ed. D.N. Freedman. New York: Doubleday, 1992
ABQ	*American Baptist Quarterly*
AHR	*American Historical Review*
AJP	*American Journal of Philology*
ANRW	*Aufstieg und Niedergang der Römischen Welt*. Ed. H. Temporini and W. Haase. Berlin: W. de Gruyter, 1972–
APF	Archiv für Papyrusforschung
BAGD	W. Bauer, W.F. Arndt, F.W. Gingrich, and F.W. Danker, *A Greek-English Lexicon of the New Testament and Other Early Christian Literature*. Chicago: University of Chicago Press, 2nd ed., 1979
BASP	*Bulletin of the American Society of Papyrologists*
BdE	Bibliothèque d' Etude
BDF	F. Blass and A. Debrunner. *A Greek Grammar of the New Testament and Other Early Christian Literature*. Translated and revised by Robert W. Funk. Chicago: University of Chicago Press, 1962
BHT	Beiträge zur historischen Theologie
BJS	Brown Judaic Studies
BRev	*Bible Review*
BSac	*Bibliotheca sacra*
BTB	*Biblical Theology Bulletin*
BZ	*Biblische Zeitschrift*
CBQ	*Catholic Biblical Quarterly*
CBQMS	Catholic Biblical Quarterly Monograph Series
CCL	Corpus Christianorum, Series latina. Turnhout and Paris, 1953
CCSA	Corpus Christianorum, Series apocryphorum

CP	*Classical Philology*
CPJ	*Corpus papyrorum judaicorum*
CQ	*Classical Quarterly*
CSCO	Corpus scriptorum christianorum orientalium. Louvain, 1903
CSEL	Corpus scriptorum ecclesiasticorum latinorum. Vienna, 1866
GCS	Die griechische christliche Schriftsteller der ersten [drei] Jahrhunderte
GRBS	*Greek, Roman, and Byzantine Studies*
HeyJ	*Heythrop Journal*
HTR	*Harvard Theological Review*
HTS	Harvard Theological Studies
ICUR	*Inscriptiones christianae urbis Romae*
ILS	*Inscriptiones latinae selectae*
JAAR	*Journal of the American Academy of Religion*
JAC	Jahrbuch für Antike und Christentum
JBL	*Journal of Biblical Literature*
JEA	*Journal of Egyptian Archaeology*
JECS	*Journal of Early Christian Studies*
JES	*Journal of Ethiopian Studies*
JFSR	*Journal of Feminist Studies in Religion*
JJurPap	*Journal of Juristic Papyrology*
JR	*Journal of Religion*
JRS	*Journal of Roman Studies*
JRT	*Journal of Religious Thought*
JSNT	*Journal for the Study of the New Testament*
JSNTSup	Journal for the Study of the New Testament, Supplement Series
JSOTSup	Journal for the Study of the Old Testament, Supplement Series
JSP	*Journal for the Study of the Pseudepigrapha*
JTS	*Journal of Theological Studies*
LCL	Loeb Classical Library
LSJ	H.G. Liddell and R. Scott, *A Greek-English Lexicon*. Rev. and augmented by H.S. Jones, with the assistance of R. McKenzie. Oxford: Clarendon, 1940
MAAR	Memoirs of the American Academy in Rome
MH	*Museum helveticum*
NIB	*New Interpreter's Bible*
NIDB	*New International Dictionary of the Bible*. Ed. J.D. Douglas and M.C. Tenney. Grand Rapids: Zondervan, 1987
NIDNTT	*New International Dictionary of New Testament Theology*. 4 vols. Ed. C. Brown. Grand Rapids: Zondervan, 1975–85
NovT	*Novum Testamentum*
NovTSup	Novum Testamentum Supplements
NTS	*New Testament Studies*
NTTS	New Testament Tools and Studies

OGIS	*Orientis graeci inscriptiones selectae*
PG	Patrologia graeca cursus completus. 162 vols. Ed. J.-P. Migne. Paris, 1857–86
Phil	*Philogus*
PGM	*Papyri Graecae magicae*
PL	Patrologia latina cursus completus. 217 vols. Ed. J.-P. Migne. Paris, 1844–64
PW	A. Pauly, G. Wissowa, and W. Kroll, *Realencyclopädie der klassischen Altertumswissenschaft*
RAC	*Reallexikon für Antike und Christentum*
RB	*Revue biblique*
REA	*Revue des études anciennes*
REG	*Revue des études grecques*
RelSRev	*Religious Studies Review*
REL	*Revue des études Latines*
SAOC	Studies in Ancient Oriental Civilizations
SA	*Studia Anselmiana*
SBLSymS	Society of Biblical Literature Symposium Series
SC	Sources chrétiennes. Paris, 1941
SecCent	*Second Century*
StPatr	Studia patristica
TDNT	*Theological Dictionary of the New Testament.* Ed. Gerhard Kittel and Gerhard Friedrich. 9 vols. Trans. Geoffrey W. Bromiley. Grand Rapids: Eerdmans, 1964–74.
ThTo	*Theology Today*
Them	*Themelios*
TUGAL	Texte und Untersuchungen zur Geschichte der altchristlichen Literatur
USQR	*Union Seminary Quarterly Review*

ACKNOWLEDGMENTS

This book is a modest revision of my 1999 doctoral dissertation submitted to Union Theological Seminary in the city of New York. I owe a special debt of gratitude to a number of people who helped make this book a reality. I want to thank Vincent L. Wimbush for all the many ways he helped me bring this project to fruition. He went beyond the call of duty in reading chapters, helping me sort through my ideas, guiding me through the maze of graduate school and into the guild of biblical studies, and encouraging me to stay the course. I will always appreciate how he opened the door for me and many others to take seriously the study of the New Testament and Christian Origins. I would also like to thank the other members of my dissertation committee – Elizabeth A. Castelli (Barnard College), Roger S. Bagnall (Columbia University), and John McGuckin (Union Theological Seminary) – who read several drafts of the dissertation and offered critical feedback that saved me from many errors. They have all continued to be generous with their time, expertise, and support as I took up the task of making my research available to a wider audience.

I am grateful for the many colleagues who either read drafts of various chapters, discussed my ideas with me, or helped me access primary source material: Brian Blount, Denise Kimber Buell, David Brakke, Elizabeth Clark, Susan Ashbrook Harvey, Robert Hill, Reinaldo Pérez, Rosamond Rodman, Carolyn Osiek, Robin Scroggs, Frederick Weidmann, Holland Hendrix, Dieter Georgi, Deirdre Good, Celia Deutsch, Frank M. Snowden, Jr., and the anonymous reviewer at Routledge. My faculty colleagues in Strong Hall at the Colgate Rochester Crozer Divinity School offered many helpful suggestions that enabled me to turn the dissertation into a book. In particular, William R. Herzog, II and Werner Lemke provided insightful and critical comments. While at Union Seminary, I benefited from the challenging feedback of many colleagues who were a part of the New Testament and Christian Origins Doctoral Seminar. In particular, Jean Pierre Ruiz and Margaret Aymer provided formal responses to my work. Of course, I accept full responsibility for any shortcomings that remain.

Betty Caroline Bolden, Drew Kadel, Seth Kasten, and Eun Ja Lee of the Burke Library at Union Theological Seminary were instrumental in helping me retrieve many valuable sources. I am also grateful to the staff of the Ambrose Swasey Library at Colgate Rochester Crozer Divinity School who went beyond the call of duty in helping me track down obscure references for completing the book. My research assistants Aaron Bouwens and Lawrence Womack provided a timely source of energy and support. John Blanpied offered editorial assistance and encouragement.

At Routledge, senior editor Richard Stoneman always had faith in this project. I am grateful for the expertise and patience of all the other editors who helped turn my humble efforts into a book, including Meg Davies who compiled the index and Kate Chenevix Trench who helped me learn that there is a time to let go.

I am deeply grateful for the financial support received from the Ford Foundation for the writing of the dissertation, and from the Research Fund for new faculty from Colgate Rochester Crozer Divinity School for the completion of the revisions.

My friend Shannon Brady Marin was a special source of encouragement throughout the writing of this project. Other friends and family have encouraged me to keep my eyes on the prize: Sharon E. Williams, Lenton Gunn, William G. Sommer, Marie T. Sergent, Valeria Sinclair Chapman, Renita J. Weems, Stacy Andres, Ericka and Doraeen Roberts, Mark Anthony White, Ganius Lee Byron, Jr., and Lorene and Paul Brown.

My husband Philip B. Davis and my children Lloyd Byron Davis and Philip Bernard Davis, Jr., through their love, patience, and good humor, help me keep all things in perspective.

Finally, I dedicate this book to the memory of my parents – the late Ganius Lee Byron, Sr., and Betty Green Byron Wilson – who, at different times and in different ways, taught me to pray, to forgive, to contend for the faith, and to trust God for everything.

GLB
Rochester, N.Y.
August 2001

INTRODUCTION

The references to Egyptians/Egypt, Ethiopians/Ethiopia,[1] and Blacks/blackness[2] in ancient Christian literature call attention to the rhetorical, polemical, and symbolic significance of ethnic groups, geographical locations, and color differences within early Christian discourses. These people and places, south of the Mediterranean, served as symbolic tropes[3] that generated and reflected an ideology of difference[4] within ancient Christian writings. In this book I examine some of the discursive uses of Egyptians/Egypt, Ethiopians/Ethiopia, and Blacks/blackness through the development of a taxonomy of what will be called *ethno-political rhetorics*.[5] These ethno-political rhetorics point to the complex web of power structures that dominated the Greco-Roman world and invariably influenced early Christian writings.

Ethno-political rhetorics, which include both pejorative and idealized representations of Egyptians, Ethiopians, and Blacks, are not necessarily directed against these actual ethnic groups, but rather refer to those *within* different Christian communities who were falling away from the "orthodox" teachings and moral standards that were being established by dominant voices within the communities.[6] In effect, Egyptians/Egypt, Ethiopians/Ethiopia, and Blacks/blackness came to symbolize the extremes within early Christianity; they represented the "most remote" manifestations of Christian identity. Christian authors used what was considered within the ancient world as wholly "other" to help shape their understandings of appropriate practices, beliefs, and values. Egyptians, Ethiopians, and Blacks provided an ideal yardstick by which various authors could advance their arguments and construct their stories about the emerging Christian communities within the empire.

So what are ethno-political rhetorics and how might an understanding of these rhetorics reshape our interpretations of ancient Christian writings? How and why did these rhetorics persist throughout the history and development of ancient Christianity? What do these rhetorics tell us about the socio-political, religious, and ideological commitments of ancient Christians? These questions will be explored throughout this book, but it is important at this point to provide a working definition of ethno-political rhetorics.

1

Ethno-political rhetorics are discursive elements within texts that refer to "ethnic" identities or geographical locations and function as political invective.[7] Ethnicity is the chief constituent component of any ethno-political rhetoric.[8] There are several ways of understanding ethnicity, but generally it is conceived of as a relationship between two contrasting individuals or groups of people.[9] It is considered a social construct that draws attention to the differences that exist within communities.[10] By drawing attention to ethnicity, one can begin to see at least one way in which group boundaries construed within early Christianity led to "insiders" and "outsiders."[11] This form of early Christian self-definition was dependent upon ethnic-othering.

Ethnic-othering was a common literary tool used to stereotype and slander those perceived as threats (e.g., religious, military, economic, etc.) within the ancient world.[12] It was a prevalent and persuasive discursive practice within Greco-Roman writings because of the existence of so-called barbarians. The Greek term *barbaros* was originally used by the Greeks to designate one who speaks a strange language.[13] The apostle Paul uses *barbaros* in this way: "If then I do not know the meaning of a sound, I will be a foreigner (*barbaros*) to the speaker and the speaker a foreigner (*barbaros*) to me" (1 Cor 14:11). The term later developed into a geographical and ethnographical reference for a foreign or strange race (i.e., anyone who was not Greek). After the rule of Augustus, Romans assigned the name *barbarus* to all tribes that had no Greek or Roman accomplishments. Most of the studies about barbarians emphasize a traditional view of antiquity, which assumes the dominance of Greeks and Romans within the empire. This in turn leads to constructing within Greco-Roman literature other peoples and cultures as "barbarian" when they present any type of threat to the empire. Greek and Roman authors used so-called barbarians as ethnographic tropes, which led to stereotypical depictions of many different ethnic groups throughout various strands of Greco-Roman literature.[14] Christian authors were also aware of different barbarian groups within antiquity and stereotyped them in their writings.[15]

In this book, I provide a systematic review of how ethnicity was used as a polemical device in early Christian writings. Ethnic differences were firmly established in the literary minds of ancient Christian authors, yet the mere use of an ethnic group or geographical locale in a text does not make it an ethno-political rhetoric. The key to understanding ethno-political rhetorics is to explore how these rhetorics function as political invective for the purpose of advancing certain teachings within early Christian communities. In the brief letter to Titus, the ethnic slur directed against the Cretans is an example of an ethno-political rhetoric:

> There are also many rebellious people, idle talkers and deceivers, especially those of the circumcision; they must be silenced, since they are upsetting whole families by teaching for sordid gain what is not right to teach. It was one of them, their very own prophet, who

said, *"Cretans are always liars, vicious brutes, lazy gluttons"* [emphasis mine]. That testimony is true. For this reason rebuke them sharply, so that they may become sound in the faith, not paying attention to Jewish myths or to commandments of those who reject the truth. To the pure all things are pure, but to the corrupt and unbelieving nothing is pure. Their very minds and consciences are corrupted. They profess to know God, but they deny him by their actions. They are detestable, disobedient, unfit for any good work.

(Titus 1:10–16)

The Cretans in this text are part of a larger discourse of political invective. The author used this ethnic group to slander certain groups who were not representing the prescribed teachings, values, and beliefs of the dominant voices within the community.[16] By appealing to assumptions that the audience must have had about Cretans, the author was able to establish boundaries for inclusion into the community.

The New Testament and other early Christian writings are replete with descriptions of different ethnic groups.[17] Many scholars are beginning to address some of the methodological issues and theoretical challenges associated with understanding ethnic identity in Greco-Roman antiquity, as well as the particular interactions among ethnic groups within Christian writings.[18] I hope to add to these discussions by organizing this book around a case study of Egyptians/Egypt, Ethiopians/Ethiopia, and Blacks/blackness. I demonstrate how the ethno-political rhetorics associated with these ethnic groups, geographical locations, and color symbols signal threats, challenges, and opponents within different early Christian communities; call attention to intra-Christian debates and controversies; and highlight the vast cultural diversity within early Christian communities that would have made such discourses possible. Although this study broaches many subject areas, it is governed by two predominate purposes: (1) to isolate *some* of the important patterns of ethno-political rhetorics within a sample of ancient texts, and (2) to suggest a hermeneutical framework for understanding the function of ethno-political rhetorics within early Christian writings.

My interest in this topic began several years ago while in graduate school. First, I was perplexed by the fact that both ancient and modern discussions about Egyptians/Egypt and Ethiopians/Ethiopia are filled with many inconsistencies. Within the writings of some ancient authors, Egypt and Ethiopia are often grouped together and viewed equally as symbols of sin. For example, Tertullian, in his treatise denouncing participation in public shows or spectacles (*spectacula*), says, "when God threatens Egypt and Ethiopia with extinction, he pronounces sentence on every sinful nation."[19] Or, they are contrasted and set apart, as in an example from the *Acts of Peter*: one of Peter's disciples recounts a dream wherein "a most evil-looking woman, who looked like an Ethiopian (*Aethiopissimam*), not Egyptian (*Aegyptiam*), but was all black (*nigram*), clothed in filthy rags."[20]

These inconsistent representations point to the confusion among the ancients themselves as well as the wide range of sources from which understandings about these ethnic groups were shaped.[21]

Within some modern discussions about Egyptians/Egypt and Ethiopians/ Ethiopia, editors and translators of the ancient sources inaccurately translate the Greek or Latin terms for these ethnic groups and geographical locations. For example, Jean Marie Courtès, in his valuable study about Ethiopians in patristic literature, summarizes the account of Perpetua struggling with the Egyptian ("*et exivit quidam contra me **Aegyptius*** [emphasis mine] *foedus specie cum adiutoribus suis pugnaturus mecum*") by saying, "Perpetua in a dream finds herself face to face with an *Ethiopian* [emphasis mine]."[22] Later, in the same essay, Courtès translates Jerome's phrase "*in extremo fluminum **Aegypti*** [emphasis mine]" as "beyond the rivers of *Ethiopia* [emphasis mine]."[23] These inconsistencies within both ancient and modern discussions highlight the need for a study that analyzes and categorizes the Greek and Latin terms for Egyptians/Egypt and Ethiopians/Ethiopia, and suggests new theories about the symbolic function of these terms in ancient Christian literature. Moreover, these inconsistent and sometimes inaccurate translations demonstrate the ideological assumptions at work in the terms themselves.[24] These ethnic groups and geographical locations represent "the other," so translators, by making mistakes or interchanging the terms, are replicating the "othering" capacity of the ancient sources.

Similar to the inconsistent and inaccurate translations of the Greek and Latin terms, I also recognized that "Egyptians" and "Ethiopians" have been used inconsistently as polemical devices when referring to the presence of "Blacks" in antiquity.[25] Once again, both ancient and modern writers exemplify these tendencies in their writings. As the example mentioned above from the *Acts of Peter* indicates, some ancient writers used the color black to describe Ethiopians. Yet, Egyptians were also considered black-skinned. For example, Herodotus describes the Colchians as "an Egyptian people" (*Aigyptioi*) because of their black skin (*melanchroes*) and woolly hair (*oulotriches*).[26] Among modern scholars, classicists, Afrocentrists, anthropologists, Egyptologists, Nubiologists, and ancient historians have provided a wealth of interpretations of Egyptians, Ethiopians, and Blacks in antiquity.[27] They describe either Egyptians or Ethiopians as Blacks depending upon their particular academic disciplinary locations.[28] Moreover, these scholars, who often review the same ancient literature, reach very different conclusions depending upon the rules and interests of their respective academic disciplines and the racial politics at work at the time of their research and writing.[29] Their disparate readings of the ancient sources and their inability to communicate effectively across disciplines provided the impetus for this interdisciplinary study.

The second factor that sparked my interest in this topic is the fact that there are many positive and negative portrayals of Egyptians, Ethiopians, and Blacks in ancient Christian literature that merit serious scholarly attention. Yet, there is an overwhelming emphasis on the positive portrayals due in large measure to the influential research of classicist Frank Snowden.[30] Snowden persuasively argued for the absence of color prejudice in antiquity by identifying many positive examples of Ethiopians as integrally involved in Greco-Roman life. In both *Blacks in Antiquity* and *Before Color Prejudice* Snowden offers a brief, yet critical review of early Christian sources.[31] From his analysis of the Ethiopian eunuch in Acts 8:26–40 Snowden concludes that consideration of race and other external conditions were of no significance in determining membership in the church.[32] Thus the early Christians used the Ethiopian as a motif in the language of conversion and as a means for emphasizing their conviction that Christianity was to include all humanity.[33]

Snowden's research generated a serious debate about the presence of Blacks in antiquity by identifying and accumulating many important literary and artistic sources that portray the multiple roles of Blacks within Greek and Roman society. Although he identified many examples of how Blacks were included in various segments of Greco-Roman life, Snowden's findings should not be accepted as the only possibility for understanding the presence of Blacks in antiquity.[34] Some of his peers critiqued the way he emphasized positive examples of Ethiopians and excluded the more grotesque representations of them.[35] Yet his highly acclaimed research became the accepted position among classicists and other scholars of antiquity, eventually influencing many studies on race relations in the ancient world.[36] William Leo Hansberry, a pioneering Africanist and one of Snowden's colleagues from Howard University, accumulated an important collection of classical texts by poets, playwrights, historians, and geographers.[37] Joseph Harris, the editor of the Hansberry papers, claims that Hansberry's interest in the sources was different from Snowden's.[38] Hansberry, unlike Snowden, acknowledged the unfavorable characterizations of Ethiopians in many of the ancient sources:

> [T]here were two streams of information emanating from the classical writers and the unfavorable characterization has had the greatest influence on the image and treatment of blacks in our own times. It was [this] characterization which motivated Professor Hansberry to persist in the study of ancient views of Africans, to correct the record and to reveal the true picture as far as that was possible.[39]

In this book I examine both positive (idealized) and negative (vituperative) representations of Egyptians/Egypt, Ethiopians/Ethiopia, and Blacks/blackness in ancient Christian literature, which provide an opportunity to explore how perceptions about ethnic and color differences influenced the discursive forms and strategies of ancient Christian authors. Numerous negative references in ancient Christian writings associate Egyptians, Ethiopians, and Blacks with sin, demons, sexual vices, and heresies.[40] For example, the author of the early second-century *Epistle of Barnabas* depicts the Christian devil as "the Black One" (*ho melas*). The author of the third-century *Passio Sanctarum Perpetuae et Felicitatis* constructs a scene in which Perpetua wrestles with an Egyptian in a dream before her martyrdom (*Passio Perpetuae* 10.6). An anonymous fifth-century desert father reports how an Ethiopian woman tempts a troubled monk: "I am she who seems so sweet to the hearts of men; but because of your obedience and the trials you have borne, God would not allow me to lead you astray. All I can do is let you smell my foul odor" (*Apophthegmata patrum* 5.5). In the fifth-century text *Life of Melania the Younger* a representative of Nestorianism took on the form of a young Black man (*Vita Melaniae Junioris* 54). In contrast to these negative references, there are several instances in which Egyptians, Ethiopians, and Blacks are idealized in ancient Christian writings. For example, in the New Testament, Luke depicts the Ethiopian eunuch as a model of virtue in Acts 8:26–40 because of his willingness to learn the scriptures and to be baptized. Another provocative example is the monastic story about Ethiopian Moses who displays his ascetic virtues at the expense of his blackness.[41] I argue that the vituperative and idealized representations function as ethno-political rhetorics that were used to prescribe the boundaries and self-definitions of early Christian communities.

My third reason for undertaking this study is the unsettling fact that scholars of the New Testament and Early Christianity have generally overlooked the significance of the references to Egyptians/Egypt, Ethiopians/Ethiopia, and Blacks/blackness for understanding the development of early Christianity. Even with the many important articles and dissertations that have been written on the Ethiopian eunuch in Acts 8:26–40[42] and the handful of studies on the presence of Egyptians, Africans, and Blacks in the Bible,[43] it is painfully obvious that most New Testament scholars have not considered discourses about these ethnic groups, geographical locations, and color symbols as critical sources for understanding early Christianity. One notable exception, however, is Vincent L. Wimbush's analysis of the desert father, Ethiopian Moses.

Wimbush contends that "the texts about Moses suggest that the ancient Christians followed a widespread trend among Greeks and Romans with respect to color symbolism."[44] On the surface these texts suggest that Black peoples were included within the circle of the elect without problem; yet upon further review, Moses appears to be "worked too hard by different communities and traditions."[45] Wimbush concludes that the texts promote the attractiveness and superiority of the ascetic life at the expense of Moses. He challenges other scholars to assess the rhetorical significance of the references to color differences as they relate to rhetorics of ascetic piety. His analysis of the Ethiopian monk, also known as Moses the Black, explores the color-coded discourses about asceticism and presents a persuasive methodological challenge for further research on how Blacks were represented in ancient Christian literature. Wimbush does not, however, explore the political factors that may have influenced the "worldly choices of renunciation of the ascetics."[46] This challenge

6

INTRODUCTION

by Wimbush motivated me to explore discourses related to Egyptians/Egypt, Ethiopians/Ethiopia, and Blacks/blackness, and to develop a theoretical framework for analyzing the intersection between ethnicity and politics in ancient Christian writings.

Long before Wimbush, Hebrew Bible scholar Charles B. Copher was the first to offer some suggestions for understanding the presence of Blacks in biblical literature. His seminal study on "biblical interpretation with reference to Black peoples" validated how passages dealing with Blacks throughout biblical and extrabiblical literature deserve serious attention.[47] His essay surveys canonical texts, rabbinical literature, New Testament and Old Testament apocrypha and pseudepigrapha, Qumran writings, patristic literature, and Muslim writings. In his interpretation of the New Testament, Copher included only Acts 8:26–39 and Acts 13:1 as passages that contain references to Blacks.[48]

In another essay, entitled "Egypt and Ethiopia in the Old Testament," Copher challenges scholars to reexamine the significance of these two nations within the Old Testament.[49] He classifies the main references to Egypt into seven categories: (1) as the name of a person, (2) in narratives of the Hebrew patriarchs and Joseph, (3) in narratives about the enslavement, Moses, and the exodus, (4) in narratives about the Hebrews having been brought out of Egypt, (5) in prophetic oracles, (6) in historical relations with Israel-Judahites-Jews, and (7) in poetical-wisdom literature.[50] He also classifies the main references to Ethiopia (Cush) into five categories: (1) as a term of identification, (2) as a geographical reference, (3) in prophetic oracles, (4) in historical relations with Judahites, and (5) in poetical-wisdom literature.[51] In this study he examines both positive and negative references to Egypt and Ethiopia, but does not analyze the complex set of factors that led to the various depictions of these places and peoples within ancient Hebrew biblical literature. In general, he pays more attention to the negative references and summarizes his findings by claiming, "there is hardly anything good said about either country."[52]

Copher has made a valuable contribution to biblical scholarship in his studies on Egyptians, Ethiopians, and Blacks in the Bible. A collection of essays written in his honor testify to his influence among many biblical scholars and theologians, as well as other scholars of religion and ancient history.[53] He was the first African American biblical scholar to begin the important task of categorizing references to Egyptians, Ethiopians, and Blacks.[54] His categories, however, are not inclusive of all the different ways Egyptians/Egypt, Ethiopians/ Ethiopia, and Blacks/blackness appear in ancient Hebrew and Christian writings. Yet he does identify several important passages that require further exploration.[55]

Robert Hood, although not a biblical scholar, was the first to provide a comprehensive analysis of the presence of Blacks and blackness in Christian traditions.[56] In *Begrimed and Black: Christian Traditions on Blacks and Blackness,* Hood identifies many ancient sources and argues that there is an ideological bias against Blacks in Christian literature that results in negative depictions of

7

Blacks (i.e., Ethiopians) as sinful, demonic, and sexually threatening.[57] He further concludes that "blackness in early Christian thought overwhelmingly conveyed social values and a moral rank subordinate to whiteness, an attitude that became a cornerstone of Western cultural views reinforced by the slave trade, economics, Egyptology, physical and social sciences, and later Christendom."[58] Hood's ambitious project offers many useful insights into understanding the presence of Blacks and blackness throughout Greco-Roman antiquity.[59] His study of selected material does not, however, take into consideration the wide range of rhetorical functions of Egyptians/Egypt, Ethiopians/Ethiopia, and Blacks/blackness in ancient Christian literature.[60] He also does not develop a clearly defensible theoretical or methodological framework for interpreting the material. Although he does an excellent job of summarizing some of the key themes related to Blacks and blackness in ancient Christian writings, his work lacks a critical assessment of gender-related factors that may be evident in the texts.[61] I hope this book offers a starting point for addressing this void.

This leads to my fourth and final reason for undertaking this project. To my knowledge, there has not been a study that takes into consideration how Ethiopian or Black women are depicted in ancient Greco-Roman sources.[62] Furthermore, no one has undertaken a systematic gender-based analysis of the rhetorical and ideological functions of Ethiopian women in ancient Christian writings. The ancients were obviously ambivalent about Ethiopian women. On the one hand they are depicted as beautiful, wise, and honorable, while on the other hand they are regarded as ugly, smelly, ill-mannered, dangerous, and demonic. In addition to this, one can detect a pattern of violence against Ethiopian women in the literature. This pattern does not necessarily reflect actual encounters with Black women in antiquity, but it certainly raises questions as to how such vituperative depictions became a common source of Christian moralizing and edifying discourse. As an African American woman, such images of Black women as "ugly," "smelly," "dirty," and "demonic" strike an emotional chord, which forces me to examine these texts and traditions with theories and methods that take into account the impact of both ethnicity and gender in early Christian writings.[63]

This book is comprised of two major parts. Part 1 (chapters 1 and 2) develops the theoretical basis for reading ethno-political rhetorics in early Christian writings and constructs a taxonomy of these rhetorics within Greco-Roman (including Christian) literature. These chapters demonstrate that early Christian authors were not alone in their use of Egyptians/Egypt, Ethiopians/Ethiopia, and Blacks/blackness as ethno-political rhetorics. They modeled the larger culture in presenting both positive and pejorative depictions of these ethnic groups, geographical locations, and color symbols. Chapter 1, drawing upon findings advanced by rhetorical criticism, ethnocriticism, and gender criticism, provides an interpretive framework for reading ethno-political rhetorics within ancient writings. Chapter 2 identifies and defines the different categories of ethno-political rhetorics related to Egyptians/Egypt, Ethiopians/Ethiopia, and

Blacks/blackness in non-Christian and Christian Greco-Roman literature.[64] I will provide several examples from each category, which are intended to be illustrative rather than exhaustive. Within non-Christian literature, I have organized the rhetorical categories around three broad understandings of difference that Egyptians, Ethiopians, and Blacks represented within the ancient world: (1) geopolitical identification, (2) moral–spiritual characterization, and (3) descriptive differentiation. Within each of these categories of difference I have identified several headings that establish the framework for understanding the many symbolic functions of these ethnic groups, geographical locations, and color symbols in ancient literature. The following table summarizes the different rhetorical categories in non-Christian literature.

Rhetorical categories (non-Christian writings)

Geopolitical identification	Moral–spiritual characterization	Descriptive differentiation
• Geographical location • Mythical idealization • Ethiopian–Scythian antithesis • Economic and military domain • Social and political status	• Character description • Color symbolism • Demons and evil • Models of "virtue" • Sexual threats	• Physical description • Name or title • Aesthetic sensibilities

These categories establish a framework for identifying the rhetorical patterns within ancient Christian literature related to Egyptians/Egypt, Ethiopians/Ethiopia, and Blacks/blackness. I argue throughout this study that ancient Christian writers did not develop their rhetorics about these ethnic groups in a cultural vacuum. Thus, in chapter 2, I also demonstrate how ancient Christian writers adopted and adjusted the ethno-political rhetorics of the empire, and even developed their own particular ethno-political rhetorics in their stories, commentaries, homilies, theological treatises, and hagiographies.[65] I have identified the following categories of ethno-political rhetorics within early Christian literature: (1) Ethiopian–Scythian antithesis, (2) allegorical exegetical interpretation, (3) sins and vices, (4) demons and evil, (5) models of "virtue", (6) heresies, (7) sexual threats, (8) military threats, (9) symbolics of geographical location, (10) name or title, (11) color symbolism, and (12) aesthetic sensibilities. These rhetorics functioned as tools of Christian self-definition. Although all of the categories listed above are to some degree reflected in the analysis of early Christian ethno-political rhetorics, I have isolated three general patterns in the literature that call attention to some of the major threats that challenged the early Christians: (1) vices and sins, (2) sexual temptations, and (3) "heresies." These broad topics comprise the scope of Part 2 of this book.

In Part 2 (chapters 3–5), I develop a taxonomy of early Christian ethno-political rhetorics related to Egyptians/Egypt, Ethiopians/Ethiopia, and Blacks/blackness within ancient Christian writings by analyzing several primary sources. In order to narrow the scope I have selected texts written during the first-through-sixth centuries CE (primarily from Rome, Asia Minor, North Africa, and Egypt) that represent different types and complexes of early Christian literature (e.g., New Testament, apocryphal, patristic, and monastic writings) and different segments of early Christian communities, and which include references to (1) Gk. *Aigyptos/Aigyptios*, Lat. *Aegyptus/Aegyptius*, or (2) Gk. *Aithiopia/Aithiops*, Lat. *Aethiopia/Aethiops*, or (3) Gk. *melas*, Lat. *niger* (sometimes *fuscus*), or (4) any combination of the above.

Chapter 3 examines apostolic and later patristic writings. Based upon a review of the use of blackness (*melas*) in the *Shepherd of Hermas* and the *Epistle of Barnabas*, I argue that color symbolism played an important role in the literary imagination of early Christian writers. This chapter also demonstrates that later patristic authors developed ethno-political rhetorics for the purpose of isolating vices and sins within their communities.

Chapter 4 examines monastic literature from late antique Egypt. In this chapter I examine ethno-political rhetorics about Ethiopians and Blacks in Athanasius's *Life of Antony* and several Sayings of the desert fathers. The ethno-political rhetorics in this chapter also draw attention to the importance of utilizing gender as a conceptual category for interpreting early Christian writings, and provide a means for utilizing womanist readings of ancient Christian sources by amplifying the marginalized voices of Ethiopian women within monastic literature.[66] Ethiopian women symbolized gender disparities, political insecurities, and aesthetic sensibilities within early Christianity.

Chapter 5 examines both New Testament and monastic writings. Luke's story about the Ethiopian eunuch (Acts 8:26–40), the "virtuous" depiction of Ethiopian Moses, and the association of the Black One (*ho melas*) with a representative of Nestorianism form the basis for exploring how early Christians went about the task of defining "insiders" and "outsiders" – orthodoxy and heresy.

Throughout Part 2, I examine the different ways that Christian authors adopted and adjusted the rhetorical strategies about Egyptians/Egypt, Ethiopians/Ethiopia, and Blacks/blackness operative within Greco-Roman antiquity. The authors deployed no uniform strategy in developing the ethno-political rhetorics that I review in this book. The depictions of these groups varied depending on the author, genre, location, and date of a given text. Three general patterns, however, are discernible. First, the Christian writers adopted fairly consistently patterns that were already established within antiquity. For example, the use of Ethiopia to represent the ends of the earth and the physical descriptions of Ethiopians were similar to such depictions in Greco-Roman writings. Second, the writers adjusted the existing discourses to fit their own particular goals for meeting the challenges within their respective communities. For example, the caricature of Egyptians and Ethiopians contained in many Roman writings was now included in the writings of church fathers, such as Augustine and Jerome. Moreover, Christians adopted the color symbolism associated with "black" as evil in Greco-Roman antiquity in their discussions about sins and vices. Third, Christian writers invented their own particular ethno-political rhetoric based upon the specific circumstances within their respective communities. For example, the authors of monastic literature from late antique Egypt revealed a particular symbolic use of Ethiopians and Blacks. In this material Egyptians were no longer at the heart of the ethno-political rhetorics; they were now in fact advancing and shaping ethno-political rhetorics about Ethiopians and Blacks to help define an understanding of the virtues of asceticism. The special military and political conditions that threatened the stability of the empire during late antiquity contributed, in some ways, to this shift in the use of the rhetoric.

The taxonomy demonstrates how the most remote people ("beyond the rivers of Ethiopia") symbolized the moral and political extremes to which Christianity could extend. Ancient Christian authors used Egyptians/Egypt, Ethiopians/ Ethiopia, Blacks/blackness as polemical devices to respond to their intra-Christian opponents. At times their ethno-political rhetorics also responded to external persecutors of their communities. By focusing on the ethno-political rhetorics related to Egyptians/Egypt, Ethiopians/Ethiopia, and Blacks/ blackness, we can isolate some of the major threats that challenged the early Christians and, more importantly, explore how Christian writers developed discourses that were derived from assumptions about ethnic difference and color symbolism operative within the ancient world.

This book systematically documents how New Testament texts, apocryphal writings, patristic commentaries and homilies, theological treatises, and desert sayings included ethno-political rhetorics about Egyptians/Egypt, Ethiopians/ Ethiopia, and Blacks/blackness as forms of political invective and cultural signifiers that addressed the problems of sinful beliefs and practices, sexual temptations and bodily passions, and heretical movements within early Christianity. Such rhetorics developed within early Christian writings as a response to the political situations, social conditions, ethnic differentiations and gender orientations within the ancient world. Discursive strategies based on the othering of marginal ethnic groups evolved within early Christianity. While most of the texts selected for analysis are from extracanonical sources, the implications for New Testament scholarship are significant.

First of all, this study challenges the general reader and interpreter of ancient Christian sources to consider the power of symbolic language related to color and ethnicity in shaping attitudes, values, worldviews, and practices of early Christians.[67] This symbolic language is steeped in ethnic and color perceptions within the ancient world. Although scholars have generated many studies on rhetoric and the New Testament, none to my knowledge have undertaken a study examining how Egyptians/Egypt, Ethiopians/Ethiopia, and Blacks/ blackness have functioned as polemical devices within ancient Christian writings.[68] Second, this study identifies and classifies some of the diverse representations of these ethnic groups, geographical locations, and color symbols through a *historical* taxonomy of ethno-political rhetorics.[69] Third, this study proposes a theoretical framework for understanding the intersection of ethnicity, gender, and politics within ancient Christian writings.

It is important to acknowledge that a project of such scope contains many inherent limitations. This book does not attempt to reconstruct or answer any questions about the actual experiences of Egyptians, Ethiopians, and Blacks within antiquity. Its purpose is to identify, accumulate, organize, and analyze some representative discourses about Egyptians/Egypt, Ethiopians/Ethiopia, and Blacks/blackness within ancient Christian literature.[70] In many ways, it is impossible to separate the discourses about these groups from their actual historical realities;[71] yet my focus is to explicate the discursive strategies within the literature. Thus, establishing the historicity of the conversations, sexual encounters, physical fights, and other bizarre interactions discussed in the texts under review is not my concern in this project.

Another limitation has to do with the choice of categories and the nomenclature used to develop the taxonomy. There is no easy way to describe adequately the various discursive representations of Egyptians/Egypt, Ethiopians/Ethiopia, and Blacks/blackness in ancient literature. The rhetorical categories proposed in the taxonomy are a suggested starting point for exploring the multiple discursive uses of these ethnic groups, geographical locations, and color symbols within ancient Christian literature. These categories do not necessarily represent all the possibilities within non-Christian and Christian literature. Moreover, some of the examples could easily fit into more than one of the categories in the taxonomy. For example, there are many instances in which color symbolism and ethnic identification or geographical location occur in the same text, as in the stories about Ethiopian Moses or the Ethiopian eunuch. Yet, in spite of these inherent limitations, the taxonomy clearly documents the multiple rhetorical functions of Egyptians/Egypt, Ethiopians/Ethiopia, and Blacks/blackness in Greco-Roman literature.

From the evidence examined in this book, it is clear that assumptions about ethnic and color differences in antiquity influenced the way Christians shaped their stories about the theological, ecclesiological, and political developments within the early Christian communities. As a result, Egyptians, Ethiopians, Blacks, and blackness invariably became associated with the threats and dangers that could potentially destroy the development of a certain "orthodox" brand of Christianity. In spite of the basic contention that Christianity was to extend to all peoples – even the remote Ethiopians, from this review of ethno-political rhetorics it appears that certain groups of Christians were marginalized and rendered invisible and silent. They were, in the words of Jerome, "blackened by their sins."[72] These groups of Christians were not solely or simply marginalized (or "blackened") because of the color of their skin or their ethnic identity (although on the surface the narratives sound as if this is the case); they were more than likely marginalized because of certain ideas and values they held about early Christianity that differed from the more dominant voices within the community. Ethnic and color difference came to *symbolize* certain theological, ideological, and even political intra-Christian controversies and challenges. The ethno-political rhetorics that have been identified in this book call attention to the power of ethnic and color-coded symbolic language to create the religious, political, social, and cultural reality of ancient Christians.

Part 1

DEVELOPING A TAXONOMY OF ETHNO-POLITICAL RHETORICS

1

INTERPRETING ETHNIC AND COLOR DIFFERENCES IN EARLY CHRISTIAN WRITINGS

In the apocryphal *Acts of Peter* Marcellus describes to Peter a dream that featured an evil-looking woman:

> And Marcellus went to sleep for a short time; and when he awoke he said to Peter, "Peter, apostle of Christ, let us boldly set about our task. For just now as I slept for a little I saw you sitting on a high place, and before you a great assembly; and a most evil-looking woman, who looked like an Ethiopian (*Aethiopissimam*), not an Egyptian (*Aegyptiam*), but was all black (*nigram*), clothed in filthy rags. She was dancing with an iron collar about her neck and chains on her hands and feet. When you saw her you said aloud to me, 'Marcellus, the whole power of Simon and of his god is this dancer; take off her head!' But I said to you 'Brother Peter, I am a senator of noble family, and I have never stained my hands, nor killed even a sparrow at any time.' And when you heard this you began to cry out even louder, 'Come, our true sword, Jesus Christ, and do not only cut off the head of this demon (*daemonis*), but cut in pieces all her limbs in the sight of all these whom I have approved in thy service.' And immediately a man who looked like yourself, Peter, with sword in hand, cut her all to pieces, so that I gazed upon you both, both on you and on the one who was cutting up the demon, whose likeness caused me great amazement. And now I have awakened and told you these signs of Christ (*signa Christi*)." And when Peter heard this he was the more encouraged, because Marcellus had seen these things; for the Lord is always careful for his own. So cheered (*gratulatus*) and refreshed (*recreates*) by these words he stood up to go to the forum.[1]

It is hard to believe that this text was written during the formative years of early Christianity. It was intended to inspire, encourage, and edify those who would receive it. What is most noticeable (and even shocking) about this text is the way "the evil-looking woman" functions within the narrative. First, she is described by ethnic and color-symbolic language: she was an Ethiopian (*Aethiopissimam*), not an Egyptian (*Aegyptiam*), but was all black (*nigram*). Second, she is described as a dancer with an iron collar about her neck and chains on her feet. Third, she is used to represent the enemy of Peter – Simon Magnus. Fourth, she is to be killed, either through decapitation or through the total dismemberment of her body – in the sight of others!

This text is usually not isolated in its entirety and is generally analyzed as only a minor subtext in the more significant unfolding drama of Peter's activities as an apostle.[2] When I have shared this text with audiences that range from seasoned biblical scholars to seminary students, to lay people in mainline Protestant churches, the responses generally include surprise, shock, anger, dismay, and silence. Most of my students cannot believe how the woman is portrayed in the text or why a Christian author would choose to tell a story that is filled with such violence toward an ethnic person. My inability to explain or justify the function of this story or the role of the ethnic woman, along with the lack of any critical commentaries or interpretations of this passage, led me to pursue the task of developing some type of interpretive framework that might account for some of the factors that converge to make such a story an acceptable part of early Christian discourses.

Three general observations about this dream of Marcellus shape the development of the theoretical framework that will be discussed in this chapter and used throughout this book. First, the author uses the woman in this text as a symbolic trope in order to communicate certain values about early Christianity. Second, the author clearly delineates the woman's ethnic identity, and clarifies this identity with color-symbolic language. Third, the interactions between the woman and the phantom person who killed her in this dream (a man who looked like Peter) raise questions about gender relations in the ancient world. In addition to these observations, this text highlights the problem I encountered in trying to come up with a theoretical framework for exploring how ethnicity might be used as an interpretive category within biblical studies. There was no one particular theory or scholar that would enable me to address all of the questions related to understanding the symbolic meanings of ethnic groups, geographical locations, and color differences in early Christian writings. Thus, for this study, I have undertaken an interdisciplinary approach that is based upon rhetorical criticism, ethnocriticism, and gender criticism. These three forms of biblical interpretation will serve as the theoretical foundation for the exploration of ethnic and color-coded discourses, which will be referred to as "ethno-political rhetorics." I will not provide an overall historical development of each of these forms of biblical interpretation; such information has already been documented in a variety of sources.[3] What is more pertinent for my purposes is to show how each of these interpretive methods opens a door for exploring the symbolic functions of Egyptians/Egypt, Ethiopians/Ethiopia, and Blacks/blackness in ancient Christian writings.

18

RHETORICAL CRITICISM

In recent years many scholars have identified the benefits of exploring discursive or rhetorical strategies within ancient Christian writings.[4] In her book entitled *Christianity and the Rhetoric of Empire: The Development of Christian Discourse*, Averil Cameron offers a compelling proposal for understanding the different ways that Christian writers adopted the discursive patterns of the larger Greco-Roman culture in their particular writings. Writing from the standpoint of a historian, Cameron examines how Christians "spoke and wrote the rhetoric of empire"; in other words, she explores the relation of Christian discourse to its context in the Roman Empire. This point will be explored more fully in Chapter 2.[5] Her understanding of Christian rhetoric, not in its technical sense, but rather in its broadest sense, "as modes of expression within which early Christianity was articulated and the power of that expression to persuade," informs my understanding of the persuasive power of ethno-political rhetorics explored throughout this book.[6] One of the most important contributions that Cameron makes in her persuasive discussion about the development of Christian discourse is the strong connection between historical events and rhetorical constructions that appear in different types of Christian writings.[7]

Elisabeth Schüssler Fiorenza argues that analyzing the "rhetoricity of the texts" yields important insights about the political intent of the author.[8] She demonstrates how the "'politics and rhetorics of othering' establish identity either by declaring the difference of the other to be the same or by vilifying and idealizing the difference as otherness."[9] Her insights draw attention to both the polemical and political commentary embedded in ancient Christian writings.

It is a well-established fact that ancient Christian writings were produced within polemical contexts that led to slander among different groups who were vying for authority. New Testament scholar Luke Timothy Johnson examines the rhetoric of slander that non-Jewish Christians directed against their Jewish opponents. Johnson argues that the power of language to shape hostile and destructive attitudes and actions toward Jews is best understood through the exercise of historical and literary imagination.[10] He analyzes the New Testament's anti-Jewish slander by outlining the historical and social context that generated anti-Jewish slander. Then he contextualizes the polemic within the conventional rhetoric of slander in the Hellenistic world.

Historian of early Christianity Robert Wilken also examines how Jews and Judaizers were the object of slander and rhetorical abuse in the sermons of John Chrysostom.[11] According to Wilken, Chrysostom's sermons were directed at Christians in his congregation who were participating in Jewish festivals and taking part in other Jewish observances in Antioch. Wilken demonstrates how Chrysostom was a model rhetor whose preaching exemplified the fourth-century standards of rhetoric of the later Roman Empire.[12] Chrysostom used hyberbole, metaphors, and similes to present the Judaizers and Jews in the worst possible light: "do not be surprised if I have called the Jews wretched. They are truly wretched and miserable for they have received many good things from God yet they have spurned them and violently cast them away."[13] Wilken accurately describes how the rhetoric of abuse found in fourth-century Christian writings was directed at religious opponents, chiefly heretics and Jews.[14] This rhetoric, influenced by sophistic invective, was instrumental in shaping the theological arguments about the status of the Jews after the death of Christ and the destruction of the temple.[15]

This present book draws upon the theoretical presuppositions of the afore-mentioned studies and offers a much-needed theoretical framework for exploring the symbolic use of Egyptians/Egypt, Ethiopians/Ethiopia, and Blacks/blackness in ancient Christian literature. Although rhetorical criticism provides a means for analyzing discursive strategies within ancient writings, it does not offer a theoretical framework for examining the impact of ethnic and color differences within early Christian writings. The next section will assess how a relatively new area of biblical criticism, known as ethnocriticism, yields interpretive possibilities for understanding such differences.

ETHNOCRITICISM

Ethnocritical studies have generally opened a new window onto ancient Christian writings. Because there are so many different scholarly approaches for interpreting and understanding ethnicity,[16] this section will summarize some of the more pertinent studies related to the New Testament and early Christianity and outline the general approach that will be used in this study. Hebrew Bible and New Testament scholars have generated many provocative studies that indicate how ancient understandings of ethnic differences filtered into religious writings.[17] Given the diverse cultural and ethnic backgrounds of the ancient world, it is no surprise that scholars are now raising questions about the ways that ethnicity or race figure in the discourses of early Christian authors.[18]

Recent studies on ethnic identity, ethnographic historiography, and ethno-criticism provide a scholarly basis for developing a theoretical framework for understanding the impact of ethnic differences within early Christianity.[19] Within antiquity, ethnic differences were highly visible and many ancient authors discussed these differences. Some have identified the ethnic, cultural, and religious identities in the book of Acts.[20] Tessa Rajak asserts that in first-century Palestine the distinction between Jews and Greeks was of great ideological importance, and it was also of political importance at times of crisis. Others have analyzed the ethnic issues in Paul's letter to the Romans. James Walters, for example, assesses the effect of early Christianity's changing relationship to the Jewish communities in Rome as a background for understanding the manner in which Jewish–Gentile issues are treated.[21] Walter's study establishes the importance of exploring questions related to ethnic identity, but he does not address how dominant ethnic perceptions and stereotypes extended beyond Jewish–Gentile relations within the ancient world.

David M. Olster offers an instructive framework for analyzing Egyptians, Ethiopians, and Blacks in ancient Christian literature. In his essay "Classical Ethnography and Early Christianity," Olster reviews the seminal study of Adolf Harnack and takes special note of Harnack's conclusions about the expression *tertium genus* (third race).[22] Olster critiques Harnack's dialectical reconstruction of Christianity's successful expansion, which viewed Christianity as a new religion that emerged along with some other Greco-Roman and Jewish religions.[23] According to Olster, the purpose of Harnack's analysis of "third race" was to "identify a separate and distinct 'Christian' religious culture that confronted and eventually overcame a competing pagan religious culture."[24] Much of scholarship has relied on the religious and cultural assumptions that Harnack established.[25]

Olster's study departs from the dialectical model of Harnack and his modern successors, and offers a new framework for understanding the use of the phrase *tertium genus*.

> One might in fact rephrase the problem of the "third race" in very different terms than Harnack and his successors. Perhaps the question is not whether Christianity was a new genus of religion in a theological or philosophical dialectic with paganism, but whether early Christians thought of themselves as a new genus of *genos* or *ethnos* in an ethnographic dialogue with classical assumptions about nation or, since the term "nation" implies some link to our own modern nationalism, race, which better renders the classical connotations.[26]

Olster argues, "it would seem more likely that Christians would use 'third race' within the broader late antique cultural context of ethnography."[27] Furthermore, Olster draws attention to the cultural dynamics of early Christianity by specifically examining ethnography's role in tying together religion, race, and culture in the earliest extant Christian apologetics.[28] He also examined some implications of Christian ethnography for the evolution of Christianity in the religious culture of late antiquity.[29] Most useful in Olster's essay is his attention to the use of ethnographic polemic within specific ancient Christian texts. For example, in his analysis of the *Epistle of Barnabas*, Olster identifies an ethnographic invective against the Jews, whereby the author of the text sought to undercut Jewish historical and racial claims to the legitimacy of their customs.[30] Olster's overall thesis is helpful for analyzing the discourses about Egyptians, Ethiopians, Blacks, and blackness in ancient Christian writings. Although he makes a defensible case for exploring ethnographic discursive strategies within ancient Christian literature, he does not account for the ethnographic invective that often uses "Egyptians" as polemical tropes.[31] Nor does he explain the meaning of the "Egyptian ethnographic tradition" that he refers to in his essay.[32]

21

Furthermore, he merely makes a passing reference to "'Egyptian' polemicists."[33] In spite of these shortcomings, Olster's work persuasively demonstrates that by the time the Christians used the title "third race" they did not do so in a cultural vacuum:[34] "The rhetoric of 'third race' was drawn from ethnography, a common and much employed genre within classical literature, whose *topoi* were common throughout contemporary, non-Christian literature."[35]

Classicist Roger S. Bagnall, in his essay entitled "Greeks and Egyptians: Ethnicity, Status, and Culture," challenges interpreters to develop conceptual clarity about the questions they raise and the methods they use regarding ethnicity in antiquity.[36] With this in mind, my focus in this study is not to analyze the ethnic identity of Egyptians, Ethiopians, and Blacks, but rather to demonstrate how ancient Christian authors used these ethnic groups as polemical devices or ethnic tropes, which at times resulted in both vituperative and idealized depictions of these people – all for the purpose of clarifying the self-definitions of early Christianity and its place within the Greco-Roman world. These polemical devices or ethnic tropes are in effect ideological constructions;[37] that is, they function symbolically and communicate certain values about the authors and their respective communities. Early Christian authors employed what have been identified as "ethnical strategies" in order to define themselves within the midst of competing threats and challenges to their emerging worldviews.[38]

Koen Goudriaan has developed a useful guide for understanding the use of ethnicity as an interpretive category. Goudriaan defines an ethnical strategy as "the policy adopted by an individual or a group for applying ethnical categories to themselves and to 'others' in a range of different circumstances."[39] Goudriaan further argues that "ethnic groups are not considered to be fixed entities with an objective existence based on inherent qualities of the people belonging to them, but as projections of the minds of those participating in ethnically coloured interaction."[40] In this regard, ethnicity is a way of organizing cultural differences. This implies that

> specific features of culture (in the broad sense) are signaled out as
> ethnically significant . . . On the basis of these traits the participants
> in a given society are divided in a "we" and a "they". The features
> that serve as boundary marks between the ethnic groups may vary
> greatly in time. For the maintenance of ethnicity it is necessary,
> however, that the boundaries themselves are kept intact.[41]

The ethno-political rhetorics identified and examined in this book are based upon a number of sophisticated "ethnical strategies" adopted by different Christian authors throughout the development of several generations and genres of ancient Christian literature.

Throughout this book I assume that ancient Egyptians, Ethiopians, and Blacks are recognizable ethnic groups within the Greco-Roman world.[42] Blacks, while presumed to be an ethnic group, are not clearly delineated as such in the literature. In many instances ancient writers referred to both Ethiopians and Egyptians as Blacks. Also, the use of Blacks overlaps into the light/dark color symbolism that existed in the ancient world. The ambiguity associated with Blacks and blackness in ancient writings calls for a systematic reinterpretation of the multiple meanings of Blacks and blackness. Henry Louis Gates, a literary and cultural critic, suggests that "blackness" has many different meanings.[43] Gates proposes that it will be necessary to move beyond the boundaries of what we understand as blackness and accept the challenge of developing and exploring new complex meanings for the future. bell hooks, another literary and cultural critic, makes a convincing case for adopting a postmodern perspective for an understanding of "blackness."[44] She asserts that "racism is perpetuated when blackness is associated solely with concrete gut level experience conceived as either opposing or having no connection to abstract thinking and the production of critical theory."[45] Her insights challenge scholars who work on understanding the presence of Blacks in antiquity to develop critical theories and methods that go beyond historical identification and consciousness raising. I agree with these scholars, that simply identifying the references to Blacks in ancient literature is not enough; it is more fruitful to explore the symbolic meanings and the possible implications within the ancient context, as well as within the postmodern era.

I have discovered at least four possible uses of black/blackness (*melas* and *niger*): (1) Black (upper case) – when clearly dealing with ethnic identity (as in Egyptians, Ethiopians, and Blacks), (2) Black (upper case) – when used as a title of a person, (3) black (lower case) – when used as an adjective to describe the color (and sometimes the ethnic identity) of a person, and (4) blackness (lower case) – when used to refer to color symbolism.

On the surface it appears that Egyptians/Egypt, Ethiopians/Ethiopia, and Blacks/blackness are used as metaphors. Several scholars have already documented how these groups, geographical locations, and color symbols are equated with metaphors of sin.[46] Yet it is my goal to go beyond this well-established interpretive framework and analyze more concretely how ethnic groups, geographical locations, and color symbols function as tropes within the discursive strategies of various Greco-Roman (including early Christian) authors.[47] In effect, I will examine how Christian authors signified Egyptians/Egypt, Ethiopians/Ethiopia, and Blacks/blackness.[48]

GENDER CRITICISM

The evil-looking women described so vividly by the author of the *Acts of Peter* helps me to see more clearly the need for gender criticism in this study. Not only is this woman described in ethnic and color-symbolic language, but she is also the object of violence within the text and used as a spectacle to show the "signs of Christ" (*signa Christi*). Feminist and womanist biblical critics have clearly identified some of the issues at stake in such violent depictions of women within biblical writings.[49] They are also exploring biblical writings for the purpose of understanding how different understandings of gender are operative.[50] The provocative Ethiopian woman in the *Acts of Peter* forces interpreters to include an additional interpretive lens that is informed by gender criticism.

In recent years gender theories have influenced many traditional academic disciplines, leading to provocative studies by classicists, historians, political theorists, and biblical scholars.[51] Some of these studies focus solely upon recovering women's experiences in ancient writings, while others are more theoretical and offer methodological suggestions for incorporating gender analysis into ancient studies. Still others, although not specifically utilizing gender theory, call attention to the importance of reading ancient texts with women and especially women of color in mind. All of these studies, in some way, have offered an important contribution to the development of feminist and womanist scholarship in particular, and early Christianity in general. My purpose is not merely to identify representations of Ethiopian women within early Christian writings, or to discuss Roman attitudes about the sexual roles of Black women.[52] Rather, I am concerned with understanding how gender is constructed in these texts and how such constructions influenced the early audiences that received them.[53] Moreover, I hope to uncover the power dynamics operating in the texts and to raise questions about the social and political environment that would have fostered the various symbolic depictions of Ethiopian and Black women identified in ancient texts.

Before going any further, I will provide a working definition of gender and discuss how gender analysis will be useful for interpreting ancient texts. Gender is generally understood as a social construction. Feminist scholar Joan Wallach Scott offers a multilayered definition of gender that serves as a heuristic foundation for the analysis of vituperative ethno-political rhetoric about Ethiopian women in monastic literature.[54] Scott defines gender as an integral connection between two propositions: (1) "gender is a constitutive element of social relationships based on perceived differences between the sexes," and (2) "gender is a primary way of signifying relationships of power."[55] The first proposition is composed of four interrelated elements: (1) "culturally available symbols that evoke multiple (and often contradictory) representations";[56] (2) "normative concepts that set forth interpretations of the meanings of the symbols, that attempt to limit and contain their metaphoric possibilities"; (3) "a notion of politics and reference to social institutions and organizations"; and (4) "gendered identities [that] are substantively constructed and relate their findings to a range of activities, social organizations, and historically specific cultural representations."[57] Scott's understanding of the process of constructing gender relationships could be used to discuss class, race, ethnicity, or any social process.[58]

Scott's second proposition about gender as a primary way of signifying relationships of power is also instructive for this study. Appealing to French sociologist Maurice Godelier, Scott argues that the concept of gender legitimizes and constructs social relationships. "It is not sexuality which haunts society, but society which haunts the body's sexuality. Sex-related differences between bodies are continually summoned as testimony to social relations and phenomena that have nothing to do with sexuality. Not only as testimony to, but also testimony for – in other words, as legitimation."[59] In analyzing gender from this perspective, Scott argues that new insights can be gained with respect to how politics constructs gender and gender constructs politics.[60] She goes on to cite an example from Edmund Burke's attack on the French Revolution, which "is built around a contrast between ugly, murderous sansculotte hags."[61]

This understanding of gender is useful for understanding the ethno-political rhetorics about Ethiopian women in monastic literature. I will argue that the sexual encounters with black and Ethiopian women described in monastic writings is used as testimony to social relations and phenomena that have nothing to do with sexuality. These women call attention to ethnic and class disparities that existed in late antiquity. The symbolic use of Ethiopian and black women was another way in which Christian authors set forth boundaries within their communities.

Political theorist Iris Young offers another useful paradigm for understanding the vituperative ethno-political rhetoric about Ethiopian women in monastic literature. She identifies a type of cultural imperialism that operates by making a group invisible while the group is also simultaneously marked out and stereotyped. This cultural imperialism requires that "dominant discourse defines them [the Other] in terms of bodily characteristics, and constructs those bodies as ugly . . . defiled, impure . . . or sick."[62] This process occurs while simultaneously projecting the physical traits of the imperialist group as the desirable norm. I will demonstrate how this type of dominant discourse is evident in the stories about Ethiopian women.

Miriam Peskowitz, in her study of ancient rabbinical texts, also analyzes discourses of gender. She asserts that "gender and sexuality are not just appropriate (or inappropriate) roles and social performances. They form categories, divisions that are given social meaning and import. They serve as marks of difference."[63] In her review of writings about Penelope, whom she describes as "a pliable icon of gender and sexuality in the Roman period," Peskowitz argues that Penelope had several, often contradictory, meanings: virtuous, devoted, dedicated, chaste, dishonest, and flirtatious.[64] Some authors used Penelope to signify certain cultural distinctions operative within Greco-Roman society. Peskowitz's cultural framework, as well as her fascinating way of establishing that multiple meanings are intended in gendered texts, helps illuminate the results of this study.

In addition to Scott and Peskowitz, womanist biblical scholars offer an important interpretive lens through which questions related to gender may surface.[65] New Testament scholar Clarice Martin, in an essay entitled "Womanist Interpretations of the New Testament: The Quest for Holistic and Inclusive

Translation and Interpretation," defines womanist biblical interpretation as
follows:

Clarice Martin

> [W]omanist biblical interpretation has a "quadrocentric" interest
> where gender, race, class, and language issues are all at the forefront
> of translation and interpretation concerns, and not just a threefold
> focus, where gender, class, and language concerns predominate
> almost exclusively, as is often the case in white feminist biblical
> interpretation and translation.[66]

According to Martin, womanist hermeneutics moves beyond feminist critiques
of patriarchy and Afrocentrist critiques of racism by challenging "all ideologies
of dominance and subordination in the biblical writers, traditioning processes,
and contemporary scholarship."[67] Its chief concern is to amplify the voices of
all persons who are marginalized within biblical texts.[68] Martin's essay is
important because the interests of women of color in general and African
American women in particular are brought to the forefront of New Testament
biblical interpretation.

In a later essay Martin provides a concise historical overview of the emergence
of womanist biblical interpretation.[69] She also outlines the role and function of
the Bible within womanist biblical interpretation and summarizes four tasks
of womanist interpreters. Martin claims that the Bible is central for African
American women and men, in spite of how it has been used and abused "by
proslavery jurists, apologists, and others in the dominant European culture of
seventeenth-, eighteenth-, and nineteenth-century America to provide the
argumentum and *invidium par excellence* in support of chattel slavery."[70] She cites
several biblical texts that have inspired generations of African Americans to
persevere and remain faithful "in the face of a multiplicity of death-dealing
forces."[71] She also indicates that womanist biblical interpreters acknowledge the
problematics of the Bible as a pervasively androcentric, patriarchal document.
One of the most important contributions of womanist biblical interpretation
is its emphasis on identifying and demystifying "the reality and effects of
multiple, interlocking ideologies and systems of hegemony and domination
inscribed within the biblical traditions and stories and within traditional male
and female (including feminist) Eurocentric critical exegetical theories and
practices."[72]

Martin acknowledges that womanist interpreters have developed a wide range
of tasks and methods based upon their training within the academic guild
and their responses to the discourses, values, and sociopolitical and religious
experiences of African American culture. She notes, however, four tasks of
womanist interpreters, which to some degree are reflected in this study of
Egyptians, Ethiopians, and Blacks.[73] First, womanist interpreters focus on the
recovery, analysis, and reconstruction of women's history in the Judeo-Christian
tradition. Second, womanist interpreters seek to reclaim the neglected histories

26

and stories of the presence and function of Black peoples within divergent biblical traditions. Third, womanist interpreters "must continue to challenge the persistent and still normative narrowness of vision of feminist theologians and biblical interpreters on the subject of race." Martin cogently expands upon this point by saying:

> The still negligible attention given to issues of ethnicity and race in feminist theological discourses and practices ignores the reality of race and ethnicity as legitimate sites of dialogic exchange and contestation in biblical interpretation and diminishes the significance of the power and the effects of the simultaneity of gender, race, and class variants in their assessment of biblical meaning.[74]

The fourth task identified by Martin is the retrieval and documentary analysis of the effective history of the Hebrew Bible and the Christian scriptures in western culture in general and on peoples of African descent in Black diasporic communities in particular.

Clarice Martin offers a much-needed challenge to scholars who examine Egyptians, Ethiopians, and Blacks within biblical narratives. She calls attention to the perspectives and roles of women, as well as the ideological and political struggles at work within the narratives and throughout the history of interpretation. Chapter 4 of this book will incorporate some of the insights from gender criticism and womanist biblical hermeneutics in assessing the use of Ethiopian and Black women in some monastic sources from late antiquity.

Hebrew Bible scholar Renita Weems, in an essay entitled "The Hebrew Women are Not Like the Egyptian Women," explores how gender, race, and ideology work together in the text about the Egyptian midwives in Exodus 1:8–22.[75] Her study of the Egyptian midwives identifies an "ideology of difference" operating in this text through which the narrator exploits the assumptions about the differences between Egyptians and Hebrews.[76] This ideology of difference is the chief component for understanding how women are used as tropes within biblical writings. As a womanist scholar, Weems has called attention to the particular reading strategies of African American women,[77] and has persuasively demonstrated how this has provided an important framework for understanding the metaphorical depictions of sexual violence in the Bible.[78]

In addition to Weems and Martin, other womanist biblical scholars are generating critical studies of biblical materials.[79] Yet most tend to focus upon canonical sources. This study will attempt to push beyond canonical boundaries and examine monastic documents from late antiquity that discuss Ethiopian and Black women.

ETHNO-POLITICAL RHETORICS: A TOOL FOR INTERPRETING ETHNIC AND COLOR DIFFERENCES IN EARLY CHRISTIAN WRITINGS

I opened this chapter with a vivid description of an Ethiopian woman. This symbolic trope from the apocryphal *Acts of Peter* led me to develop a theoretical basis for understanding how ethnic and color differences signal political and ideological meanings within ancient Christian writings. Because of the lack of any concrete methodological strategies for understanding the meaning of such tropes in ancient texts, a theory of ethno-political rhetorics has been developed through the use of rhetorical criticism, ethnocriticism, and gender criticism. These three forms of biblical interpretation enable the reader to identify the discursive elements in texts that are based upon the symbolic power of ethnic and color differences operative within the ancient world. In the following chapter I construct a taxonomy (or classification) of ethno-political rhetorics in Greco-Roman (including Christian) literature and demonstrate that early Christian authors were not alone in their use of Egyptians/Egypt, Ethiopians/Ethiopia, and Blacks/blackness as ethno-political rhetorics.[80] They modeled the larger culture in presenting both positive and pejorative depictions of these ethnic groups, geographical locations, and color symbols.

2

EGYPTIANS, ETHIOPIANS, BLACKS, AND BLACKNESS IN GRECO-ROMAN LITERATURE

For the most part . . . taxonomies are regarded – and announce themselves – as systems of classifying the phenomenal world, systems through
which otherwise indiscriminate data can be organized in a form wherein
they become knowable.

(Bruce Lincoln, *Discourse and the Construction of Society*)

INTRODUCTION

This chapter classifies a wide range of ethnic discourses related to Egyptians/
Egypt, Ethiopians/Ethiopia, and Blacks/blackness contained in Greco-Roman
literature (both Christian and non-Christian). Several scholars have made
attempts to categorize the numerous references to these ethnic groups,
geographical locations, and color symbols in Greco-Roman literature, yet none
have developed a comprehensive framework for understanding the different
rhetorical functions of the references.[1] Furthermore, there has been no attempt
to examine or explain how ancient Christian authors appropriated different
Greco-Roman discursive strategies related to Egyptians, Ethiopians, and Blacks
in their writings. Therefore, I develop a taxonomy that classifies and accounts
for the different rhetorics related to Egyptians/Egypt, Ethiopians/Ethiopia, and
Blacks/blackness within Greco-Roman literature and isolates some possible
functions of the rhetorics within ancient Christian writings.

Averil Cameron has effectively demonstrated in her book *Christianity and the
Rhetoric of Empire* that an examination of Greco-Roman rhetorics provides a
means for understanding the complex and dynamic development of ancient
Christian rhetorics.[2] She suggests that "rather than a single Christian discourse,
there was . . . a series of overlapping discourses always in a state of adaptation
and adjustment, and always ready to absorb in a highly opportunistic manner
whatever might be useful from secular rhetoric and vocabulary."[3] The taxonomy
of rhetorics about Egyptians/Egypt, Ethiopians/Ethiopia, and Blacks/blackness
developed in this chapter indicates that Christian authors did not create their
exegetical interpretations and theological treatises in a cultural vacuum. They

were influenced by the cultural values expressed in the literature of Greco-Roman authors. They used, as Cameron would say, secular rhetoric and vocabulary to persuade their audiences. Thus, before we can examine the Christian texts that contain ethno-political rhetorics about Egyptians/Egypt, Ethiopians/Ethiopia, and Blacks/blackness, we must first provide an overview of the different ways these ethnic groups, geographical locations, and color symbols appeared in Greco-Roman writings.

The taxonomy in this chapter is an effort to identify and organize the primary sources so that the many symbolic representations become accessible to the reader. This taxonomy is similar in many respects to taxonomies generated by classicists and literary theorists that classify the different types of invective within Greco-Roman and Christian literature.[4] These scholars have determined that organizing the primary sources according to their rhetorical functions yields important insights about the extent to which language can shape the social, religious, and political understandings communicated in different types of literature.

Given the many, diverse rhetorical functions of Egyptians/Egypt, Ethiopians/Ethiopia, and Blacks/blackness in Greco-Roman literature, it is necessary to develop a general schema for organizing the common overarching themes within the literature. The numerous rhetorical functions identified in this chapter have been organized into four major categories: (1) geopolitical identification, (2) moral–spiritual characterization, (3) descriptive differentiation, and (4) Christian self-definition. The first three categories focus on representations within non-Christian Greco-Roman literature. The fourth classification identifies the different ways that Christian authors either adapted the rhetorics from their Greco-Roman contemporaries or invented their own specific rhetorics for the purpose of shaping their self-definition. The next section provides several representative examples of each type of rhetoric contained in both Christian and non-Christian Greco-Roman literature.[5] A brief summary of each major category and its constituent parts will be provided.

RHETORICAL CATEGORIES

Non-Christian Writings

Geopolitical identification

Geographical references to Egypt/Egyptians and Ethiopia/Ethiopians are widespread throughout Greco-Roman literature. Ancient geographers, historians, philosophers, and moralists referred to these places and people for shaping an understanding of the boundaries of the inhabited world.[6] In many instances, the lands of Egypt and Ethiopia were idealized as mythical places. Greco-Roman authors also signaled social, political, and economic concerns of the empire by symbolically referring to Egyptians and Ethiopians in their writings. Ethiopians were also included within a well-known Ethiopian–Scythian formulaic expression to indicate geographical extremes. The geopolitical identification of Egypt/Egyptians and Ethiopia/Ethiopians was a common discursive strategy within Greco-Roman literature. Beyond the mere identification of geographical location, these places and people carried multiple layers of meaning within the ancient Greco-Roman writings. In this section, five categories have been identified: (1) geographical location, (2) mythical idealization, (3) Ethiopian–Scythian antithesis, (4) economic and military domain, and (5) social and political status.

Geographical location

The land of Egypt was a popular geographical destination within the ancient world.[7] Many of the ancient sources offer examples of travelers who sought wisdom and higher learning from the philosophers and priests of Egypt. According to Plutarch, the wisest among the Greeks (e.g., Solon, Thales, Plato, Eudoxus, Pythagoras, and Lycurgus) came to Egypt (eis Aigypton) and consorted with the priests.[8] Classical geographers provided detailed accounts of their explorations and observations about Egypt.[9] Herodotus visited Egypt in about 450 BCE, and spent several months traveling throughout the country.[10] The second of his nine books of "History" is devoted entirely to Egypt. Diodorus Siculus visited Egypt in 59 BCE.[11] He writes of the myths, kings, and customs of that country in the first book of his voluminous historical work. The geographer Strabo, who traveled the land of Egypt with his friend Aelius Gallus (the governor of Egypt under the rule of Augustus), provides the oldest systematic account of the geography of Egypt in the seventeenth book of his treatise on geography.

Although travel and tourism were common activities in Greco-Roman Egypt,[12] very few ancient geographers or historians were able to travel to Ethiopia. Therefore, many of the geographical descriptions and historical summaries about Ethiopia serve more to stimulate the literary imagination of the reader than to record actual events.[13] The most characteristic feature of Ethiopia in early Greek writings is its remote geographical location.[14] As reflected in the minds of the elite Greco-Roman authors, Ethiopia represented the "end of the earth" (eschatou tēs gēs). Both Homer and Herodotus identified Ethiopia as a region in the southern part of the world far removed from the center of Greek culture.[15] But Ethiopians were found not only in the southern part of the Greco-Roman world; they could also be found in the East and in the West. Homer claims that these dark-skinned remote people lived either toward the setting sun or toward the rising sun.[16] This statement seems to have been the genesis for the widespread confusion among the ancients regarding the exact geographical location of Ethiopians.[17] Herodotus noted physical differences between eastern and western Ethiopians: those from the East had straight hair and those from the West had woolly hair, thick lips, and a different type of speech.[18] Philostratus says Ethiopia covers the western wing of the entire earth under the sun.[19]

Mythical idealization

The mythical veneration of Egyptians and Ethiopians is well attested in the writings of ancient Greek authors.[20] Homer considered Ethiopians blameless people who were held in high esteem by the gods: "For Zeus went yesterday for a feast to the incomparable (*amymonas*) Ethiopians at the Ocean, and all the gods followed him."[21] Homer also depicted Egyptians as skilled healers: "there [in Egypt] everyone is a physician, wise above human kind; for they are of the race of Paeëon."[22] The Greek historian Herodotus (490–424 BCE) also venerates Egyptians and Ethiopians. In his description of the expeditions of Cambyses in Book 3 of his history of the ancient world, Herodotus claims that the long-lived Ethiopians (*makrobious Aithiopas*)[23] are the "tallest and finest of all humans (*megistoi kai kallistoi anthrōpōn pantōn*)."[24] As for Egypt, Herodotus considered it the original home of all religion and presented a vivid picture of the manners and customs of the Egyptians.[25] He also claimed that the Egyptians deemed themselves to be the oldest nation on earth or the firstborn of all humans (*prōtous genesthai pantōn anthrōpōn*).[26] Diodorus records that the first appearance of humans on earth took place in Egypt:

> When in the beginning the universe came into being, humans first came into existence in Egypt (*kata tēn Aigypton*), both because of the favorable climate of the land and because of the nature of the Nile ... When the world was first taking shape, *the land [of Egypt]* could better than any other have been the place where humanity came into being because of the well-tempered nature of its soil; for even at the present time, while the soil of no other country generates any such thing in it alone certain living creatures may be seen coming into being in a marvellous fashion.[27]

Latin authors generally did not venerate Ethiopians and Egyptians in the same way as Greek authors. By the Roman period, Ethiopians and Egyptians were described in a more pejorative sense. For example, Cicero calls Ethiopians stupid and Juvenal expresses contempt for them through color-symbolic language: "Let the straight-legged man laugh at the club-footed, the white man at the Ethiopian."[28] One exception to the negative portrayal of Ethiopians can be found in the first century CE text by Pliny the Elder. Pliny emphasized the wisdom (*sapientes*) of the Ethiopians[29] and discussed their skill with the bow and arrow.[30]

Ethiopian–Scythian antithesis

Throughout ancient Greek literature the white, straight-haired, blue-eyed Scythian of the north was contrasted with the black, woolly-haired Ethiopian of the south to indicate the extreme boundaries of the ancient world.[31] Both Scythia and Ethiopia were used to refer to the ends of the earth.[32] According to Frank Snowden, the Ethiopian–Scythian formula had appeared as early as Hesiod and had been "a frequent, if not favorite, Hellenic illustration of the boundaries of the north and south as well as of the environmental theory."[33] Menander (fourth century BCE) used this formulaic expression to express the equality of humankind:

> The man whose natural bent (*gegonōs*) is good,
> His mother, though Ethiopian (*Aithiops*),
>   has made him nobly born.
> "A Scyth (*Skythēs*)," you say? Pest!
>   Anacharsis was a Scyth (*Skythēs*)![34]

Menander may have been influenced by Antiphon the Sophist who had insisted that both barbarians and Greeks are by nature born alike in all things.[35]

Aristotle also utilized this formulaic expression in his writings.[36] He departed, however, from the inclusive and universal view of humanity by claiming that Ethiopians are considered to be less intelligent than Scythians. In *De generatione animalium*, after describing Scythians and Thracians who have straight hair (*euthytriches*), Aristotle makes a reference to the woolly hair (*oulotriches*) of Ethiopians, and associates this with their brains: "Ethiopians (*Aithiopes*) and people who live in hot regions have woolly hair, because both their brains (*enkephaloi*) and the environing air are dry (*zēroi*)."[37]

Economic and military domain

Ancient Roman literature is filled with many examples of a recognizable level of contempt for the native Egyptians. Once Augustus (Octavian) took control of the empire in 30 BCE, Egypt became an exploited and conquered territory under the personal domain of the emperor.[38] He added "Egypt" to the empire through calculated military force. When Augustus took over Egypt, he also claimed the kingdom of Meroë, south of the first cataract, which was occupied by Ethiopians. Many from "both races" (i.e., Egyptians and Ethiopians) were killed as a result of the military campaigns of Augustus. In the *Res gestae*, Augustus set forth a summary of his deeds and accomplishments as the new leader of the Roman Empire; he summarized his dealings with Egypt and Ethiopia as follows:

> By my command and under my auspices two armies were led almost
> at the same time, one into Ethiopia, the other into that part of

Arabia which is called Felix; and large forces of the enemy belonging
to both races were killed in battle, and many towns captured. In
Ethiopia the army advanced as far as Napata, the nearest station to
Meroë; in Arabia to the borders of the Sabaei to the town of Mariba.
Egypt I added to the empire of the Roman people.[39]

Mainly because of trade and economic reasons, Egypt was kept under the
direct authority of the emperor,[40] and provided approximately one-third of the
annual grain supply of Rome.[41] It was too rich and valuable a territory to entrust
to the standard mode of administration. Thus Augustus treated Egypt as his own
territory. He assigned Gaius Cornelius Gallus, an equestrian, to serve as its first
governor,[42] and imposed severe taxes on the land.

The *Kandakē* (Queen) of Ethiopia was a major threat to the Romans. Strabo
describes how she and her army captured the Thebaid.[43] Gallus crushed the
attack and established the first cataract as Rome's southern frontier.[44] Cassius
Dio summarizes another encounter between Gaius Petronius and the Ethiopians:

> About this same time *the Ethiopians (hoi Aithiopes)*, who dwell *beyond
> Egypt (hyper Aigyptou)*, advanced as far as the city called Elephantine,
> with the *Kandakē* as their leader, ravaging everything they encoun-
> tered. At Elephantine, however, learning that Gaius Petronius, the
> governor of Egypt, was approaching, they hastily retreated before
> he arrived, hoping to make good their escape . . . for Petronius,
> finding himself unable either to advance farther, on account of the
> sand and the heat, or advantageously to remain where he was with
> his entire army, withdrew, taking the greater part of it [the army]
> with him. Thereupon the *Ethiopians (tōn Aithiopōn)* attacked the
> garrisons, but he again proceeded against them, rescued his own
> men, and compelled the *Kandakē* to make terms with him.[45]

Social and political status

The social and legal status of Egyptians was a point of confusion for many Greco-
Roman authors. The citizens of the three Greek cities (Alexandria, Ptolemais,
and Naukratis) had privileges that distinguished them from the remainder of
the Egyptian population.[46] Roman citizenship was not given to an Egyptian
unless he or she first held the citizenship of Alexandria. Alexandria, which the
Romans called *Alexandria ad Aegyptum*, became the political and economic
capital of Roman Egypt.[47] Pliny the Younger provides an important example
of the overall confusion among the ancients relating to citizenship status of the
Egyptians:

> I was reminded by people more experienced than I am that, since
> the man is an *Egyptian (Aegyptius)*, I ought not to have asked for

Roman citizenship for him before he became a citizen of Alexandria. I had not realized that there was any distinction between *Egyptians* and other aliens, so I had thought it sufficient to inform you only that he had been given his freedom by an alien and that his patron had died some time ago.[48]

The Romans determined citizenship based on their categories of legal status: First, those who held Roman citizenship; second, the citizens (*astoi*) of the three Greek cities of Egypt; and third, non-citizens or "Egyptians."[49]

Moral–spiritual characterization

Egyptians, Ethiopians, and Blacks/blackness were often used within Greco-Roman writings to symbolize immoral behavior. In this regard, color symbolism became a useful means for communicating values about good and evil or right and wrong behavior. Ethiopians and Blacks were used not only to symbolize evil and demonic activity, but also, by some Greco-Roman authors, to exemplify the virtuous. In addition, Egyptians, Ethiopians, and Blacks were often used as symbols of sexual vice. In this section, five categories have been identified: (1) character description, (2) color symbolization, (3) demons and evil, (4) models of "virtue," and (5) sexual objects.

Character description

The color black (*melas*) was associated with immorality throughout Greco-Roman literature. The Greek poet Pindar (b. 522 BCE) uses the term *melaina* to describe the *hardened heart* (*melainan kardian*) that had turned away from God.[50] According to Aristotle (fourth century BCE), Egyptians and Ethiopians possessed a character trait of cowardice (*deilos*) because of their black (*melanes*) complexion:

> Those who are too *black* (*agan melanes*) are cowards; this applies to *Egyptians and Ethiopians* (*Aigyptious, Aithiopas*). But the excessively white are also cowardly; witness women. But the complexion that tends to courage is in between these two.[51]

Plutarch, a first-century CE moralist, advises a young man not to spend his time with those prone to evil: "Do not taste of black-tails (*melanourōn*)"; that is, "do not spend your time with blackened men (*melasin anthrōpois*), because of their malevolence (*kakoētheian*)."[52] The ancient geographer Strabo considered the Egyptians "savage" (*oxy*) and "not inclined to be civil (*apolitikon*)."[53] The Jewish philosopher and exegete Philo (20 BCE – 50 CE) indicated how elite Jewish authors adopted the Greco-Roman tendency of displaying negative attitudes against Egyptians. In his work entitled *Flaccus*, Philo described a situation in which a number of Jewish elders were dragged into the theater and scourged with a whip before an Alexandrian mob that had flocked together to watch the spectacle.

> There are differences between the scourges used in the city, and these differences are regulated by the social standing of the persons to be beaten. The Egyptians (*Aigyptious*) actually are scourged with a different kind of lash and by a different set of people, the Alexandrians (*Alexandreas*) with a flat blade, and the persons who wield them also are Alexandrians (*Alexandreōn*).[54]

In addition to Philo, the Jewish historian Josephus (37–ca. 97 CE) similarly demonstrated how Egyptians (*Aigyptioi*) were held in negative regard by Greeks, Romans, and elite Jews. In his rebuttal to Apion, who had labeled his Jewish adversaries *Aigyptioi*, Josephus says:

> That he should lie about our ancestors and assert that they were *Egyptians by race* (*to genos Aigyptious*) is by no means surprising. He told a lie, which was the reverse of this one about himself. Born in the Egyptian oasis, more Egyptian than them all, as one might say, he disowned his true country and falsely claimed to be an Alexandrian, thereby admitting the ignominy of his race. *It is therefore natural that he should call persons whom he detests and wishes to abuse Egyptians. Had he not had the meanest opinion of natives of Egypt* (*Aigyptious*), *he would never have turned his back on his own nation* (*to genos*) [emphasis mine].[55]

Josephus further discussed the bad reputation of the Egyptians:

> In their relation to us, Egyptians (*Aigyptioi*) are swayed by one of two feelings: either they feign to be our kinsmen in order to gain prestige, or else they drag us into their ranks to share their bad reputation (*kakodoxias*).[56]

Color symbolism

Greco-Roman authors also described moral attributes in terms of white/black color symbolism. For example, in a Latin collection of legends from the third century CE, Pseudo-Callisthenes provides an account of Alexander the Great's visit to one of the Candaces in her palace in Meroë in the fourth century BCE. He found her to be "of wondrous beauty," but she was reported to have said of her people during the conversation, "We are whiter and brighter in our souls than the whitest of you."[57] An anonymous third-century epitaph of a black slave from Antinoe in Roman Egypt says:

among the living I was very *black* (*melanteros*), darkened by the rays of the sun. But beauty is less important than nobility of soul; and my soul (*psychē*), ever blooming with the whiteness (*leukois*) of flowers, attracted the goodwill of my prudent master and embellished the *blackness* (*melainan*) of my physical appearance.[58]

This epitaph was hardly written by the slave. It is evidence of the master's social perceptions, which are imposed on the slave – even when dead! Another example comes from the fourth-century CE Latin poet Ausonius, who makes a connection between the dark complexion and "white soul" of his grandmother, Aemilia Corinthia Maura. He discusses how she received her name and emphasizes that her name was not a reflection of her inner soul.

Her name was given her in play, because of her *dark* (*fusca*) complexion she was called Maura in old days by her girl-friends. But she was not dark in her soul (*atra animo*), which was whiter (*candidior*) than a swan and brighter than untrodden snow.[59]

The association of whiteness and blackness with moral attributes became a common rhetorical strategy throughout many types of ancient writings.[60]

Demons and evil

Demons represent the most widespread depiction of Ethiopians, Egyptians, and Blacks in Greco-Roman literature.[61] Demons (Gk. *daimōn*) in the ancient world denoted gods and lesser deities, intermediary beings, spirits of the dead, or in some cases ghosts.[62] They are in many instances understood as representatives of the underworld. Suetonius uses both Egyptians and Ethiopians to describe scenes from the underworld: A nocturnal performance in which scenes from the lower world were represented by Egyptians and Ethiopians.[63] Lucian describes a long-haired demon "blacker than darkness" (*melanteros tou zophou*):

He was filthy and long-haired and blacker than darkness (*melanteros tou zophou*) itself. Standing over me, he made an attempt on me, attacking from all sides to see if he could conquer me, changing himself now into a dog, now into a bull or lion. But I had ready the most horrible Egyptian curse, and speaking in the Egyptian tongue I drove him away and bound him in a corner of a dark room.[64]

When the emperor Domitian wanted to terrorize his more important subjects, he would invite them to dinner in a room decorated in black and entertain them with dances by slave-boys painted black like ghosts.

And first he set beside each of them a slab shaped like a gravestone, bearing the guest's name and also a small lamp, such as hang in tombs. Next comely naked boys, likewise painted black, entered like phantoms, and after encircling the guests in an awe-inspiring dance took up their stations at their feet.[65]

Models of "virtue"

Egyptians, Ethiopians, and Blacks were not always associated with demons in Greco-Roman literature. There are some examples in which they are considered virtuous figures. In one of Martial's epigrams, a certain black girl is represented as desirable. She was called "blacker than night" (*nocte nigriorem*) and preferred over a certain girl who was whiter than a washed swan (*loto candidior puella cygno*):

> A certain girl wants me (envy me, Procillus),
> one whiter than a washed swan,
> than silver, than snow, than lilies, than privet.
> But I want a certain girl, one *blacker* than night,
> or ant, or pitch, or crow, or cricket.
> Already you were thinking of the cruel rope.
> If I know you well, Procillus, you will live on.[66]

Sexual threats

Ethiopian males were viewed as sexual objects by many Roman authors and poets. The Roman satirist Juvenal, who was exiled to Syene in Egypt by Domitian, describes the consequences of women having adulterous relations with Ethiopian males:

> But how often does a gilded bed contain a woman that is lying in? So great is the skill, so powerful the drugs, of the abortionist, paid to murder mankind within the womb. Rejoice, poor wretch; give her the stuff to drink whatever it be, with your own hand: for were she willing to get big and trouble her womb with bouncing babes, you might perhaps find yourself the father of an *Ethiopian* (*Aethiopis*); and some day a *coloured* (*decolor*) heir, whom you would rather not meet by daylight, would fill all the places in your will.[67]

According to Pliny the Elder, a general would send a "black with an extremely large phallus" to a lady, who would regard him as a precious gift.[68] Pliny also describes the ways in which African males were used as political pawns among Roman aristocrats. For example, there was a consul who feared that his wife would find sexual interest in his political enemy while he was away serving the emperor in a foreign land. He sent his wife an African male to keep her occupied, to prevent her interest from wandering to his political enemy.[69]

Descriptive differentiation

Greco-Roman authors were consumed with describing the unique physical attributes of Egyptians, Ethiopians, and Blacks. In most cases the physical descriptions were not intended to communicate any negative regard for these ethnic groups. Yet, in some instances the physical descriptions did serve to communicate ideas and values about the aesthetic sensibilities that were operative within ancient Mediterranean culture. There are also many examples in which the terms "Ethiopian" or "Black" are used as names of individuals. In this section, three major categories have been identified: (1) physical description, (2) name or title, and (3) aesthetic sensibilities.

Physical description

Greco-Roman literature is filled with physical descriptions of Egyptians, Ethiopians, and Blacks.[70] The chief characteristics for Ethiopians mentioned throughout the literature include black skin (*melanchrous*), woolly hair (*oulotriches*), thick lips (*procheilos*), flat nose (*simotēs*), and bow-legs (*crura in orbem*). Homer describes Eurybates, the cohort of Odysseus, as having a dark complexion (*melanochroos*) and woolly hair (*oulokarēnos*).[71] Philostratus concludes that Ethiopians are "black men (*anthrōpous melanas*) – a feature not found in other continents – and we meet in them with races of pygmies (*ethnē Pygmaiōn*) and of people who bark in various ways instead of talking, and other wonders of the kind."[72]

Sextus Empiricus (third century CE) contrasts the snub-nose of the Ethiopian with the hook-nose of the Persian: "the Ethiopian preferring the blackest and most snub-nosed, and the Persian approving the whitest and most hook-nosed . . ."[73] While some ancient authors describe Ethiopians as the tallest and most beautiful people of all (*megistoi kai kallistoi anthrōpōn pantōn*),[74] others describe them as pygmies (*pēcheis*). For example, Philostratus (third century CE) describes Nile-dwelling pygmies as follows:

> About the Nile the pygmies (*pēcheis*): they are sporting children no taller than their name implies; and the Nile delights in them for many reasons, but particularly because they herald its coming in great floods for the *Egyptians (Aigyptiois)*.[75]

The *Appendix Virgiliana* (first century CE) provides one of the most detailed descriptions of an African woman.[76] Eight physical traits are mentioned:

> African in race (*Afra genus*), her whole figure proof of her country – her hair tightly curled, lips thick, *color dark (fusca colore)*, chest broad, breasts pendulous, belly somewhat pinched, legs thin, and feet broad and simple.[77]

The Greek physician Galen (second century CE), in his textbook on anatomy, included a list of ten traits he claimed were associated with Ethiopians: (1) thick lips, (2) broad nostrils, (3) frizzy hair, (4) black eyes, (5) furrowed hands and feet, (6) thin eyebrows, (7) pointed teeth, (8) smelly skin, (9) long penis, and (10) great merriment.[78] He further claimed that Ethiopians had defective brains.[79] Although several scholars question whether this list of physical characteristics should be attributed to Galen, anthropologist St. Clair Drake claims that Galen's views would have been available to sanction and reinforce pejorative attitudes about and discriminatory behavior toward Ethiopians within early Christianity.[80]

Greek and Latin writers also described Egyptians as black or dark-skinned. For example, Herodotus described Egyptians as black in two sections of Book 2 of his *Histories*. The first occurrence is as follows:

> The Dodonaeans called the women doves because they were foreigners, and seemed to them to make a noise like birds. After a while the dove spoke with a human voice, because the woman, whose foreign talk had previously sounded to them like the chattering of a bird, acquired the power of speaking what they could understand. For how can it be conceived possible that a dove should really speak with the voice of a man? Lastly, by calling the dove black the Dodonaeans indicated that the woman was an Egyptian.[81]

The second occurrence is in his discussion about the Colchians, in which he describes them as

> an Egyptian race . . . My own conjectures were founded, first, on the fact that they are black-skinned and have woolly hair, which certainly amounts to but little, since several nations are so too.[82]

Ammianus Marcellinus, Latin historian and friend of the emperor Julian, provides a vivid physical description of Egyptians:

> Now the men of *Egypt* are, as a rule, *somewhat swarthy* (*subfusculi*) and *dark* of complexion (*atrati*), and rather gloomy-looking, slender and dried-up, excitable in all their movements, quarrelsome, and demanding.[83]

In Lucian's second-century CE text entitled *The Ship or the Wishes*, Lycinus describes a young Egyptian shipbuilder (*Aigyptios naupēgos*):

> This fellow is not only *dark-skinned* (*melanchrous*), but thick-lipped (*proxeilos*) and too thin in the leg. He spoke in a slovenly manner, one long, continuous prattle; he spoke Greek, but his accent and

intonation pointed to his native-land. His hair coiled in a plait behind shows he is not freeborn.[84]

These examples indicate how Greco-Roman authors were not consistent in their descriptions of Egyptians and Ethiopians. They often associated dark or black skin with either group of people.

Name or title

The color-symbolic term "black" was also used as a name or title within Greco-Roman literature. A second-century BCE army list gives the names of two Ptolemaic soldiers called Apollonios, qualifying one as Black (*melas*) and the other as White (*leukos*).[85] Classicist A.M. Devine, in a brief philological essay, examines the use of *melas* in this example, and concludes that it does not signify racial overtones or indicate that Apollonios was a Black person.[86] Another classicist, Alan Cameron, also provides several examples of the use of *melas* and *leukos* with respect to ancient nicknames.[87] He claims that in an examination of color-coded names a focus on racial connotations misses the point.[88] Cameron suggests that it is more important to determine whether the author intended to indicate the *color* of Apollonios's skin.[89] He concludes that *melas* and *leukos* function as nicknames instead of ethnic markers. The validity of Cameron's findings are questionable in light of other examples of nicknames in the ancient world.[90]

Aesthetic sensibilities

Ethiopians and Blacks, in a very striking way, point to the aesthetic sensibilities operative within Greco-Roman culture, especially in narratives that describe the physical attributes of women. Within Greco-Roman writings, beauty or attractiveness is generally symbolized by whiteness, while ugliness or undesirability is symbolized by blackness. The anonymous third-century epitaph of a black slave cited above exemplifies these color-coded aesthetic sensibilities:

> among the living I was *very black* (*melanteros*), darkened by the rays of the sun. But beauty is less important than nobility of soul; and my soul (*psychē*), ever blooming with the whiteness (*leukois*) of flowers, attracted the goodwill of my prudent master and embellished the *blackness* (*melainan*) of my physical appearance.[91]

Christian Writings

Christian self-definition

The Greco-Roman rhetorical categories identified above are reflected to some degree in early Christian writings. This is not to say that Christian writers adopted without revision the discursive strategies of other Greco-Roman authors; on the contrary, Christians adapted and adjusted the discourses, and even developed their own particular rhetorics about Egyptians/Egypt, Ethiopians/Ethiopia, and Blacks/blackness. These rhetorics functioned within Christian literature as invective and encomium, praise and blame, idealization and vilification. There was no simple or consistent pattern within the literature. One can identify, however, some persuasive discursive strategies of othering within the literature that appealed to commonly held assumptions within the ancient world about the ethnic and color difference of Egyptians, Ethiopians, and Blacks.[92]

This ethnic-othering was established as an acceptable means of discourse because of values about ethnic difference and color symbolism that dominated the Greco-Roman ethos and worldview. Greco-Roman authors were consumed with ethnic difference.[93] Polemical discussions about different ethnic groups were common in the Mediterranean world.[94] Many scholars have identified the verbal wars that took place between Jews and Gentiles in the ancient world, especially within the New Testament.[95] Yet studies about Egyptians, Ethiopians, and Blacks as polemical devices in ancient Christian literature have not received adequate attention. This section will document some examples of how Christian authors adapted and transformed some of the widespread symbolic representations of Egyptians/Egypt, Ethiopians/Ethiopia, and Blacks/blackness within Greco-Roman discourses and even advanced their own original forms of ethno-political rhetorics.

Ethiopian–Scythian antithesis

Within the New Testament, the letter of Colossians includes the formulaic Ethiopian–Scythian antithesis. However, instead of comparing Ethiopians to Scythians, the author of this text compares barbarians and Scythians:

> In the renewal there is no longer Greek and Jew, circumcised and uncircumcised, *barbarian (barbaros)*, *Scythian (Scythēs)*, slave and free; but Christ is all and in all![96]

The author of this text was more than likely elaborating upon the baptism formula used by Paul to demonstrate that being baptized into Christ negates differences based on status, ethnic identity, and gender:

> for in Christ Jesus you are all children of God through faith. As many of you as were baptized into Christ have clothed yourselves with Christ. There is no longer Jew or Greek, there is no longer slave or free, there is no longer male and female; for all of you are one in Christ Jesus. And if you belong to Christ, then you are Abraham's offspring, heirs according to the promise.[97]

Allegorical exegetical interpretation

Some of the church fathers used allegory to interpret Scripture. Most of these authors were concerned with explaining the meaning of the black bride of Solomon in Song of Songs.[98] Origen, in his interpretation of the bride, says the following:

> We ask in what way is she *black* (*melaina*) and in what way *fair* (*kalē*) without whiteness. She has repented of her sins; conversion has bestowed beauty upon her and she is sung as 'beautiful'. If you repent, your soul will be 'black' because of your former sins, but because of your penitence your soul will have something of what I may call an Ethiopian beauty.[99]

The sixth-century writer Gregory of Elvira summarizes the problem of the symbolization of color with respect to the black bride of Solomon by saying:

> I admit to being confused. How can the Church say she is *black and beautiful*, whereas she who is black cannot be beautiful? How can she be black if she is beautiful, or beautiful if she is black? But ponder the mystery of the word, and see with what depth of meaning the Holy Spirit speaks.[100]

The story about the marriage of Moses to a black Ethiopian woman (Num 12:1–16) garnered much attention from many of the patristic writers. Origen interpreted this text as a symbolic union of the spiritual law (Moses) and the church (the Ethiopian woman) – a foreshadowing of the universal church.[101]

Sins and vices

Some Christian authors used Egyptians and Ethiopians to symbolize sins and vices.[102] For example, Tertullian says that "when God threatens Egypt and Ethiopia with extinction, he pronounces sentence on every sinful nation."[103] Origen compared Gentile converts to the black bride of Solomon; though once blackened by sin, they were now whitened by the grace of God.[104] This argument was repeated by Jerome:

> At one time we were *Ethiopians* (*Aethiopes*) in our vices and sins. How so? Because our sins had *blackened* (*nigros fecerant*) us. But afterwards we heard the words: "Wash yourselves clean!" And we said: "Wash me, and I shall be whiter (*dealbabor*) than snow." We are *Ethiopians* (*Aethiopes*), therefore, who have been transformed from *blackness* into whiteness (*candorem*).[105]

In addition to the metaphor of sin, many of the vices that plagued early Christians were associated with the color black (*melas*). For example, in the second-century CE text *Shepherd of Hermas*, the daughters of the vices are dressed in black garments:

> "Hear, also," said he, "the names of the women who have *black garments* (*himatia melana*). Of these also four are more powerful. The first is Unbelief, the second Impurity, the third Disobedience, and the fourth Deceit; and those who follow them are called Grief, Wickedness, Licentiousness, Bitterness, Lying, Foolishness, Evil-speaking, Hate. The servant of God who bears these names shall see the Kingdom of God, but shall not enter into it."[106]

The author of the *Shepherd of Hermas* also uses the black mountain (*orous tou melanos*) to describe those who have turned against the faith:

> From the first mountain, *the black one* (*tou melanos*), are such believers as these: apostates and blasphemers against the Lord, and betrayers of the servants of God. For these there is no repentance, but there is death, and for this cause they also are *black* (*melanes*), for their way (*genos*) is lawless (*anomon*).[107]

Demons and evil

Egyptians, Ethiopians, and Blacks are represented as demons or the devil throughout Christian writings from the first century CE through late antiquity. In the late first-century text *Epistle of Barnabas*, the devil appears as the Black One (*ho melas*):

> Wherefore, let us pay heed in the last days, for the whole time of our life and faith will profit us nothing unless we resist, as becomes the sons of God in this present evil time, against the offences which are to come, that *the Black One* (*ho melas*) may have no opportunity of entry.[108]

> But the way of the *Black One* (*ho melas*) is crooked and full of cursing, for it is the way of death eternal with punishment, and in it are the things that destroy their soul: idolatry, forwardness, arrogance of power, hypocrisy, double-heartedness, adultery, murder, robbery, pride, transgression, fraud, malice, self-sufficiency, enchantments, magic, covetousness, the lack of the fear of God.[109]

In the *Acts of Peter* (180–200 CE), a female demon is described as "a most evil-looking woman, an *Aithiops* not *Aigyptios*, but altogether *melas*."[110] In another section of the *Acts of Peter*, Satan is a black (*melas*) enemy of Christ, the source of wickedness and abyss of darkness, who shoots poisoned arrows at the souls of innocent Christians.[111] The Black One (*ho melas*) also appears as a name for demons in late antique papyri.[112]

Within several early Christian writings the devil is also associated with the Egyptian (*ho Aigyptios*). For example, in the early third-century martyrdom text *Passio Perpetuae et Felicitatis*, Perpetua in a dream fights with the Egyptian (*ho Aigyptios*) opponent who was identified as the devil (*ho diabolos*). Most interpretations of this text focus upon Perpetua's transformation into a male.[113] Yet there is also much significance in the use of *ho Aigyptios* within the text.[114] Closer inspection of her dream indicates that the Egyptian opponent functioned within the text as a rhetorical device to advance the importance of martyrdom.

> Then there came forth against me a certain *Egyptian* (*Aigyptios tis*), horrible in appearance, along with his assistants, ready to fight with me. There came also to me comely young men as my assistants and helpers. I was smoothed down and I became male. And they began to rub me down with oil as is customary for a contest. And I saw the *Egyptian* (*ton Aigyption*) rolling in the dust.[115]

Ethiopians and Blacks are personified as demons throughout monastic literature.[116] One well-known example is Antony's encounter with the devil, who appeared in the form of a black boy (*melas pais*).[117] Another example is contained in the story of Abba Apollo who was in charge of a large monastery in the Thebaid. In this story a small Ethiopian declares, "I am the demon of arrogance."[118]

Models of "virtue"

In the New Testament, the Ethiopian eunuch in Acts 8:26 is depicted as a model of ancient Christian virtue. Luke uses this figure, who would have been considered "other" or "foreign" to his audience, to demonstrate that Christianity could break through cultural and ethnic differences.

In later ascetic writings, the desert father Ethiopian Moses is another model of ancient Christian virtue. He is venerated as a model of virtue because of his extreme acts of humility and self-control in the face of challenge and chastisement:

> The archbishop, wishing to put him to the test, said to the clerics, "When Father Moses comes into the sanctuary, drive him out, and go along with him to hear what he says." So the old man came in and they rebuked him and drove him out, saying, "*Go away, Ethiopian* (*Hypage exō Aithiops*)." He left and said to himself, "Rightly have they treated you, *ash skin, Black one* (*spododerme, melane*). As you are not a human, why should you come among humans?"[119]

The collectors and editors of such stories use color-symbolic language to demonstrate that a black-skinned Ethiopian can achieve ascetic virtue in spite of his ethnic and color difference.[120] In both of these examples, general attitudes within the larger Greco-Roman society influenced the polemical use of these Ethiopians.

Heresies

Ambrose, the fourth-century bishop of Milan (375–97 CE) set up a striking association between the "black" church and the heretical movements Manichaeism and Arianism. Ambrose claims that the church (*ecclesia*) was formerly "black (*fusca*) in broad daylight," but later "shone brightly in the night." Now she is white, having been cleansed of the Manichaean and Arian heresies: she receives the dual illumination of the Old and New Testaments, which she unites and fulfills.[121]

Another example of the association of Blacks with heretical sects is found in the fifth-century text entitled the *Life of Melania the Younger*:

> Just then the Devil threw the souls of simple people into great trouble through the *polluted doctrine of Nestorius*. Therefore many of the wives of senators and some of the men illustrious in learning came to our holy mother in order to investigate the orthodox faith with her. And she, who had the Holy Spirit indwelling, did not cease talking theology from dawn to dusk. She turned many who had been deceived to the orthodox faith and sustained others who doubted; quite simply, she benefited all those who chanced to come to her divinely-inspired teaching. Thus the Devil, the enemy of truth, was very jealous both on account of those who came to her for edification and on account of her uncle's salvation. He changed into a *young black man* (*melana neaniskon*) and came to her, and said the following: "For how long do you destroy my hopes through your words? Know, then, that if I am strong enough to harden the hearts of Lausus and the emperors . . . if not, I inflict on your body such tortures that you will fear even for your life, so that you may be kept silent by necessity."[122]

Sexual threats

The sexual danger that Ethiopians presented to the desert fathers is well attested in the monastic literature from the fourth through sixth centuries CE. For example, Palladius, in a work entitled "Of Fornication," describes devils who appear in the form of Ethiopians. These Ethiopians incite a monk to yield to his sexual passions.[123] In another example, Cassian describes an Ethiopian who appears outside a monk's cell and shoots an arrow into its occupant; overcome by sexual passion, the monk runs about as if in a frenzy.[124]

Ethiopian women were also depicted as sexual threats within the ascetic and monastic literature from Egypt of the late fourth and early fifth centuries. The need to control sexual passions took on an increased level of intensity when Ethiopian women were involved. The physical descriptions of the Ethiopian women within these texts are more detailed and graphic than the physical descriptions of Ethiopian men. A notable example follows:

> Twenty days passed when, suddenly, he saw the work of the devil appear before him, "and it stood before him in the form of an *Ethiopian woman* (*magnitudinis Aethiopem*), smelly and disgusting (*turpissimum*) in appearance, so much so that he could not bear her smell. She then said to him, 'In the hearts of men I smell sweet, but because of your obedience and your labor, God does not permit me to lead you astray, but I have let you know my smell.'" When the man returned to his father he said that he no longer wished to go into the world for he had seen the work of the devil and had smelled her foul odor.[125]

This example indicates how Ethiopian women were often associated with body odors. Body odor became a distinguishing feature within monastic writings for indicating the boundaries between the pure and polluted, the insiders and outsiders among the desert dwellers. The stench of the Ethiopian woman became a symbol for the enduring sexual threat she represented to the monks.

Two other examples shed light on how Ethiopian women were depicted in monastic writings. Palladius, in the *Lausiac History*, provides an account of a monk who was tempted by the sensuous vision of an Ethiopian girl gathering ears of corn.[126] In the *Apophthegmata patrum* a monk, surrounded by fifty demons, performed indecent sex acts with two Ethiopian women.[127] These and other examples provide an important lens through which the intersection of ethnicity and gender in the writings of the desert fathers can be analyzed.

Military threats

Rufinus of Aquileia's description of a group of Ethiopians leads one to believe that they were a powerful military force in the early fifth century.

> A . . . story is told of a general who went to . . . inquire whether he would overcome the *Ethiopians*, who at that time had fallen on Syene – which stands on the frontier of the Thebaid – and had devastated the surrounding country. John said to him, "If you march against them, you will take them by surprise and defeat them and subdue them and you will find favour with the emperors." And that is what actually happened, the event proving as John had predicted. He also

47

said, "The most Christian Emperor Theodosius will die a natural death."[128]

Palladius also identifies the military threat of the nomadic group of Ethiopians known as Blemmyes. He says in the *Dialogue on the Life of St. John Chrysostom* that he "was kept under guard near the Blemmyes or the Ethiopians at a place called Syene."[129] In the *Lausiac History*, Palladius wrote about the monasteries of Tabennesi in the Thebaid, which were crowded with refugees who had fled from the Blemmyes (*ethnos tōn Blemmyōn*) who were plundering Upper Egypt.[130]

Symbolics of geographical location

In the New Testament, Matthew includes a geographical reference to Egypt (Matt 2:13–15). Within this context, it appears that Egypt was a place of refuge for Joseph and his family and was a fulfillment of prophecy.[131]

> Now after they had left, an angel of the Lord appeared to Joseph in a dream and said, "Get up, take the child and his mother, and flee *to Egypt* (*eis Aigypton*), and remain there until I tell you; for Herod is about to search for the child, to destroy him." Then Joseph got up, took the child and his mother by night, and went *to Egypt* (*eis Aigypton*), and remained there until the death of Herod. This was to fulfill what had been spoken by the Lord through the prophet, *"Out of Egypt* (*ex Aigyptou*) I have called my son."[132]

Throughout Acts 7, Luke uses the land of Egypt in Peter's speech as a symbolic reminder of God's plan of salvation for the people of Israel.[133] In particular, Acts 7:22 states that "Moses was instructed in all the wisdom of the Egyptians (*pasē(i) sophia(i) Aigyptiōn*)."[134] The brief letter of Jude also includes a reference to the land of Egypt: "Now I desire to remind you, though you are fully informed, that the Lord, who once for all saved a people out of the land of Egypt (*ek gēs Aigyptou*), afterward destroyed those who did not believe."[135] These geographical references to Egypt within the New Testament take on symbolic meaning within these texts for both theological and discursive purposes. The experiences of the people of Israel in the land of Egypt is central for understanding God's plan of salvation for the early Christians. In a much later monastic text, Egypt is used to describe the birthplace of a repentant sinner known as Mary: "My homeland, father, was Egypt (*Aigypton*). I lived with my parents but when I was only twelve years old I spurned their care and went into Alexandria."[136]

Ethiopia and Ethiopians also take on symbolic geographical meaning in Christian writings. For example, Luke's reference to the Ethiopian eunuch in Acts 8:27 is used as the fulfillment of Acts 1:8c, which suggests that

Christianity is to extend to the ends of the earth (*eschatou tēs gēs*). Augustine also viewed Ethiopians as those who dwelled at the ends of the earth (*finibus terrae est*) and he used Ethiopians (*Aethiopes*) to symbolize the inclusive (universal) nature of the catholic church.

> The Catholic Church has been foretold not to be in any particular quarter of the world, as certain schisms are, but in the whole universe, by bearing fruit and growing even unto the very *Ethiopians* (*Aethiopes*), indeed the remotest and blackest (*teterrimos*) of men.[137]

Name or title

There are several examples throughout early Christian writings in which "Egyptian," "Ethiopian," or "Black" are used as names or titles. In the New Testament Luke refers to Simeon as *Niger*.[138] In Acts 21:37–39 Luke also depicts a Roman tribune as misidentifying Paul for the Egyptian (*ho Aigyptios*) insurrectionist who had been known for starting riots:

> Just as Paul was about to be brought into the barracks, he said to the tribune, "May I say something to you?" The tribune replied, "Do you know Greek (*Hellēnisti*)? Then you are not *the Egyptian* (*ho Aigyptios*) who recently stirred up a revolt and led the four thousand assassins out into the wilderness?" Paul replied, "I am a Jew (*Ioudaios*), from Tarsus in Cilicia, a citizen of an important city; I beg you, let me speak to the people."[139]

Why did Luke present Paul in this way?[140] Was this a reference to an actual historical situation,[141] or was Luke utilizing a particular rhetorical strategy within this narrative that reflected general social attitudes about ethnic difference? I contend that Luke's use of ethnic markers in this text (*Hellēnisti*, *Aigyptios*, and *Ioudaios*) signal, among other things, a polemical strategy in which "the Egyptian" is used as a foil to establish the importance of Paul and his mission within early Christianity. In the *Epistle of Barnabas* the Black One is used as a generic name or label for some form of evil within the community.[142] Ethiopian Moses or Moses the Black is another example of the use of an ethnic name or title.[143]

Color symbolization

Color symbolism is used in the New Testament to refer to those who represent the threat of sin. The author of the brief letter of Jude instructs his readers about "certain intruders" (*tines anthrōpoi*) who have entered the community.[144] The author does not specifically refer to *melas* in this text, but the intruders are associated with darkness (*skotos*):

These are blemishes on your lovefeasts, while they feast with you without fear, feeding themselves. They are waterless clouds carried along by the winds; autumn trees without fruit, twice dead, uprooted; wild waves of the sea, casting up the foam of their own shame; wandering stars, for whom the deepest darkness (*skotos*) has been reserved forever.[145]

Among patristic writers, darkness became a major theme for discussing the presence of sin. Light came to the Gentiles once they turned from their life of sin:

Very glistening are the pearls of Ethiopia, as it is written, Who gave thee *to Ethiopia {the land} of black men*. He that gave light to the Gentiles, both to the Ethiopians and unto the Indians did His bright beams reach. The eunuch of Ethiopia upon his chariot saw Philip: the Lamb of Light met the dark man from out of the bath. While he was reading, the Ethiopian was baptized and glistened with joy, and journeyed on! He made disciples and taught, and out of black men he made men white {as snow}. And the *dark Ethiopic women* became pearls for the Son; He offered them up to the Father, as a glistening crown from the Ethiopians.[146]

Aesthetic sensibilities

Among Christian authors the Ethiopian symbolized aesthetic values that were deeply embedded in Greco-Roman culture. Monastic authors of late antique Egypt were especially obsessed with aesthetic values of beauty and attractiveness. In many of the *Sayings of the Desert Fathers* the monks were tempted and seduced by "very good-looking and beautiful women."[147] Usually, these women were presumed to be white women; but in some instances, the authors indicated the attractiveness of the black or Ethiopian woman. In one example, an Ethiopian woman is represented as the opposite of beauty: "she recognized her husband, but he could not recognize her; so much her beauty had disappeared to the point where she looked like an *Ethiopian woman*."[148]

Summary

From the foregoing taxonomy of rhetorical categories, it is clear that there was a rich socio-political, cultural, and literary climate within which ancient Christian authors developed their ethno-political rhetorics about Egyptians/ Egypt, Ethiopians/Ethiopia, and Blacks/blackness. This taxonomy identifies only a few representative examples of the various types of rhetorics within Greco-Roman literature as a way of establishing the complex symbolic functions of references to these ethnic groups, geographical locations, and color symbols.

Moreover, this taxonomy documents the fact that Greco-Roman writers were aware of the otherness of these ethnic groups and geographical locations, and likewise associated the color black and blackness with evil and demonic activities. Both virtuous and vituperative depictions of these peoples, places, and color symbols were operative within the discursive strategies of various authors.[149] It is difficult to assess the level of first-hand experience Greco-Roman authors may have had with these groups. What is more important for this study is that there was a pattern among the ancient writers that emphasized the rhetorical utility of these ethnic groups for advancing certain values and ideas within their communities. The various rhetorical tropes identified in this chapter provide a springboard for a review of early Christian rhetorics about Egyptians/Egypt, Ethiopians/Ethiopia, and Blacks/blackness.

The taxonomy developed in this chapter also documents how ancient Christian authors adapted, and even exaggerated at times, the patterns that existed in Greco-Roman literature. In many instances Christian authors generated their own particular rhetorics that became useful for defining threats and dangers within their respective communities. A taxonomy of ethno-political rhetorics related to Egyptians/Egypt, Ethiopians/Ethiopia, and Blacks/blackness in ancient Christian literature enables scholars to better understand the controversies and challenges that shaped the development of early Christianity. The second part of this book will examine more closely the use of ethno-political rhetorics in early Christian writings.

Part 2

READING ETHNO-POLITICAL RHETORICS IN EARLY CHRISTIAN LITERATURE

3

"WE WERE ETHIOPIANS IN OUR VICES AND SINS": ETHNO-POLITICAL RHETORICS DEFINING VICES AND SINS

At one time we were Ethiopians in our vices and sins. How so? Because our sins had blackened us. But afterwards we heard the words: "Wash yourselves clean!" And we said: "Wash me, and I shall be whiter than snow. We are Ethiopians, therefore, who have been transformed from blackness into whiteness."

(Jerome, *Homily 18 on Psalm 86*)

INTRODUCTION

Jerome (348–420 CE) reflects a general polemical use of Ethiopians in ancient Christian literature. In his homily on Psalm 86, Jerome casts Ethiopians as symbols of vices and sins. In this psalm several nations are mentioned, which Jerome interprets by way of allegory. He uses "Ethiopians" in this sermon as a springboard for launching an understanding of "the calling of the Gentiles" (*aduocationem gentium*):

So far, the psalmist has been speaking almost enigmatically, but now he speaks more plainly of the calling of the Gentiles, for notice what he says: "Of Philistia, Tyre, the people of Ethiopia (*populus Aethiopium*): 'These were born there.' " [1] He designates Philistines to distinguish them from the Jews, for we are the Philistines. "Tyre." Tyre connotes tribulation, or SOR. *"The people of Ethiopia": black and cloaked in the filth of sin* (*niger, et in peccatorum sordibus inuolutus*). "The people of Ethiopia." We find the same typology in the verse: "Let Ethiopia extend its hands to God." [2] "Of Philistia, Tyre, the people

55

of Ethiopia." Now for the meaning: . . . "And the people of Ethiopia." At one time we were *Ethiopians, Ethiopians in our vices and sins* (*Aethiopes uitiis atque peccatis*). How so? *Because our sins had blackened us* (*quoniam peccata nos nigros fecerant*). But afterwards we heard the words: "Wash yourselves clean!"[3] And we said: "Wash me, and I shall be whiter than snow."[4] We are Ethiopians, therefore, who have been *transformed [from blackness] into whiteness [candorem]*. "Of Philistia, Tyre, and the people of Ethiopia: 'These were born there.'" Where were they born? "Glorious things are said of you, O city of God!" These were born there: in the city of God.[5]

After Jerome provides a brief explanation of the function of Philistia and Tyre in the text, he proceeds to establish a typology for understanding the people of Ethiopia:[6] "'the people of Ethiopia': black and cloaked in the filth of sin." He finds in this psalm a heuristic key for explaining the value of penance and spiritual transformation for early Christians. He pulls his audience into the sermon by saying, "at one time we were Ethiopians – Ethiopians in our vices and sins." Jerome not only equates Ethiopians with vices and sins; he also embellishes this sermon with color-symbolic language that links the sin of *Aethiopes* with *nigros*: "our sins had blackened us" (*peccata nos nigros fecerant*). He uses these words to exhort his audience to spiritual transformation from "blackness" (*niger*) to "whiteness" (*candor*).[7] For Jerome, those who have strayed from the faith, regardless of their ethnic identity or social location, are labeled "Ethiopians" (*Aethiopes*) and "blackened" (*nigros fecerant*) by their sins (*peccata*).[8]

Jerome was not the only patristic writer to use Ethiopians as polemical devices. In other major regions of the empire Tertullian, Origen, Augustine, and many others used Ethiopians as tropes within their commentaries, homilies, and theological treatises to shape an understanding of vices and sins within the early church.[9] In this chapter, I consider several representative examples of this phenomenon in order to examine how the discursive uses of Ethiopians and Blacks within these patristic writings had both theological and political implications. The patristic authors routinely reflected in their writings the prevailing attitudes among Christians that equated sin with blackness and salvation with whiteness. In addition, some patristic fathers referred to the color "black" or "the Black One" not only as interpretation of the Scriptures ("Old Testament"), but as symbols for discussing political realities related to the barbarian invasions threatening the empire.

In some cases the discussion about vices and sins in these commentaries, homilies, and theological treatises refers to specific political situations that troubled the respective audiences of these texts. One example of this may be found in a letter from Jerome, written in 396 CE, in which it was apparent that he was aware of the barbarian threat to the empire by the Goths during the fourth and fifth centuries:[10]

We have long felt that God is offended, but we do nothing to placate him. It is *because of our sins that the barbarians are strong, through our vices that the Roman army is defeated* [emphasis mine]; and as if this were not enough of disaster, almost as much destruction has been wreaked by civil wars as by the sword of the enemy. Wretched were the Israelites, in comparison with whom Nebuchadnezzar is described as a servant of God; unhappy are we, who displease God so much that his anger rages against us through the fury of the barbarians. Hezekiah repented, and one hundred and eighty five thousand Assyrians were wiped out by one angel in a single night. Jehoshaphat sang praises to the Lord, and the Lord repaid him with victory. Moses fought Amalek not with a sword but with prayer. If we want to be raised up, let us cast ourselves down. For shame! How unbelievably stupid we are! The Roman army, conqueror and master of the world, is overcome by these barbarians, trembles before them, is terrified to look at them, when they cannot even walk properly and think themselves good as dead as soon as they touch the ground.[11]

Jerome's consolatory letter, which was written to Heliodorus on the occasion of his nephew's death, extended beyond the normal bounds of consolation to reflections on wider societal matters.[12] Apparently aware of the potential downfall of the empire, Jerome viewed the threat of the barbarians as God's response to vices and sins.[13]

In the sermon cited above, Jerome refers to a specific group of barbarians – Ethiopians – as symbols of sin. He uses "Ethiopians" and white/black color dualism to symbolize the vices and sins within his community. Jerome appealed to Ethiopians and the color black to encourage his audience not only in devotion to the church, but also in devotion to the empire. From these two texts of Jerome, one can see how spiritual concerns and political concerns were not mutually exclusive.

Several scholars have identified how Ethiopians and Blacks are associated with sins or vices in Christian writings.[14] Some have even suggested that the blackness of Ethiopians was used as a "metaphor for sin."[15] My focus is to move beyond the "metaphor for sin" motif that isolates Ethiopians and Blacks. Because many patristic authors mention both Ethiopians/Ethiopia and Egyptians/Egypt, and also draw upon assumptions about black/white color symbolism, I will broaden my examination of the sources to examine the rhetorical function of the different references to these ethnic groups, geographical locations, and color symbols for achieving the community formation goals of some patristic authors. In this chapter, I explore how Egyptians/Egypt, Ethiopians/Ethiopia, and Blacks/blackness were used as symbolic tropes in narratives about vices and sins in a representative sample of patristic writings from major urban regions in the East and the West ranging chronologically from the postapostolic period well into late antiquity.[16] But, before I undertake a review of the ethno-political rhetorics, I first want to provide a historical summary of the development of apostolic literature and patristic exegesis in early Christianity. After this background information, I will examine two "apostolic texts" (The *Epistle of Barnabas* and the *Shepherd of Hermas*), and then the texts from two leading church fathers (Tertullian and Origen).

HISTORICAL BACKGROUND: APOSTOLIC AND PATRISTIC LITERATURE IN THE EAST AND WEST

The extant writings generated during what is considered the postapostolic period (ca. 70–135 CE), which are not contained in the New Testament, are known as the "apostolic fathers."[17] These writings were produced during a critical transitional stage in the history of early Christianity. They reflect significant aspects of the character of early Christianity as it was defining itself in the midst of internal conflicts and external persecutions of the late first and second centuries CE. The postapostolic period was a time of great diversity, with many expressions of Christianity vying for legitimacy. The texts generated during this period contain significant Jewish influences and themes. Before the middle of the second century, Christian thought was actually Jewish-Christian and expressed itself in language and symbols that were derived from various forms of Judaism.[18] Christians during this period were more than likely Jews who were holding on to many of their customs and traditions as they attempted to adapt to Christianity. This Jewish–Christian synthesis is evident in texts like the *Epistle of Barnabas* and the *Shepherd of Hermas*, which will be examined later in this chapter.

The postapostolic period was also a time when Christian communities were undergoing internal self-definition. They had not developed systematic doctrine, established a canon of Scriptures, agreed upon forms of government and organization for the church, or established standards of orthodoxy. In addition to these internal developments, early Christian communities were also struggling to define themselves vis-à-vis the Greco-Roman culture and society into which they were expanding.[19] These internal and external factors influenced the discursive strategies of the writings from this period.

The later patristic period was very different from the postapostolic period. Many of the leading patristic writers, mainly from North Africa, Alexandria, and Rome, used Egyptians/Egypt and Ethiopians/Ethiopia in their theological treatises, homilies, and exegetical writings as discursive devices to symbolize the consequences of sin (*hamartia*). The later patristic writers, unlike the earlier apostolic fathers during the first and second centuries, centered their rhetorics about Egyptians/Egypt and Ethiopians/Ethiopia upon biblical passages that mentioned these peoples and places. I will focus upon three regions in this chapter. First, in North Africa church fathers such as Tertullian in the late second and early third centuries used typological interpretation as the key to their biblical hermeneutics.[20] Typology equipped the North African theologians and exegetes with a means for using Scriptures to speak to doctrinal, ecclesiastical, and political concerns within their communities. Typology focused on types and figures from the Scriptures, but leaned toward the historicity of Old Testament stories, which runs counter to allegorical interpretation.

Second, in Alexandria, patristic writers applied mainly an allegorical interpretation to Scriptures. With allegorical interpretation every word in Scripture had a precise symbolic intention. The most significant aspect of allegorical interpretation is that the interpreter could say one thing in order to signify another. Philo, Clement, and Origen were leading proponents of this method in Alexandria. (Origen's allegorical interpretation of the black bride in the *Song of Songs* will be reviewed later in this chapter.)

Finally, in Rome, Jerome was one of the most important translators and interpreters of Scriptures. One of his major achievements was his Latin translation of the Old Testament, known as the Vulgate, which he made directly from the Hebrew (ca. 398–405 CE).[21] Although he relied mostly on Origen for his earliest commentaries,[22] he justified this preoccupation with Origen's writings by referring to other famous Latin literary figures who had relied on Greek models.[23] He also claimed that he wanted to expose the Latin reader to the treasures of eastern exegesis.[24] In his later commentaries on the major and minor prophets, Jerome employs a typological form of exegesis. His method is based on utilizing Old Testament facts and figures as *typoi* for teachings about different aspects of the early church. For example, in his commentary on Ezekiel 4:16–17 the desire for bread in Jerusalem becomes a symbol of the desire for spiritual bread and water in the church.[25]

Patristic writers from North Africa, Alexandria, and Rome employed allegory and typology in their interpretations of scriptures.[26] At times they used Egypt/Egyptians and Ethiopia/Ethiopians to symbolize vices and sins within their communities. Moreover, they often appealed to assumptions about color symbolism that were operative in ancient Christianity to help explain the meaning of these places and people.[27]

One of the central tenets of ancient Christianity was its egalitarianism, which effectively relativized religious, social, economic, gender, and ethnic differences. Based upon the teachings of Paul and subsequently developed in several other New Testament writings, the ancient Christians established a formula for inclusion into the community.[28] Those included in the egalitarian community of the early Christians were presumably the ones who were able to clothe themselves in the message of Christ and renounce their former social and cultural realities. While some have argued that Ethiopians became an important symbol of Christianity's ecumenical mission,[29] this theme of universal inclusivity was not as simple as it appeared.

Patristic writers were forced to reconcile how those of different ethnic cultures and backgrounds could come together under one common religious identity. They turned to the Old Testament for answers. Informed with assumptions about ethnic difference, early church fathers used Scriptures that dealt with Egyptians/Egypt and Ethiopians/Ethiopia to develop responses to the vices and sins that threatened their communities. These responses often included color-symbolic language about Blacks and blackness.

The ethnic-othering of Egyptians/Egypt, Ethiopians/Ethiopia, and Blacks/blackness became an effective rhetorical strategy for defining vices and sins among early Christian authors. Discourses about these ethnic groups and the related color symbolism used to describe them highlighted the internal tensions within Christian communities, as well as some of the political concerns within the larger society. Ethno-political rhetorics provided the language for shaping an understanding about the composition and development of early Christianity. The awareness of ethnic and color differences reflected and informed the mentality and consciousness of the ancient Christians. This chapter provides a few representative examples of how such ethno-political rhetorics functioned within patristic writings as signs of sins and vices. The next section examines two apostolic writings that use "the Black One" (*ho melas*) and related terms as polemical devices: the *Epistle of Barnabas* and the *Shepherd of Hermas*.

APOSTOLIC FATHERS

Sources

Epistle of Barnabas

The *Epistle of Barnabas* offers a point of entry into the exploration of the use of black or blackness (*melas*). The Black One (*ho melas*) is referred to twice in this letter. The first occurrence, in chapter 4, provides warnings for the lawless (*anomos*). The second occurrence, in chapter 20, discusses the way that leads to death (*thanatos*). Both of these sections of *Barnabas* are related in that they serve to shape the self-understanding of the community during what were considered the last days (*eschatais hēmerais*). In *Barnabas* 4.9 the author says:

> Therefore, we ought to pay attention in the last days, for the entire time of our life and faith will not benefit us unless we fight against, in this present lawless time, the offences that are to come, as becomes the children of God, in order that the *Black One* (*ho melas*) may not creep in among us.[30]

The author introduces the Black One as a threat that should be cut off from the community.[31] The sense of eschatological urgency in this passage is similar to that found in another apostolic writing known as the *Didache*:

60

Watch over your life: "Let your lamps" be not quenched "and your loins" be not ungirded, but be "ready," for you do not know "the hour in which our Lord will come." But gather together frequently seeking the things that are profitable for your souls, for the whole time of your faith shall not profit you unless you are found perfect at the last time.[32]

Based upon evidence in the letter, *Barnabas* seems to have been written sometime between 70 and 115 CE.[33] Assuming that the letter was written near the end of this time period, it was the product of a tumultuous time of crisis for the Jewish community in Alexandria. Within this community there were many new adherents to Christianity who were seeking a message of hope in the final days.[34] The author claims that Jesus gave the covenant to the "new people" (*ton laon ton kainon*),[35] in contrast to an "evil angel" (*angelos ponēros*) who had deceived the Jews.[36]

In general, scholars who have attempted to examine the function of *melas* within this epistle have focused on the association of *ho melas* (the Black One) with *ho diabolos* (the devil).[37] A close reading of the text reveals, however, that *ho diabolos* is not specifically mentioned in chapter 4 of *Barnabas*. The author assumes that the reader will make the association between "the Black One" and "the devil" based on commonly held understandings about evil within the community. In *Barnabas* 2.10, the author says, "We ought to consider carefully, brothers and sisters, our salvation, in order that the Devil (*ho ponēros*) may not gain a deceitful entry into us and hurl us away from our life."[38]

In chapter 20 the author connects the way of the Black One with the way of death (*hodos thanatou*):

> But the way of the *Black One* (*hē tou melanos hodos*) is crooked and full of cursing, for it is the *way of death* (*hodos thanatou*) eternal with punishment, and in it are the things that destroy their soul: idolatry, audacity, arrogance of power, hypocrisy, double-heartedness, adultery, murder, robbery, pride, transgression, fraud, malice, self-sufficiency, enchantments, magic, covetousness, the lack of the fear of God; persecutors of the good, haters of the truth, lovers of lies, knowing not the reward of righteousness, who "cleave not to the good," nor to righteous judgment, who attend not to the cause of the widow and orphan, spending wakeful nights not in the fear of God, but in the pursuit of *vice* (*ponēron*), from whom meekness and patience are far and distant, "loving vanity, seeking rewards," without pity for the poor, working not for him who is oppressed with toil, prone to evil speaking, without knowledge of their Maker, murderers of children, corrupters of God's creation, turning away the needy, oppressing the afflicted, advocates of the rich, unjust judges of the poor, *altogether sinful* (*panthamartētoi*).[39]

Here the author includes an extended list of vices that *ho melas* is known to bring into the community. The polemical intent is evident in the way *ho melas* functions with the detailed list of vices, which emphasizes the "altogether sinful" activities that were known to destroy the soul.

In Greco-Roman antiquity, vice lists were generally connected to lists of virtues. These lists were a common feature of Greco-Roman moral and ethical treatises.[40] In *Barnabas* the list of virtues is contained in chapter 19. The virtues, in contrast to the vices, are indicated as "the way of light" (*hē hodos tou phōtos*).[41] Both lists are introduced in chapter 18 in the discussion about the "Two Ways."[42] These lists usually indicated certain behaviors that led to life and certain threats that led to death and destruction. The use of nations or color-coded terms is not a standard feature of virtue and vice lists. Generally, some term for evil (*ponēros*) was contrasted with some form of good or right behavior (*kalos*). The forms of the lists varied, ranging from a simple list,[43] to a chain,[44] to a dialogue.[45]

The Black One (*ho melas*) had many possible meanings. It could mean "darkness," "blackness," or "gloom."[46] It could also refer to the Evil One (i.e., Satan) or to "death." In the writings of Homer, death (*thanatos*) is often qualified as *melas*.[47] Within *Barnabas*, the way of the Black One is also linked to the way of Darkness (*skotos*), overseen by "angels of Satan" (*angeloi satanas*), which ultimately leads to the way of death:

> Now let us pass on to another lesson and teaching. There are two Ways of teaching and power, one of Light (*tou phōtos*) and one of Darkness (*tou skotous*).[48] And there is a great difference between the two Ways. For over the one are set light-bringing angels of God, but over the other angels of Satan. And the one is Lord from eternity and to eternity, and the other is the ruler of the present time of lawlessness (*anomias*).[49]

In this text, the way of Darkness is contrasted to the way of Light, overseen by light-bringing angels of God.[50] A similar pattern is present in the *Didache*, written around the same time as *Barnabas*: "There are two Ways, one of Life and one of Death, and there is a great difference between the two Ways."[51] Chapter 5 of the *Didache* also discusses the way of Death:

> But the Way of Death is this: First of all, it is wicked and full of cursing, murders, adulteries, lusts, fornications, thefts, idolatries, witchcrafts, charms, robberies, false witness, hypocrisies, a double heart, fraud, pride, malice, stubbornness, covetousness, foul speech, jealousy, impudence, haughtiness, boastfulness. Persecutors of the good, haters of truth, lovers of lies, knowing not the reward of righteousness, not cleaving to the good nor to righteous judgment, spending wakeful nights not for good but for wickedness, from

whom meekness and patience is far, lovers of vanity, following after reward, unmerciful to the poor, not working from him who is oppressed with tóil, without knowledge of him who made them, murderers of children, corrupters of God's creatures, turning away the needy, oppressing the distressed, advocates of the rich, unjust judges of the poor, *altogether sinful (panthamartētoi)*; may ye be delivered, my children, from all these.[52]

This imagery of two ways, symbolized by light and darkness, was also common to the Gospel of John and 1 Thessalonians.[53]

The two references to *ho melas* (the Black One) in *Barnabas* function as a type of ethno-political rhetoric that pointed to vices and sins within the community. The rhetoric was not intended to denounce actual Black persons within the community; rather it functioned as a type of intra-Christian polemic against those who were being swayed by other doctrines and understandings of the faith. The Black One called attention to the vices and sins that threatened the weaker members of the community and it also pointed to the way of death that destroyed the soul.

In addition to this intra-Christian polemic, the author of *Barnabas*, aware of persecutions in Alexandria, also used this text to instruct his community about the political threats that dominated second-century Alexandria. Based on the allegorical symbolism contained throughout the letter, scholars generally favor an Alexandrian provenance for the epistle.[54] Further support for an Alexandrian provenance is the reference to *Barnabas* in one of the major writings of Clement of Alexandria.[55]

Alexandria was a major center for cultural and intellectual activity. It was also an international hub for travel, trade, and political activity. Blacks were more than likely a common sight in this city. They were transported to Alexandria as a result of the military conflicts between the Romans and Nubians.[56] Frank Snowden offers many examples of the presence of Blacks in Greco-Roman antiquity and suggests that they participated in various aspects of Alexandrian culture and society.[57] The presence of Ethiopians or "Black Ones" within the larger society may have influenced how the author shaped the rhetorics about *ho melas* within *Barnabas*. A brief discussion about the general content and form of the text will help clarify the functions of the ethno-political rhetorics.

Scholars have generated a long history of debate as to whether *Barnabas* is a letter, homily, treatise, or tractate.[58] Although it neither contains an elaborate opening or closing, nor explicitly mentions the author, addressees, or the specific situation that occasioned its writing,[59] it does contain the basic framework of an ancient letter.[60] The opening contains both a greeting and a general outline of the purpose and intentions of the author (1.1–8).[61] The body of the letter is divided into two sections. The first section (2.1–16.10), outlining various aspects of Jewish ritual life, opens with the general purpose for the letter: "seeing then that the days are evil *(ponērōn)*, and that the worker of evil himself is in power, we ought to give heed to ourselves, and seek out the ordinances of the Lord."[62] A brief transition is provided in 17.1–18.1. Here the author summarizes the previous section and prepares to discuss another lesson and teaching (*gnōsin kai didachēn*). The second section (18–20) discusses the Two Ways. The letter closes with final words of encouragement to be on guard against the Evil One (*ho ponēros*), followed by a brief benediction (21.9).[63]

Barnabas contains a strong attack against Judaism.[64] Throughout this letter the author denounces major aspects of Jewish ritual observance such as fasting (chap. 7), animal sacrifices (chap. 8), circumcision (chap. 9), food laws (chap. 10), Sabbath rest (chap. 15), and the temple (chap. 16). In addition, the text was written to warn Christians against certain Jewish conceptions of the Old Testament. The author also indicates that he is passing on tradition.[65] Although many scholars argue that the author was Jewish, most claim that he was more than likely a Gentile convert who was still informed by the concerns of the Jewish community in Alexandria.[66] I argue that *Barnabas* contains an intra-Jewish-Christian polemic used to inform a Jewish-Christian audience of the threat of persecution. The community was being encouraged to live out the last days by avoiding the way of the Black One (*hē tou melanos hodos*).[67] The reference to *ho melas* is possibly a reference to *ho ponēros* (the evil one), which could refer to the devil, or more specifically to the Roman emperor Trajan, who would later be responsible for wiping out the Jews in Alexandria.[68]

The context of persecution is important for understanding *Barnabas*. The Jewish revolt of 115–17 CE is the most probable backdrop for this epistle. It is evident throughout the epistle that the author was transposing the internal tensions of the Jewish Diaspora community into the new historical situation of the Christians.[69] The ethno-political rhetorics about *ho melas* helped shape the community's self-understanding with respect to its intra-Christian opponents and external enemies.

David M. Olster proposes an ethnographic reading of *Barnabas* by asserting that the author was concerned with "denying the Jews' racial claim to the Christian God."[70] Olster further argues, "the author of *Barnabas* not only endeavored to undercut Jewish customs and racial legitimacy. He also desired to disenfranchise the Jews and appropriate their history and claims to a God."[71] In this way *Barnabas* maintained that the God of the Christians never had a covenant with the Jews. Olster identifies the parallel between *Barnabas* and the diatribe against Apion, the chief opponent of the Jews to whom Josephus devotes an entire book.[72]

> You will say, "But surely this people (*ho laos*)[73] received physical circumcision as the seal of their covenant?" Why every Syrian and every Arab is physically circumcised, and so are the idol priesthoods. But does this make them members of the Jews' covenant? Even the very Egyptians (*hoi Aigyptioi*) practice physical circumcision![74]

According to Olster, the author of *Barnabas* attacked the Jews' "cultural plagiarism" by using an ethnographic invective similar to that found in Josephus's response to Apion.[75] Gentile Christians claimed Jewish history as their own and redefined themselves as "a race adopted by its God."[76] Olster's reading correctly identifies an example of ethnographic polemic operative within *Barnabas*, but his analysis ignores the references to the Black One in the letter. Based upon the foregoing review of *ho melas*, I conclude that the color symbolism in *Barnabas* points to intra-Christian struggles and controversies, as well as external threats of persecution that plagued the Jewish-Christians in Alexandria. *Ho melas* does not refer directly to "Blacks" as an ethnic group in *Barnabas*. But the author of this text may have been influenced by either the real or imaginative "presence" of Ethiopians and Blacks in Alexandria and used *ho melas* as a trope within the ethno-political rhetorics about vices and sins.

Shepherd of Hermas

The *Shepherd of Hermas* provides a useful picture of the second-century church at Rome.[77] This complex document, which contains five visions, twelve mandates (or commandments), and ten similitudes (or parables), was more than likely written over a long period of time by multiple authors.[78] Several studies dealing with economic issues, language patterns, ecclesial concerns, and prophetic tendencies within the *Shepherd of Hermas* offer important assessments of various aspects of this document.[79] None of these studies, however, addresses the symbolic color references to black or blackness that are found in the ninth similitude and fourth vision. Before I begin an examination of the function of *ho melas* in the *Shepherd of Hermas*, a general outline of the text is in order.

The *Shepherd of Hermas* contains apocalyptic, prophetic, and paraenetic material. The manuscript evidence suggests an original separation between *Visions* 4 and 5.[80] *Visions* 1–4 comprise a unit that contains a strong apocalyptic orientation toward an imminent tribulation. This unit features an elderly woman (*tēn presbyteran*) as the revelatory agent of the church (*hē ekklēsia*).[81] Starting with *Vision* 5[82] and continuing through *Similitude* 10, a shepherd appears to Hermas as a revelatory agent or angel of repentance (*angelos tēs metanoias*) who dictates the mandates and similitudes.[83] This section presupposes a past persecution that produced apostates.

Ho melas and related terms occur ten times in the ninth similitude. *Ho melas* is used mainly in the sections that describe the women clothed in black robes (9.15.1–3), the black mountain (9.19.1), and the stones used in building the tower (9.30.2). *Similitude* 9 recapitulates the theme of the tower introduced in *Vision* 3 and develops the theme of persecution (*thlipsis*) introduced by the ancient lady in *Vision* 4. There are several apocalyptic symbols in the third and fourth visions. The tower introduced in *Vision* 3 is an allegory for the church (Herm. *Vis.* 3.3.3). The building of the tower is central for this eschatological document:

Foolish man! Do you not see the tower yet building? When the tower is finished and built, then comes *the end* (*telos*); and I assure you it will be soon finished. Ask me no more questions. Let you and all the saints be content . . . with my renewal of your spirits.[84]

The construction of the tower symbolizes the time that is allowed for those who have sinned to come to repentance:

I asked her: "Why has the tower been built on the water, Lady?" . . . Hear, then, why the tower has been built upon the water: because your life was saved and shall be saved through water, and the tower has been founded by the utterance of the almighty and glorious Name, and is maintained by the unseen power of the Master.[85]

The fourth vision contains a warning of the great persecution (*thlipsis*) that is to come, symbolized by a beast (*thērion*):

Go then and tell the Lord's elect ones of his great deeds, and tell them that this *beast* [*thērion*] is a type of the great *persecution* [*thlipsis*] that is to come. If then you are prepared beforehand, and repent with all your hearts towards the Lord, you will be able to escape it, if your heart be made pure and blameless, and you serve the Lord blamelessly for the rest of the days of your life. "Cast your cares upon the Lord" and he will put them straight.[86]

Vision 4.1.10 lists the four colors contained on the head of the beast: black (*melan*), the color of flame and blood (*pyroeides kai haimatōdes*), gold (*chrysoun*), and white (*leukon*).[87] The meaning of these colors is described in 4.3.1–5. Black (*to melan*) symbolized the current world with its trials and persecutions.[88] "The color of flame and blood" means that this world must be destroyed by blood and fire. "Gold" represents those who have fled from this world. "White" symbolizes the world to come, in which the elect of God shall dwell, for those who have been chosen by God for eternal life will be without spot (*aspiloi*) and pure (*katharoi*).[89]

The nature of the persecution referred to in this vision has been debated among scholars.[90] Some argue that there was an actual external political crisis, while others view the persecution as a "perceived" crisis that has to do with the social identity of Christians in the face of Nero's persecution and the destruction of Jerusalem.[91] According to Carolyn Osiek, the crisis affecting the community behind the *Shepherd of Hermas* is a "perceived" crisis that was brought about by internal as well as external factors.[92] Thus the color black on the beast's head (the current world with its trials and persecutions) is a symbolic way of referring to the struggles within the community and the "perceived" crisis that is at stake in terms of self-definition and identity. In this regard the *Shepherd of Hermas* functions as a type of community-building propaganda.

The ninth similitude recapitulates and reinterprets the theme of the tower introduced in the visions and emphasizes the theme of penitence. In *Similitude* 9.19–29 the shepherd (*poimēn*) shows Hermas twelve mountains, each of which has a different purpose and appearance. These mountains are metaphors for describing different believers and leaders within the Christian community.[93] Most of the mountains are represented by thorns and thistles (*akanthas kai tribolous*), herbs (*botanas*), creeping things (*ta erpeta*), wild beasts (*thēria*), and trees (*dendra*). The author emphasizes white/black color symbolism in the sections about the first and the twelfth mountains. The first mountain (Herm. *Sim.* 9.19.1) is "black as pitch" (*melan hōs asbolē*) and the twelfth one is white (*leukos*).[94]

> From the first mountain, *the black one* (*ho melas*), are such believers as these: apostates and blasphemers against the Lord, and betrayers of the servants of God. For these there is no repentance, but there is death, and for this cause they also are *black* (*melanes*), for their way (*genos*) is lawless.[95]

> And from the twelfth mountain, *the white one* (*ho leukos*), are such believers as these: They are as innocent babes (*nēpia brephē*), and no evil enters into their heart, nor have they known what wickedness (*ponēria*) is, but have ever remained in innocence. Such then shall live without doubt in the kingdom of God, because by no act did they defile the commandments of God, but remained in innocence all the days of their lives in the same mind.[96]

These two extremes represent those who had been influenced by evil and those who were innocent and had never known wickedness.

The mountains are also connected to the tower that is being built.[97] As mentioned earlier, the eschatological symbol of the building of the tower signifies the time when repentance is possible.[98] The author utilizes an ethno-political discursive strategy in the discussion about the stones that are to comprise the tower.

> The stones that are taken from the plain and put into the building of the tower instead of those which are rejected, are the roots of *the white mountain* (*tou orous tou leukou*). Since then all the believers from the white mountain were found guiltless, the lord of the tower commanded these to be brought from the roots of this mountain for the building of the tower. For he knew that if these stones go into the building of the tower they will remain bright (*lamproi*) and none of them will become *black* (*melanēsei*). But if he had added them from

the other mountains he would have been obliged to visit the tower again, and to purge it, for all these have been found *white* (*candidi*),[99] both past and future believers, for they are of the same *way* (*genos*). Blessed is this *way* (*genos*) because it is *innocent* (*akakon*).[100]

In this case, the ethno-political discursive strategy is steeped in color-symbolic language that is used to shape an understanding of the significance of repentance. The shepherd is considered the angel of repentance (*nuntius paenitentiae*)[101] and exhorts his audience to amend themselves while the tower is still being built.[102] The stones that make it into the tower at this point represent the past and future believers of the same blessed way (*genos*). The author is using *genos* as a symbolic term to distinguish those within the community who were righteous and innocent believers.[103] Such believers were able to stand firm in the face of threat and persecution. This blessed way (*makarion to genos touto*) is in direct opposition to the lawless way (*to genos anomos*), that is, those from the black mountain.

The symbolic language about *genos* in the *Shepherd of Hermas* is similar to that in the New Testament. For example, the author of 1 Peter 2:9 identifies the chosen people of God as follows: "But you are a chosen way (*genos*), a royal priesthood, a holy nation (*ethnos hagion*), God's own people (*laos*), in order that you may proclaim the mighty acts of him who called you out of darkness (*ek skotous*) into his marvelous light (*phōs*)."[104] Both 1 Peter 2:9 and *The Shepherd of Hermas* demonstrate that within early Christianity there was a tradition of ethnic-othering that reflected the color-coded literary imaginations of the authors of these texts.

One key to understanding the author's use of *melas* in the *Shepherd of Hermas* lies in the socio-political conditions that prompted this apocalyptic myth. The social and political threats within the larger society were major challenges to the Christian identity of this community. The function of *melas* is related to the function of apocalyptic literature in general. Such literature calls attention to persecution (*thlipsis*). The nature of the persecution is difficult to determine with certainty. But the author has appealed to apocalyptic language and themes to communicate to his audience strategies for enduring the threats of persecution.

One final point can be made about the color-symbolic language in *Similitude* 9. The socio-political reality calls for an ethical exhortation revealed through a description of women and maidens. Those who bear the names of these stronger maidens or virgins (*parthenōn*) will be able to enter the Kingdom of God. Those who bear the names of the women clothed in black garments represent those who shall see the Kingdom of God, but shall not enter into it.

"Explain to me, Sir," said I, "the names of the virgins, and of the women who are clothed in *black robes* (*ta melana himatia*)." "Listen," said he, "to the names of the stronger virgins who stand at the corners. The first is Faith, the second is Temperance, the third is Power, the fourth is Long-suffering, and the others who stand between them have these names: Simplicity, Guilelessness, Holiness, Joyfulness, Truth, Understanding, Concord, Love. He who bears these names and the name of the Son of God, 'shall be able to enter into the Kingdom of God.'" Hear, also, said he, "the names of the women clothed in *black robes* (*ta melana himatia*). Of these also four are more powerful. The first is Unbelief, the second Impurity, the third Disobedience, and the fourth Deceit; and those who follow them are called Grief, Wickedness, Licentiousness, Bitterness, Lying, Foolishness, Evil-speaking, Hate. The servant of God who bears these names shall see the Kingdom of God, but shall not enter into it."[105]

Summary

Both *Barnabas* and the *Shepherd of Hermas* demonstrate that color symbolism played an important role in the imaginations of early Christian writers. The anonymous authors of these texts used *melas* to warn, instruct, and encourage their audiences to endure internal and external threats that challenged their identity and stability. Within both the Christian community in Alexandria and the Christian community in Rome, internal battles, competing loyalties, apostasy, fear, insecurity, and double-mindedness were major problems. *Melas* became a strategic trope for identifying these concerns within the community.

In the Alexandrian Jewish-Christian context of *Barnabas*, *melas* served as a polemical device for instructing the community about vices. In the Roman Jewish-Christian context of the *Shepherd of Hermas*, *melas* and related terms served as a way of signifying the perceived threats to the community. Both documents highlight the diversity of early Christianity and the complex modes of communicating its beliefs and values.[106] The references to blackness in these texts do not refer to Blacks or Ethiopians as particular ethnic enemies of the communities. The symbolic language about blackness was a part of a rhetorical strategy that functioned within the writings as a form of resistance to the perceived internal and external threats to the communities.

During the postapostolic period, the emerging Christian movement was struggling to define itself vis-à-vis its Jewish roots and, increasingly, vis-à-vis the Greco-Roman culture and society into which it was expanding.[107] These texts are valuable indicators of how the "apostolic fathers" responded to their intra-Christian opponents. They defined their Christian opponents with a color-symbolic ethno-political rhetoric that effectively marginalized them as a lawless people (*genos anomos*).

The eschatological urgency and apocalyptic language of these second-century writings provide a heuristic key for understanding the use of *melas*. In order to understand their ethno-political rhetorics it is important to be sensitive to the functions of apocalypse as literature. John J. Collins says:

> The legacy of the apocalypses includes a powerful rhetoric for denouncing the deficiencies of this world. It also includes the conviction that the world as now constituted is not the end. Most of all it entails an appreciation of the great resource that lies in the human imagination to construct a symbolic world where the integrity of values can be maintained in the face of social and political powerlessness and even of the threat of death.[108]

Apocalypses employed heavy symbolism and dualistic language to draw attention to social and political conditions. Such texts sustained their readers and audiences during times of fear and uncertainty. The Christian communities during the postapostolic period were struggling to define themselves. The authors of these texts appealed to color-symbolic language to emphasize the importance of maintaining moral standards and commitments even in the face of persecution.

The next section will focus on patristic writings from the late second through the fifth centuries CE. In these writings, which mostly feature exegetical interpretations of scriptures that mention Egyptians and Ethiopians, another type of ethno-political rhetoric is developed.

PATRISTIC WRITINGS

Sources

Tertullian, De spectaculis 3

Tertullian (160–225 CE), in his treatise entitled *De spectaculis*, provides an excellent framework for understanding the symbolism related to Egypt and Ethiopia in the writings from the early church fathers. This treatise belongs to the early years of Tertullian's literary activity (ca. 197–200 CE) in North Africa, before his association with Montanism.[109] Tertullian wrote this treatise because he was concerned that "people in our own ranks" (*nostrorum detractatus*) were attending the public shows or spectacles (*spectacula*).[110] He acknowledged that the scriptures did not specifically comment on this matter.[111] But with the sensibilities and methods of a sophist,[112] he found in Psalm 1:1 support for his argument that Christians should avoid the spectacles.[113]

Tertullian seeks to prove that "these things (*spectacula*) are not compatible with true religon and true obedience to the true God."[114] In sum, the spectacles are to be avoided because of their idolatrous character.[115] The first two chapters of this treatise establish the *opinionem ethnicorum* (Gentile opinion) on the matter.[116] In chapter 3 Tertullian deals specifically with people within his own community (*nostrorum detractatus*) who put forth the same arguments as the Gentiles (*ethnicorum*). His adversaries within the North African church demanded a scriptural response to the spectacles.[117] Tertullian was unable to find any specific passage that dealt with the topic of the spectacles. Therefore, he relied on Psalm 1:1 as a textual springboard for his response to his opponents.[118] Thus, after his tortured exegesis of Psalm 1:1,[119] Tertullian generalizes about the spectacles from particular examples: "When God reminds the Israelites of discipline and upbraids them, His words apply undoubtedly to all."[120] Next, Tertullian draws upon an image of Egypt and Ethiopia:

> [W]hen He threatens destruction to *Egypt and Ethiopia* (*Aegypto et Aethiopiae*), He certainly cautions every sinful nation against judgment to come. Thus, if we reason from a special case to the general type that every sinful nation is an *Egypt and Ethiopia* (*Aegyptus et Aethiopia*), in the same manner we reason from the general class to a special case that every spectacle is a gathering of the ungodly.[121]

In this example, which is possibly an allusion to Ezekiel 30,[122] Tertullian is not actually calling Egypt and Ethiopia sinful. Rather, he is using these places to symbolize the sinfulness of the spectacles. Egypt (*Aegyptus*) and Ethiopia (*Aethiopia*) represented any sinful nation (*omnem gentem peccatricem*).[123] Tertullian was a master at using biblical language and imagery in his writings, which is evident in *De spectaculis*.[124] Tertullian shaped an ethno-political rhetoric about Egypt and Ethiopia in order to respond to opponents within his community who were being influenced by "pagan" activities and practices.[125] He assumes that his audience would understand the association of Egypt and Ethiopia with the sinfulness of the spectacles.

Tertullian refers to Egypt and Ethiopia in many of his other writings. I contend that his use of these nations as polemical devices is influenced by his participation in the debates among his contemporaries as to whether Christians constituted a "third way" (*tertium genus*) – that is, a new religious identity next to Jews and Greeks.[126] Thus, in his treatise *Ad nationes*, Tertullian says:

> But, you say, it is on the score of religion and not of nationality that we are considered to be third; it is the Romans first, then the Jews, and after that the Christians. What about the Greeks then? Or supposing that they are reckoned among the various Roman religions (since it was from Greece that Rome borrowed even her deities), where do the *Egyptians* (*Aegyptii*) at any rate come in, since they possess a religion which, so far as I know, is all their own and full of secrecy?[127]

I find Tertullian's use of *Aegyptii* in his discussion about Greeks, Romans, and Jews an important clue that he viewed Egyptians as a distinct *ethnos*. Thus his use of Egyptians (and Ethiopians) in *De spectaculis* may have been influenced by the symbolic language about nations that was used within North African

Christian communities. Tertullian may have also used Egyptians and Ethiopians in this treatise because of his awareness of these groups as ethnic others within North Africa.[128] He used these groups as symbolic tropes in his treatise on the spectacles in order to respond to his detractors and to define the sinful activities that threatened to weaken his community.

Origen, Commentarium and Homiliae in Canticum Canticorum

One of the most important figures in the development of ancient Christian exegesis was Origen (ca. 185–254 CE). In his treatise entitled *De principiis*, or *On First Principles*, Origen describes the different levels involved in interpreting scriptures. He regards the scriptures as inspired in every respect and arranged by God in a series of levels.[129] The first or "corporeal" level is the literal meaning of the text. The second level is the moral meaning.[130] The highest level is the spiritual or theological meaning. According to Origen, the spiritual level, which is always present but veiled, contains the essential truths of Christianity. The exegete elucidates this meaning through allegorical interpretation. Origen argues that some passages include metaphors or figures that could only be interpreted allegorically. Origen calls these figures *typoi* and explains their function:

> God has arranged that certain stumbling-blocks, as it were, and offences, and impossibilities should be introduced into the midst of the law and the history in order that we may not, through being drawn away in all directions by the merely attractive nature of the language, either altogether fall away from the true doctrine, as learning nothing worthy of God, or by departing from the letter come of the knowledge of nothing more divine.[131]

Origen encouraged the exegete to investigate the meanings of words within scriptures.[132] Such an investigation into the "spiritual" or "theological" meanings of key words would serve to develop a true understanding of the church. In my view, the meanings of words not only delineate the spiritual and theological foundations for the church, but also have the potential to expose socio-political and cultural concerns within the author's world. Such is the case with the provocative set of words in the Song of Songs with respect to the black bride of Solomon: "I am black and beautiful (*Melaina eimi kai kalē*), O daughters of Jerusalem, like the tents of Kedar, like the curtains of Solomon. Do not gaze at me because I have been blackened (*memalanōmenē*), because the sun has gazed on me."[133]

Origen's allegorical interpretation of the black bride raises many questions about his discursive strategies with respect to Blacks and blackness. In both his commentary and homily on Song of Songs 1:5–6, Origen associates the black bride with the Gentile church. He also associates the black bride with sins and vices. (Unfortunately, since Origen's commentary and homilies do not survive in the original Greek, I must examine the Latin translations of these texts made by Jerome and Rufinus.[134])

Origen opens Book 2 of the commentary by equating the black bride with the Gentile church:

> This Bride who speaks represents the Church (*ecclesiae personam*) gathered from among the Gentiles (*ex gentibus congregatae*); but the daughters of Jerusalem to whom she addresses herself are the souls who are described as being most dear because of the election of the fathers, but enemies because of the Gospel.[135] Those are, therefore, the daughters of this earthly Jerusalem who, seeing the Church of the Gentiles, despise and vilify her for her ignoble birth; for she is baseborn in their eyes, because she cannot count as hers the noble blood of Abraham and Isaac and Jacob, for all that she forgets her own people and her father's house and comes to Christ.[136]

The bride is used here as a symbolic trope to indicate the Gentile church that did not have the same beginnings or noble birth as the people of Israel. Origen goes on to discuss how the bride responds to being labeled black; that is, "as one who has not been enlightened by the patriarch's teaching."[137] The bride responds to this accusation by saying:

> I am indeed *black* (*nigra*), O daughters of Jerusalem, in that I cannot claim descent from famous men, neither have I received the enlightenment of Moses' Law. But I have my own beauty (*pulchritudinem*), all the same. For in me too there is that primal thing, the Image of God wherein I was created; and, coming now to the Word of God, I have received my beauty.[138]

The beauty of the bride is found in her openness to receiving the Word of God. Her beauty is further exemplified through her penitence and faith.

> I am that *Ethiopian* (*Aethiopissa*). I am *black* (*nigra*) indeed by reason of my lowly origin (*ignobilitate*); but I am beautiful (*formosa*) through penitence (*paenitentiam*) and faith (*fidem*). For I have taken to myself the Son of God, I have received the Word made flesh; I have come to Him who is the Image of God, the Firstborn of every creature and who is the brightness of the glory and the express Image of the substance of God, and I have been made fair (*formosa*).[139]

After this, Origen refers to several other passages related to Ethiopians and Blacks within the Old Testament and other Jewish writings that foreshadow the Gentile church being viewed as black.[140]

Another way of interpreting the association of "blackness" with sin within patristic writings is through the theme of *obscuratio*, or the darkening of the heart (*kardia eskotisthē*).[141] This theme is contained within the New Testament in Paul's letter to the Romans:

> For the wrath of God is revealed from heaven against all ungodliness and wickedness of those who by their wickedness suppress the truth. For what can be known about God is plain to them, because God has shown it to them. Ever since the creation of the world his eternal power and divine nature, invisible though they are, have been understood and seen through the things he has made. So they are without excuse; for though they knew God, they did not honor him as God or give thanks to him, but they became futile in their thinking, and their senseless minds (*kardia*) were *darkened* (*eskotisthē*).[142]

Obscuratio does not have meaning only for the individual, but also for the Gentile church. The Gentile church is "black" by reason of the obscurity of her origins as differing from the synagogue.[143]

In Origen's first homily, the black bride says:

> "*I am black and beautiful* (*Nigra sum et speciosa*), O ye daughters of Jerusalem." Address yourself to the daughters of Jerusalem, you member of the Church, and say: "The Bridegroom loves me more and holds me dearer than you, who are the many daughters of Jerusalem; you stand without and watch the Bride enter the chamber." [Let no one doubt that *the Black One* (*nigram*) is *beautiful* (*formosam*), for all she is called *black* (*nigram*). For we exist in order that we may acknowledge God, that we may tell forth songs of a song, that we may be those who have come from *the borders of Ethiopia* (*Aethiopiae finibus*), from the *ends of the earth* (*extremo terrae*), to hear the wisdom of the true Solomon.][144]

In his homilies Origen remains consistent in his interpretation of the black bride as representative of the Gentile church. These homilies were prepared around 244 CE, only a few years after his *Commentary*, which was written sometime between 240 and 244 CE.[145] In his first homily, Origen compared Gentile converts to the black bride of Solomon; though once blackened by sin, they were now whitened by the grace of God. He also identifies sins and vices with foul odors:

> If the Bridegroom has touched me, I too become of a good odor, I too am anointed with perfumes; and His perfumes are so imparted to me that I can say with the apostles: We are the good odor (*bonus odor*) of

Christ in every place.[146] But we, although we hear these things, still *stink of the sins and vices* (*peccatis vitiisque foetemus*) concerning which the penitent speaks through the prophet, saying: My sores are putrefied and corrupted because of my foolishness.[147] Sin has a putrid smell, virtue exhales sweet odors.[148]

Summary

In his review of the early church fathers, Frank Snowden concluded that "Ethiopians were by all means to be embraced, for the Church, in the words of Augustine, was to reach even the Ethiopians, the remotest and blackest of men."[149] Snowden used Augustine's text to support his contention that Ethiopians were included in the economy of salvation as generally understood among early Christians. However, a closer examination of Augustine and other church fathers such as Tertullian, Origen, and Jerome suggests that ethnopolitical rhetorics based upon the symbolic use of Egyptians/Egypt, Ethiopians/Ethiopia, and Blacks/blackness were operative in some of their writings.

A general pattern is discernible in which these ethnic groups, geographical locations, and color symbols symbolized vices and sins that threatened the Christian faith. Thus, those who strayed from the faith became "Ethiopians" and were "blackened by their sins." According to the sources reviewed in this section, the only solution out of this *blackened* state was repentance (*metanoia*) from sins. Penitence, in many instances, was represented as a cleansing that left the reformed sinner white and pure with – in the words of Origen – a kind of Ethiopian beauty (*Aethiopici decoris*).

A patristic tradition of spiritualizing blackness and whiteness developed in the third through fifth centuries CE. This color-symbolic spiritualizing also included references to Egyptians and Ethiopians. St. Paulinus of Nola, writing in the late fourth and early fifth centuries, demonstrates how this spiritualizing weaves back and forth between references to color symbols or ethnic groups and references about sin.

> Let us avoid not merely committing sin but even thinking of it, as we would hold our noses to avoid the infectious emanation and the foul stench from a rotting corpse. Solomon warns us that sin is to be feared and loathed like the appearance of a snake, and says it is armed with lion's teeth. He speaks the truth, for sins with bestial maw savagely devour the soul conquered by the sick pleasure of the body and appropriated after defeat by the serpent for his meal. That serpent devours "*the peoples of the Ethiopians (Aethiopum populos),*" not those roasted by the sun, but those whom *sin has* blackened (*uitiis nigros*) and guilt has made *black as night* (*nocticolores*). Such are the *Ethiopians* that the serpent devours, and among them the condemned Satan finds food to eat. God used the single word

"earth" to describe both the sinner and serpent's food, and so the man who devours sins is devoured by the dragon.[150]

Paulinus indicates that he is not referring to actual Ethiopians in this text by saying "not those roasted by the sun." He makes it clear that "the peoples of the Ethiopians" symbolize "those whom sin has blackened and guilt has made black as night."

CONCLUSION: ETHNO-POLITICAL RHETORICS DEFINING VICES AND SINS

This chapter draws attention to patristic sources and isolates how Egyptians/ Egypt, Ethiopians/Ethiopia, and Blacks/blackness were cast as symbols of vices and sins. Within the postapostolic writings such as *Barnabas* and the *Shepherd of Hermas*, *melas* was used as a color referent to indicate the evil within the world that should be avoided. *Ho melas* was not necessarily a reference to actual Blacks or Ethiopians, even though these peoples may have been the inspiration for such discourses. Discourses about the Black One and blackness symbolized threats to the respective communities to whom these writings were addressed. These threats involved both internal and external crises that challenged the communities to heighten their awareness of social and political events as well as of their own identity and self-understanding.

Among the church fathers, Blacks/blacks as well as Egyptians/Egypt and Ethiopians/Ethiopia served as ethnic tropes in their commentaries, homilies, and theological treatises. Equipped with scriptures and allegorical methods for interpretation, church fathers developed ethno-political rhetorics to convince their audiences of the threats within their communities, as well as the challenges that existed in the larger Greco-Roman society. Tertullian used Egyptians/Egypt and Ethiopians/Ethiopia to symbolize the sins of the early church and the vices that caused his followers to stray from the faith. Origen was more concerned with using the black bride described in the Song of Songs to symbolize the value of penitence and faith. His allegorical interpretations of the bride in both his commentary and homilies reflect the influence of white/black color symbolism that was operative in the ancient world.

4

"STIRRING UP THE PASSIONS": ETHNO-POLITICAL RHETORICS DEFINING SEXUAL THREATS

A certain father when he went out to become a monk was a virgin, and he did not even know that a whore existed among the children of men. And when he was dwelling in his cell the devils began to stir up in him the *passion of fornication*, and lifting up his eyes he saw the devils going around him in the forms of *Ethiopians*, and they incited him to yield to the passion.

(Palladius, *Apophthegmata patrum* 579)

INTRODUCTION: ETHIOPIANS AND BLACKS IN MONASTIC LITERATURE

In the previous chapter, I explored how some early Christian writers used Egyptians/Egypt, Ethiopians/Ethiopia, and Blacks/blackness to symbolize the perceived vices and sins that threatened their Christian communities during the second and third centuries CE. In this chapter, I examine several monastic stories from the fourth and fifth centuries CE that exemplify how Ethiopians and Blacks became symbolic tropes in narratives about sexual immorality (*porneia*).[1] These tropes were a part of ethno-political rhetorics that emphasized the importance of early Christian asceticism.[2] They also served to shape the theological, cultural, and ideological understandings of monastic Christianity of late antique Egypt.

Ethno-political rhetorics about Ethiopians (both males and females), often vituperative in nature, became a handy pedagogical tool for instructing and encouraging the monks in their cultivation of discipline (*askēsis*) and self-control (*enkrateia*). In many instances vituperative rhetorics about Ethiopians, which employed various forms of sexual slander, were part of a larger discursive strategy of political invective based on dominant values and perceptions about

77

ethnic and color difference in Greco-Roman Egypt.[3] In this chapter, I isolate the invective and discuss some of the reasons why this type of rhetoric became so popular in monastic sources from late antiquity.

I also analyze the symbolic discourses about Ethiopian women in monastic literature. Ethiopian women in the stories of the desert fathers symbolized the multifaceted threats that both gender and ethnic difference represented to those constructing the religious and ideological boundaries within late antique Christian literature. These women symbolized the dangerous sexual vices that challenged the piety and self-control of the monks. While the references to Ethiopian women in monastic literature are sparse compared to references to women in general, I argue that their use by Christian authors of late antiquity was part of a sophisticated discursive strategy of vituperation that signaled a complex web of power relationships among a circle of Christians in late antique Roman Egypt. Ethiopian women functioned in the texts as markers of difference that symbolized the acceptable standards, social roles, and norms within certain types of monastic culture.

Ethiopian women were consistently portrayed in extremely compromising positions in Christian monastic sources.[4] For example, an anonymous author reported a story of a monk who performed indecent sex acts with two Ethiopian women.[5] In another example, Ethiopian women were hit, slapped, and driven away from the desert monks because of their lingering "foul odors" (*fetorem*).[6] One monk, Pachon, after resisting an Ethiopian maiden by boxing her on the ear, maintained that her stench (*dysōdias*) stayed on his hand for two years afterward.[7] Ethiopian women became the interpretive site for attitudes about women, sexuality, the body, and other cultures within the stories about the desert fathers and their ascetic virtues (e.g., *enkrateia*, *sōphrosynē*). Furthermore, the way that Christian writers (especially the monastic authors) signified Ethiopian women has implications for understanding how Black women are signified in contemporary discussions about politics and morality.[8] Many contemporary stereotypes about Black women can be traced back to ancient Christian writings.

It is important to note the distinction I make between Egyptians and Ethiopians in this chapter. Thus far throughout this book, I have assumed that ancient Christian writers used Egyptians/Egypt, Ethiopians/Ethiopia, and Blacks/blackness as ethnic, geographical, or color-symbolic tropes. Thus a clear pattern of political invective was discernible against all three categories in Christian writings from the first, second, and third centuries CE. But by the fourth century CE, with the expansion of monastic literature from late antique Egypt, "Ethiopians" (*Aithiopes*) were perceived as the "ethnic other" by the authors of Egyptian monastic literature.[9] According to William Y. Adams, Nubians (i.e., Ethiopians) represented barbarity as opposed to Egyptian civilization; they became "a kind of human yardstick" by which the superiority or inferiority of the Egyptians could be measured.[10] Because of this perception of otherness, Egyptian authors adopted the rhetorical strategies of the larger culture and used "Ethiopians" as ethnic tropes to accomplish their persuasive goals.

At times, the monastic writers also used the amorphous terms *melas* or *niger* to describe individuals who represented threats to the monks.[11] One desert father describes color differences between Egyptians and Ethiopians as follows: "Those who inhabited the border regions between Egypt and Ethiopia were less black than the Ethiopians, but more black than the Egyptians."[12] The use of black (*melas* or *niger*) is not actually an ethnic designation in the same way as Ethiopian (*Aithiops*), but for the Egyptians, both Ethiopians and Blacks represented the extreme departure from the Roman ideal somatic norm.[13] Thus Ethiopians and Blacks, as well as the color black or blackness, became an integral part of the ethno-political rhetorics about sexuality in monastic writings.

[handwritten marginalia: Degree of blackness]

There are at least two possible explanations why "Egyptians" of late antiquity were able to employ the same ethno-political rhetorical strategies that had developed during the early period of Christianity.[14] The first explanation is based on the socio-political climate of ancient Egypt.[15] In the early years of the empire this province was heavily monitored and controlled by Augustus and his prefects mainly for trade and economic reasons. The Romans identified *both* Egyptians and Ethiopians as ethnic-others. By late antiquity, however, the socio-political climate changed drastically as the city of Alexandria became a major center of political activity, economic commerce, intellectual training, and theological controversy.[16] Now many leaders within the province of Egypt (especially the city of Alexandria) adopted the dominant Roman attitudes about ethnic-othering that had prevailed during the earlier years of the empire. Many of the authors of the monastic literature had spent some time in Alexandria and invariably adopted aspects of the culture of this influential city. Alexandrian bishops such as Athanasius, Theophilus, and Cyril were instrumental in creating the theological and political documents that shaped monastic culture. Thus, within many ascetic writings *"Egyptians" used Ethiopians* as tropes to define an understanding of the ascetic life.

A second possible explanation for the way Egyptians used Ethiopians as symbolic tropes in monastic literature involves the elevated status of Egypt as the place of the holy man.[17] It became one of the chief centers for those seeking to cultivate the ascetic way of life (*askēsis*).[18] According to Peter Brown, "it was in Egypt that the theory and practice of the ascetic life reached its highest pitch of articulateness and sophistication."[19] John Cassian, writing in the early fifth century, describes the general popularity of Egypt:

> We quickly decided to go *to Egypt* and to visit the greatest possible number of holy men in the remotest areas of the desert of Thebais. Their renown had spread throughout the world and our urge was not so much to rival them as to get to know them.[20]

The ascetic communities of the desert brought about a privileged position for the Greek-influenced Egyptian monks. Within these communities Ethiopians, when compared to Egyptians, were considered different, and likewise inferior.

I argue that Ethiopians are not simply included within monastic literature to discuss sexual vices that were known to distract the monks. Rather, the Ethiopians in the sources under review carry symbolic meanings that indicate how some Christian monastic writers defined themselves in relationship to different types of threats in late antique Roman Egypt. The sexual threat of the Ethiopian described in ascetic literature represents a type of ethno-political rhetoric that calls attention to military and political challenges that threatened the stability of Christian communities in Roman Egypt. The discursive use of Ethiopians (and Blacks) requires analysis so that the reader can better understand how social and political concerns influenced the construction of an influential branch of Christianity. But before I undertake an analysis of specific texts containing these ethno-political rhetorics, it is important to provide an overview of the historical context out of which these rhetorics arose.

HISTORICAL BACKGROUND: MONASTICISM IN LATE ANTIQUE EGYPT

The fourth century CE witnessed the growth of a new expression of Christianity known as monasticism.[21] By the fifth century CE, monasticism was firmly established throughout the Christian world and had become one of the main social forces within the eastern provinces of the empire. Withdrawal (*anachōrēsis*) into the desert (*erēmos*) was a way of rejecting the values of the inhabited world (*oikoumenē*).[22] The desert became the place for prayer, reflection, and action. The monks made a city in the desert and generated some of the most influential writings of late antiquity.[23]

The literature from this period reflects the diversity of monastic expressions among the desert monks and other ascetics who adhered to the teachings of various monastic traditions. Monastic movements emerged in many different geographical regions, such as Syria, Palestine, North Africa, Asia Minor, and Egypt.[24] An examination of all of these regions is beyond the scope of this study, but the monastic activity in Egypt is central.

Scholars have generally identified three types of monasticism in late antique Egypt.[25] The first type, practiced mainly in Lower Egypt, was known as *anchoritic* because of its adherence to a solitary, hermitic way of life. Antony (251–356 CE) is the model of this form of monasticism. He is reported to have heard a passage from the Gospel of Matthew as a direct call for him to retreat into the desert.[26] His struggles and ultimate victories over the demons became a source of inspiration and emulation for other monks. The collected *Sayings of the Fathers* is based on oral tradition that transmitted the experiences of Antony and many other anchoritic monks.

A second type of monasticism, practiced mainly in Upper Egypt, known as *coenobitism*, was characterized by communities of ascetics who came together around a central leader. Pachomius (290–347 CE), who formed a community at Tabennisi in the Thebaid, became known as the founder of this form of monasticism.[27] Having been influenced by Palamon (an anchorite monk) and the Christians at Thebes, Pachomius sought to establish a monastery and rule based upon a communal lifestyle and the structures of the church. He founded the Koinonia for the purpose of establishing in Christianity a community withdrawn from the world.[28]

A third form of monastic life was centered in Nitria and Scetis. This form was a combination of the first two, where several monks lived together, often as disciples of an "Abba." Close to the major urban city of Alexandria, these locales became the ideal place for someone like John Cassian to make his first contact with the desert.[29] It was chiefly through the writings of Cassian that the tradition of early desert monasticism reached the West.[30] This was a "scholarly" and sophisticated Greek-influenced form of monasticism that evolved around an educated group of ascetics, of whom Evagrius Ponticus (345–99 CE) was the most famous.[31] Many of the Sayings recorded by Cassian, Palladius, and Rufinus came from this tradition. These writers knew the desert and often had first-hand accounts of the oral tradition of the Sayings.

These three expressions of monasticism were not mutually exclusive, nor do they reflect completely the complex development of Egyptian monasticism.[32] There could be anchoritic monks in both upper and lower Egypt, just as coenobitic monasticism was practiced in many different parts of the Egyptian desert. Pachomian monasteries were located in the cultivated land of the valley, and the inhabitants of these monasteries sometimes took over abandoned villages.[33]

The tripartite description also prompts a view of monasticism as an expression of Christianity that developed in the desert among illiterate, indigenous Egyptians. Although some of the monks were more than likely Copts of low economic status, there were also many monks in the cities and villages through-out Egypt who were Hellenized elites with economic privilege and advanced social standing within their communities.[34] The flight to the desert for many of the monks should not be perceived solely as some dramatic physical departure from the world.[35]

During the fourth and fifth centuries a new genre of Christian writings emerged from the desert. These writings about saints, known as hagiography, represented the sayings, lives, rules, and letters of the desert monks. This literature, intended for use as spiritual guidance and direction, came to exercise great influence over people who wanted to cultivate a lifestyle that would distance them from the social and political turmoil within Greco-Roman Egypt. The spiritual response of the ascetics was, in part, a reflection of the socio-political crisis that characterized this period of history.[36]

James E. Goehring argues that the literature from the desert contains many references to social and economic interaction with the inhabited world.[37] In fact, the flight into the desert (anachōrēsis) also refers to those in Egypt who were trying to flee heavy taxes and other economic burdens.[38] Goehring challenges the interpreter of this material to consider how the expansion in the desert was part of a larger set of political, social, and religious developments in the Roman Empire. Without a doubt, the authors of the texts under review in this chapter must have been aware of the socio-political climate of the empire. They used their hagiographic writings about the desert monks, not only for spiritual purposes, but also as economic and socio-political commentary. In many ways monasticism was a response to the economic and political realities of late antiquity.[39]

can ~ separate politics from religion

Peter Brown claims that the literature of the early Egyptian ascetics reflects the response of those "who found themselves driven into the desert by a crisis in human relations within a world that had become unbearable."[40] This interpretation suggests that *anachōrēsis* involved a literal flight to some distant locale known as the desert (*erēmos*) with no return to, or engagement with, the inhabited world (*oikoumenē*).[41] The monks lived in the cities, villages, and countryside, and often served as spiritual guides to many travelers throughout the desert.[42] Thus the monastic writings contained the stories of those who were in close contact with the inhabited world and were in many ways frustrated with the social and political developments within the world.[43]

At the same time as the monastic experiments were forming and developing in the desert of Egypt, wars were threatening the stability of the land and its people. As the breadbasket of the empire, Egypt was a desired land, often under military occupation and subject to threats by various sub-Saharan nomadic tribes.[44] It is beyond the scope of this chapter to explain or define all the military and political threats in Roman Egypt during late antiquity.[45] Yet it will be useful for my purposes here to describe briefly one military group identified in Greco-Roman writings that may have influenced the symbolic use of Ethiopians and Blacks in monastic literature.

EXCURSUS: The Political and Military Threat of the Blemmyes

Roman Egypt was constantly defending its boundaries in late antiquity. One constant threat came from its Nubian neighbors in the desert, generally referred to in the classical sources as Blemmyes (*Blemmyes*).[46] According to ancient geographer Strabo, the Blemmyes, along with Troglodytes, Noubai, and Megabari, were Ethiopians (*Aithiopes*) who lived toward the south (*pros noton*):

> And the remaining parts (of the land), those toward the south, are inhabited by Troglodytes, *Blemmyes*, Noubai, and Megabari, those *Ethiopians* who live above Syene. These are nomads and are neither numerous nor warlike, although they were thought to be so by the ancients because often, like robbers, they would attack defenseless people.[47]

Dionysios, another ancient geographer who lived in Alexandria during the reign of Hadrian (117–38 CE), also described the location of the Blemmyes in his geographical tractate known as *Orbis descriptio*:

> In the corners live the *Ethiopians* (*Aithiopĕes*), the farthest away of the mainland, direct on the ocean by the valleys of distant Kerna over which the hill tops of *the sun-burned Blemmyes* (*aithaleōn Blemmyōn*) tower, from where the waters of the plentiful Nile flow forth. From Libya it flows eastward abundantly, it is called "Siris" by the *Ethiopians* (*Aithiopōn*), but the inhabitants of Syene have renamed the twisting (river) "Nile."[48]

Dionysios's work was translated into Latin during the second half of the fourth century by Rufius Festus Avienus. In his translation, entitled *Orbis terrae*, Avienus provides one of the most vivid physical descriptions of the Blemmyes:

> The *Blemmyes* (*Blemmyes*) have large stature, *black skin* (*nigri cute*), and slender waist. Moreover, their arms and legs are marked by protruding muscles. They always run barefooted over the sand, without leaving so much as a footprint.[49]

These ancient texts validate the geographical origins and physical characteristics of the Ethiopian warriors known as the Blemmyes.

The Blemmyes invaded Egypt several times from the mid-third to the late sixth century CE. During the reign of Decius (249–51 CE) they attacked the southern frontier of Egypt.[50] They continued to exercise their military strategy and power leading Diocletian (284–305 CE) to enter into a treaty with them toward the close of the third century.[51] Their threat to southern Egypt is evident in the ways that different communities within the desert sought protection from them.[52]

Classicists and historians have all agreed that the Blemmyes were a persistent menace to the land of Egypt; yet they have disagreed on the extent to which the ancient sources can be relied upon in constructing the historical background of the relationship of Egypt with the nomadic tribe from the south.[53] My own review of the primary sources – even with their limitations and problems – leads me to conclude that the Blemmyes or some groups like them were a political and military threat that forced the Romans to adjust their military strategies and devise special pacts with this group.[54] Pliny, for example, claims that Ethiopia had been in a series of wars with Egypt:

> Ethiopia was worn out by alternate periods of dominance and subjection in a series of wars with Egypt, having been a famous and powerful country even down to the Trojan wars, when Memnon was king; and the stories about Andromeda show that it dominated

Syria and the coasts of the Mediterranean in the time of King Cepheus.[55]

By the fifth century CE, both the Blemmyes and Nobades had formed an alliance in opposition to the growing influence of Christianity. During the reigns of both Theodosius II (405–50 CE) and Marcian (450–57 CE) the Blemmyes raided Christian communities, and sometime during this period attacked the Christian settlement at Kharga.[56] Emperor Marcian authorized a military campaign against the Blemmyes, which was successful in bringing them under control. They were still permitted to make their annual pilgrimage to the temple of Isis at Philae.[57]

I am assuming that the authors of the monastic sources were aware of the presence of the black-skinned Blemmyes or some groups like them in the desert. This is not to say that they saw the Blemmyes on a day-to-day basis. Such information relating to the encounters between Egyptians and Blemmyes is neither sufficiently documented nor necessary for my purposes.[58] But I want to suggest that the "presence" of the Blemmyes or other sub-Saharan nomadic groups who dwelled around the regions of Syene and Scetis, and their perceived threat, may have influenced the authors of the monastic writings to include the pejorative references to Ethiopians and Blacks within their ethno-political rhetorics defining sexual threats. Although the texts under review in this chapter use the terms *Aithiops* and *melas*, it is plausible that the authors may have had the Blemmyes (*Blemmyes*) in mind as they developed the different stories about the desert monks.

The Blemmyes and Ethiopians shared similar physical characteristics that made it difficult to distinguish between the two groups.[59] The ethno-political rhetorics identified in monastic writings about Ethiopians and Blacks may have been a subtle way of responding to the political and military threat that the Blemmyes or other groups like them presented within the desert. I will argue that political and military threats in the desert may have been a backdrop for the stories about sexual immorality in monastic writings, especially those from Upper Egypt. Palladius, for example, wrote that the monasteries of Tabennesi in the Thebaid were crowded with refugees who had fled from the Blemmyes (*ethnos tōn Blemmyōn*) who were plundering Upper Egypt.[60] In his *Dialogus*, Palladius also claims that he was "under guard in the neighborhood of the Blemmyes, a tribe of the Ethiopians, at a place called Syene."[61] According to Rufinus the Ethiopians raided the Thebaid border town of Syene and caused a Roman general to ask the monk John of Lycopolis whether he would prevail against them.[62] Many of the texts under review in this chapter originated from the milieu of Syene, and from the period after nomadic tribes devastated that area.[63] The way the monastic writers developed ethno-political rhetorics about Ethiopians and Blacks served to encourage the monks to avoid sexual temptations and political turmoil with the enemies from the south.

SEXUALITY AND THE BODY: THE ETHIOPIAN AS OBJECT OF SEXUAL PASSION

Introduction

The piety and ideological worldview of the desert fathers are defined in part through the symbolic representations of Ethiopians in monastic sources. A sense of sexual danger is evident throughout the writings of the desert fathers. What is most obvious in these texts is the vilification of Ethiopians (and sometimes "Blacks") for the purpose of defining the contours of virtuous ascetic behavior. According to Peter Brown, the ascetic literature of Egypt of the fourth and fifth centuries produced many vivid anecdotes concerning sexual seduction and heroic sexual avoidance.[64] In this literature the body became the focus of many stories about sexual temptations and lusts.

The monastic writers were not concerned only with sexuality in their discourses about various trials and temptations of the monks. They were also concerned about articulating, shaping, and defending a certain view of the world. In order to renounce the world, which was filled with political strife and change, control of bodily passions was paramount. In many of the stories Ethiopians are used as tropes or foils, leading one scholar to identify the "anti-black sentiment" in many of the monastic sources.[65] The "Ethiopian" became a dramatic trope for signifying what Geoffrey Galt Harpham calls "the signs of temptation" within the desert.[66] In this literature Ethiopians – both men and women – personified the most powerful forms of sexual temptations and vices that challenged the austere and ascetic life of the monks. The following section will provide three examples of how Ethiopians (and sometimes Blacks) were used to set forth the boundaries of proper sexual behavior for the desert monks.

Sources

Athanasius, Vita Antonii 6

The *Vita Antonii* was written by the Alexandrian bishop Athanasius (295–373 CE) shortly after Antony's death in 356 CE.[67] This text is one of the most representative examples of early Egyptian monastic literature, and according to Averil Cameron, it served as required reading for educated Christians.[68] According to the heading of the prologue in the Latin version by Evagrius, this document was addressed "to monks in foreign parts (*ad peregrinos fraters*)." This description most likely refers to monks in the West who had requested that Athanasius give some account of the life of Antony for the sake of their edification and emulation. Athanasius responded to this request by providing a biography of Antony's life.[69] This *Vita* provides the story of his birth, his call to the monastic life, his many encounters with demons, his miracles and visions, and his ultimate death.[70]

85

The theological concerns of Athanasius are apparent throughout the *Vita*. His controversies with the Arians inform many of the chapters in this text. During the mid-fourth century, followers of Arius were bidding for the support of Egyptian monastics, and the *Vita* preserves notice of the Arian contention that Antony shared their doctrine:

> When on one occasion the Arians gave out the lie that his views were the same as theirs, he showed that he was vexed and angry with them. Answering the appeal of both the bishops and all the brethren, he came down from the mountain, and entering Alexandria, he denounced the Arians . . . Wherefore, do not have the least thing to do with the most godless Arians: there simply is no fellowship of light with darkness [2 Cor 6:14]. You must remember that you are God-fearing Christians, but they by saying that the Son and Word of God the Father is a creature, are in no respect different from the pagans who worship the created in place of God the Creator.[71]

We also learn from this text that Athanasius participated in a literary climate that associated sexual immorality with Blacks.[72] After a brief summary of his birth and youth (chap. 1) and his call and first steps into the ascetic life (chaps. 2–4), Athanasius provides a section on Antony's early conflicts with demons (chaps. 5–7). It is in chapter 6 of this section about demons that Antony is challenged by the spirit of fornication (*pneuma porneias*), who appears in the image of a black boy (*melas pais*). In order to assess the rhetorical strategy involved with the use of *melas pais* in chapter 6, it is first necessary to look at some ethnographic clues contained throughout the *Vita*.

Athanasius begins the *Vita* with a statement about Antony's ethnic, economic, and religious background: "Antony was an Egyptian by birth (*genos Aigyptios*). His parents were well born and prosperous, and since they were Christians, he also was reared in a Christian manner."[73] By opening this document with an ethnic-geographic marker, Athanasius is establishing the importance of Antony's ethnic background, which will become significant later when he has to conquer the *melas pais* in chapter 6.[74] As mentioned earlier in this chapter, Egyptians considered themselves ethnically different from the dark-skinned Ethiopians in the Nile Valley. Athanasius appealed to these ethnic differences in the *Vita* in order to show the importance of renouncing the passions of the flesh.

In Athanasius's text, chapter 6 opens with a dragon (*drakōn*) as the chief opponent of Antony.[75] This dragon suddenly alters himself into the image of a *melas pais*. The text is as follows:

> Finally, then, when the dragon was unable by this strategy to defeat him, but instead saw himself being thrust from Antony's heart,

Dragon
as
black
boy

86

gnashing his teeth (as Scripture says),[76] he altered himself, taking
on the likeness of his mind.[77] It later appeared to him in the image
of a *black boy* (*melas pais*). And as if succumbing, he no longer
attacked by means of thoughts (for the treacherous one had been
cast out), but now using a human voice, he said, "I tricked many,
and I vanquished many, but just now, waging my attack on you and
your labors, as I have upon many others, I was too weak." Then
Antony asked, "Who are you who is saying these things to me?"
Immediately he replied with a pitiful voice, and said, "*I am a friend
of fornication* (*egō tēs porneias eimi philos*).[78] I set its ambushes and I
worked its seductions against the young – I have even been called
a *spirit of fornication* (*pneuma porneias*). How many who wanted to live
prudently (*sōphronein*) I have deceived! How many of those exercising
self-control (*enkrateuomenous*) I won over when I agitated them! I am
the one on whose account the prophet reprimands those who fall,
saying, 'you have been led astray by a spirit of fornication.'[79] For it
was by my devices that they were tripped. I am he who so frequently
troubled you and so many times was overturned by you." And
Antony gave thanks to the Lord, and responding boldly to him,
said: "You, then, are much to be despised, for you are *black of soul*
(*melas ton noun*), and like a morally weak child. From now on you
cause me no anxiety, for the Lord is my helper, and I shall despise
my enemies."[80] Hearing these things, *the Black One* (*ho melas*)
immediately fled, cowering at the words and afraid even to approach
the man.[81]

When the black boy enters the story the subject matter shifts to emphasize
the threat of fornication, a challenge to all those aspiring to live the ascetic life.[82]
Several commentators who have reviewed this passage suggest many theories for
understanding the function of *melas* within the text. For example, Courtès
describes this account as Antony being brought into a theater and forced to
wrestle with a huge "Ethiopian" before an audience comprising whites and
blacks.[83] In his study of the politics of asceticism David Brakke claims that
Athanasius underscores Antony's mastery of his bodily desires through a sexual
temptation that draws on the "racial and sexual stereotypes held by Christians
in late Roman society."[84] He goes on to say that the representation of the devil's
evil with a black person "draws on the color prejudices of some Egyptians of the
Roman period."[85] Brakke's remarks begin to approach the complex relationship
between ascetic piety and color symbolism in the *Vita Antonii*, but his analysis
focuses more on the symbolism of "the boy" who is tempting Antony with
pederasty.[86] He sums up Antony's encounter with the devil as follows: "by
tempting Antony with pederasty, the devil offers him what Athanasius
considered an anomalous sexual relationship of pure desire, lacking any generally
accepted social function in Egyptian society of the late Roman empire."[87] In

both of these cases the interpreters are not able to bring any clear resolution to the use of *melas* in this text.[88] They allow their own presuppositions about racial prejudices to filter into their analyses. A review that summarizes how ascetic values are transmitted at the expense of ethnic others will yield new possibilities for interpreting this text.

First of all, this scene is used to represent Antony's first victory over the devil (*kata tou diabolou*).[89] Spiritual warfare with the demons was a major concern of the desert monks and much of the instruction in the hagiographic material addressed how to struggle against the demons.[90] One of the chief ways the devil could distract or conquer a monk was through his thoughts (*logismoi*). A fifth-century *Vita* spuriously attributed to Athanasius emphasizes the need to be vigilant against the devil's attempts to control the thoughts: "Therefore it is necessary always to be watchful (*grēgorein*). For he does battle by means of external acts, and subdues by means of internal thoughts (*logismois*). And he does much more by means of the internal; for night and day he approaches spiritually."[91]

Fornication is not always associated with Blacks in hagiographic writings. In the *Apophthegmata patrum* there are several examples in which the monks are challenged to control their sexual passions without reference to Blacks or any other ethnic groups.[92] These examples tend to be short, simple descriptions of sexual encounters and their consequences. The face-to-face confrontation that Athanasius constructs between the black boy and Antony is much more developed than other examples and deserves further exploration for the ethnographic polemic used in this text.

Chapter 5 of the *Vita* describes how the devil first attempted to distract Antony from the ascetic life through his thoughts. However, these thoughts related to money, property, fame, and the care of his younger sister and were not powerful enough to divert Antony from his ascetic resolve. After this, the devil tried to incite Antony to lust by masquerading as a woman. This scheme also failed because Antony chose to fight back through more fervent prayer and fasting.

In chapter 6 Athanasius has the devil move beyond the realm of thoughts and seduces Antony to stray from his commitments. This lover of fornication speaks to Antony and informs him of the powers of the sexual vice of fornication. At this point Athanasius uses an image of a black boy to highlight how Antony will conquer the representative of fornication.[93] He portrays the black boy as weak (*asthenēs*), treacherous (*dolios*), deceitful (*ēpatēsa*), pitiful (*oiktras*), and fearful (*phobētheis*). Moreover, the color black (*melas*) is used to describe the inner character of the boy: "you are black in your soul" (*gar melas ei ton noun*).[94]

Athanasius was concerned with the values and practices associated with prudent living (*sōphrosynē*) and self-control (*enkrateia*). Fornication or sexual immorality was one of the major stumbling blocks to these virtues. After the encounter with the black boy, Antony is determined to practice asceticism in earnest through the mortification of his body.

Antony, having learned from the Scriptures that the wiles of the Evil One are manifold, practiced asceticism in earnest, bearing in mind that even if he could not beguile his heart by pleasure of the body, he would certainly try to ensnare him by some other method; for the demon is a lover of sin. So he more and more mortified his body and brought it into subjection, lest having conquered on one occasion, he should be the loser on another. He resolved, therefore, to accustom himself to a more austere way of life.[95]

Throughout the *Vita*, Athanasius emphasizes the moral virtues of Antony and presents him as the model anchorite. In chapter 6 the *melas pais* is used as a foil for establishing the importance of the severest form of asceticism.

Athanasius's admittedly idealized portrait of Antony is established by the vituperative rhetoric against the *melas pais* in chapter 6. The *melas pais* is used to signal the threat of fornication that tempted Antony and other monks of the desert. Athanasius employed an ethnographic trope that he knew would be familiar to his audiences. He demonstrated that Antony's example and resolve to take up the ascetic life in earnest (*syntonōs ekechrēto tē askēsei*) would be more exemplary and compelling when presented as a victory over an ethnic other – *melas pais*.

melas – black pais – boy

Palladius, Apophthegmata patrum 579

The *Apophthegmata patrum* (*Sayings of the Desert Fathers*) were originally spoken to individuals on specific occasions and subsequently recorded and compiled for the edification of monks within various monastic communities. The *Sayings* often took the form of short, instructive wisdom speech. These speeches or stories, based on early oral traditions in the Coptic language, deal with a wide variety of subjects pertaining to the quest for the spiritual life devoted to God. The *Sayings* represent conversations or words (*rhēma*)[96] that emerged from the everyday life of the monastic movements of Scetis[97] or Syene in upper Egypt. Most of the *Sayings* followed a general pattern: a monk seeking to live the ascetic life is identified; the monk is presented with a vice or temptation, usually in the form of demons; an experienced monk offers advice about how to overcome the temptation; the monk reflects on the advice received; the monk confronts the temptation; and the monk resolves to continue on the path of *askēsis*. This general pattern is present in a *Saying* about fornication attributed to the fifth-century desert father Palladius.

Palladius (ca. 364–420 CE) traveled throughout the desert of Egypt for several years, collecting first-hand accounts from the monks who dwelled there. He undoubtedly heard many of the *Sayings* of the desert fathers and constructed his own version of the stories so that his audience would understand the challenges or constant threats to the ascetic life. One of the most pervasive challenges for the monks was fornication. In the following text Palladius describes how devils in the forms of Ethiopians stir up "the passion of fornication" in a desert father who wanted to become a monk:

> A certain father when he went out to become a monk was a virgin, and he did not even know that a whore existed among the children of men. And when he was dwelling in his cell the devils began to stir up in him the *passion of fornication*, and lifting up his eyes he saw the devils going around him in the forms of *Ethiopians*, and they incited him to yield to the passion; then he rose up straightway and prayed, and said, "O Lord, help me," and when he had said these things immediately a stone fell from the roof, and he heard as it were a sweet voice, and he seemed to enjoy a short respite from the *thoughts of fornication*. And he rose up and came to one of the old men and related the matter to him, and the old man answered and said, "I do not know what this means"; and he sent him on to Abba Poemen, and that brother related the matter unto him also. Then the old man said unto him, "The stone that you saw fall is the Calumniator, and that voice that you heard is *lust*. Take heed unto thy soul, and make supplication unto God, and behold, you shall be freed from this war"; and Abba Poemen taught him how to *contend against devils*, and having prayed, he dismissed him, and that brother came to his cell. And he made entreaty and supplication unto God, and God granted him to attain to such a gift [of excellence] that, when that brother died, He was pleased that there should be revealed unto him whether it was well with his soul or not.[98]

The few scholars who have identified and commented on this text have for the most part merely acknowledged the "anti-black" sentiment expressed in the use of the Ethiopians.[99] Unlike Antony, who encountered the devil in the form of a black boy, the unnamed monk in this story was challenged by many devils in the form of Ethiopians who stirred up the passion of fornication. The Ethiopians in this case do not speak or assume any active role; the author uses them to emphasize the significance of the threat of fornication. This story is an example of how monastic authors drew upon a well-established "other" in order to communicate the importance of contending against the devils.

Pelagius, Apophthegmata patrum 5.4

In the sixth century Pelagius, a deacon of Rome and later Pope (556–61 CE), translated into Latin a section of the *Lives of the Desert Fathers* that deals with fornication. In this text, Abbot Apollo counsels a young man to return to his cell so that he can cultivate a better understanding of how to fight against the assaults of the adversary or demon of lust (*daemone fornicationis*). The young man had initially sought counsel from an older monk about the thoughts of fornication (*cogitationes fornicationum*) that had invaded his mind.

> There was a certain brother who was earnest and anxious after good living. And being sorely harassed by the *demon of lust* (*daemone fornicationis*), he came to a certain old man and related to him his imaginings. But on hearing these things, and himself being free, the old man was indignant, and declared that the brother was miserable and unworthy to wear the habit of a monk, inasmuch as he admitted such thoughts to his mind. And the brother, hearing this, despaired of himself: and he left his own cell and took the road back to the world.[100]

As the story continues, Abbot Apollo, by providence of God, met the young man and counseled him on how to manage the demon of fornication:

> But by God's providence the abbot Apollo met him: and seeing him perturbed and in heavy sadness, questioned him, saying, "My son, what is the cause of your deep sadness?" At first the brother, in the shame of his soul, could answer him nothing: but after the old man had asked him many questions as to what had befallen him, he confessed, saying, "*Thoughts of lust* (*cogitationes fornicationum*) do challenge me: and I confessed it to this old man, and according to him there is now no hope of salvation for me: and so in deep despair I am going back to the world." But when the abbot Apollo heard this, like a wise physician he began asking many questions and counseled him, saying, "Think it no strange thing, my son, nor despair yourself. For even I, at my age, and in this way of life, am sorely challenged by just such thoughts as these. Therefore do not be found without this kind of testing, where the remedy is not so much in one's anxious thought as in God's compassion. Today at least grant me what I ask of you, and go back to your cell." And the brother did so. But the abbot Apollo on leaving him made his way to the cell of that old man who had brought him to despair: and standing outside he entreated God with tears, saying, "Lord, who sends temptation when it is needed, turn the *battle* (*bello*) wherein that brother has suffered against this old man that by experience he may learn in his old age what length of time has never taught him: to have compassion on those who are harassed by temptations of this sort." His prayer ended, he saw an *Ethiopian* (*Aethiopem*) standing close to the cell and shooting arrows against the old man: and as if pierced by them, the old man was running about like a man drunk with wine. And when he could endure it no longer, he came out of his cell and down that same road which the young man had taken,

going back to the world "For no man can endure the *assaults of the adversary* (*insidias adversarii*), neither can any extinguish or restrain the fire that leaps in our nature, unless God's grace shall give its strength to human weakness. In this salutary judgment upon us, let us pray to God with all supplication, that He will turn aside the scourge that is fallen upon thee, for He makes sore and binds up; He wounds and His hands make whole: He humiliates and exalts; He kills and makes life; He brings down to hell and brings back." And so saying, he made his prayer, and immediately, the old man was freed from the *warfare* (*bello*) that had been brought upon him. And the abbot Apollo counseled the old man to ask of God for the tongue of the wise that he might know when it was time to speak.[101]

This story on the surface is intended to teach the monks about the importance of having compassion for those who are struggling with temptations. Another meaning, however, could be intended through the reference to *Aethiopem*. The Ethiopian signals the threat of sexual immorality, as well as social, cultural, political, and military threats that challenged the monks.

Apollo was sorely concerned that the old man did not extend compassion to the young man who needed some sound advice on how to deal with his passions. After convincing the young man to go back to his cell, Apollo went to the cell of the old man and prayed to God with tears (*cum lacrymis*). Apollo prayed that the old man would learn "to have compassion on those who are harassed by temptations of this sort." After the prayer, Apollo saw an Ethiopian standing close to the cell and shooting arrows against the old man. The Ethiopian in this text caused the old man to go back into the world.

This *Saying* does not follow the general outline given above in the section on Palladius. In this case Abba Apollo helped an older man who was expected to know already how to contend against the demons. The Ethiopian in this extended story is not directly connected with the demon of fornication. Multiple meanings are intended in this text. First, the Ethiopian symbolizes the constant spiritual warfare (*bello*) that all desert monks must endure. Second, the Ethiopian reflects the basic military image of Ethiopians, who were known for fighting with bows and arrows.[102] Third, the Ethiopian indicates the author's awareness of ethnic differences within the desert. These differences were instrumental in forming the ethno-political rhetoric in this hagiographic text.

The references to *bello* are significant in this *Saying*. Spiritual warfare was an ongoing aspect of the ascetic life. Pelagius uses the term twice – first, during Apollo's opening prayer: "turn the *bello* wherein that brother has suffered against this old man that by experience he may learn in his old age what length of time has never taught him: to have compassion on those who are harassed by temptations of this sort"; second, after Apollo's closing prayer: "the old man was freed from the *bello* that had been brought upon him." These prayers indicate how important it is for the monks to endure spiritual warfare against the demons.

In addition to the spiritual lessons contained in this *Saying*, there are also political, military, and ideological meanings buried within the prayers and personified in the description of the Ethiopian. The warfare (*bello*) of the monks may have also involved encounters with different military groups in the desert. In this regard the Ethiopian opens a window onto the complex military battles that were an important element of the socio-political milieu out of which this *Saying* emerged. The monks could not totally isolate themselves from these conflicts and battles that occurred within the desert.[103] Thus the vivid description of an Ethiopian shooting arrows into the cell of the old man was a symbolic reflection of the Ethiopians who were waging battles in the desert. Although this text opens with a focus on fornication, what evolves throughout the narrative is a well-crafted, subtle commentary on the military threats in the desert.

Finally, the symbolic Ethiopian in this text is part of an ethno-political rhetoric that communicates values about the social reality of the desert monks and ideological values of the author or editor of this story. The monks did not lead such cloistered lives that they were unaware of wider societal concerns that were developing in their midst. Furthermore, the author used the image of "an Ethiopian shooting arrows" to emphasize the consequences of not having compassion on those who are battling with thoughts of fornication. This symbolic image was effective because of the understandings about ethnic difference that existed in ancient Egypt.

Summary

The examples in this section highlight how Ethiopians and Blacks were used as tropes in ascetic writings to symbolize both spiritual and political threats that challenged the desert monks and those who sought to emulate them. Lust, fornication, and other sexual vices were personified in the forms of Ethiopians and Blacks, and even given voice to seduce their targets. Clearly, a discursive strategy has been identified within several monastic stories. The authors of this material knew that, given the socio-political climate of late antique Roman Egypt, Ethiopians and Blacks were very much present in the minds of the Egyptian ascetics in the desert.[104] No other ethnic groups are isolated within the monastic literature of late antique Egypt in the same fashion as Ethiopians and Blacks. An exploration of the ethno-political rhetorics vilifying Ethiopians and Blacks in these texts provides a new framework for understanding the complex religious and socio-political milieu that influenced the writing of these documents. The rhetorics functioned in at least two ways: (1) to reinscribe the monastic insistence that the "flesh" and "passions" are problems that should be mortified through the cultivation of *askēsis*, and (2) to demonstrate an affinity with Romans who saw Ethiopians and Blacks as a political and military threat.

Ethiopians and Blacks became an ethnic-other in these writings. They were presented in the form of demons as a way of exemplifying the importance of constant spiritual warfare against the passions of the flesh. They were also used by monastic authors to demonstrate that those who cultivated the ascetic life were nevertheless good Romans who shared similar values about certain groups of Ethiopians who were considered a menacing threat to Roman Egypt.[105] The renunciation of sexual vices by the desert monks was a corollary to the renunciation of political threats to the empire. The authors strategically used ethno-political rhetorics about Ethiopians and Blacks to help shape a monastic worldview that reflected the social and political realities affecting both desert and city dwellers.

SEXUALITY AND GENDER: THE ETHIOPIAN WOMAN AS OBJECT OF LUST AND TEMPTATION

Introduction

In an essay on early Christian ascetic women, Gillian Clark identifies some of the notable differences between male and female ascetics.[106] She provides many examples to show how women presented a special challenge to the monks in the desert. For the male ascetics, even the presence of a woman was held to be particularly distracting and a threat to the spiritual progress of the monks.[107] John of Lycopolis, a desert monk who had not seen a woman in forty years, says, "it is not in our interest to have our dwellings near inhabited places, or to associate with women. For a meeting of this kind gives rise to an inexpungeable memory, which we draw from what we have seen and from what we have heard in conversation."[108] Another monk, Sisoes, desired to go to the desert, for it was considered the place where there were no women.[109] John Cassian points out that even mothers are to be avoided: "first you think about your mother or your sister; then about some religious woman you have met; then about some other woman."[110] These examples led Gillian Clark to conclude that "the construct of woman as sexual temptress, as desire personified, was apparently so powerful that even men committed to a life of prayer could not think of women as fellow human beings with the same commitment."[111]

Peter Brown also emphasizes the pervasive fear of women within monastic literature.[112] Brown even identifies the misogyny in the texts and cites several examples of negative representations of women: A monk dipped his cloak into the putrefying flesh of a dead woman, so that the smell might banish thoughts about her; a dutiful daughter repelled the advances of a young monk by warning him that he could not imagine the strange and terrible stench of a menstruating woman; a novice carried his elderly mother across a stream, his hands prudently wrapped in his cloak: "for the flesh of all women is fire."[113]

Brown asserts "among the monks, male and female bodies came to be presented as equally charged with sexual feeling, because both were equally subject to an exacting obligation to preserve their virgin state."[114] Thus the body (i.e., the

94

"virgin" body) of the monk was used as a boundary to define the place of the
ascetic movement. Brown argues that the misogyny of much ascetic literature
was part of a wider strategy of defining the place of the ascetic movement in late
Roman society. One purpose of this literature was to keep the "world" and the
"desert" at a safe distance from each other. Thus women were used symbolically
in the stories about the desert fathers as a distancing strategy to establish
boundaries between the city and the desert. Brown concludes that the leaders of
the Egyptian church wanted to ensure that the monks remained in the prestige-
filled, and relatively safe, zone of the desert.[115]

Both Clark and Brown identify how "women" carried symbolic meaning in
the monastic sources. However, they do not offer any clues for understanding
the use of Ethiopian (or black) women and girls within monastic sources. Brown
persuasively highlights the "nightmarish sexual encounters" within many
monastic texts, yet omits from his discussion texts that contain symbolic color-
coded descriptions of Ethiopian (or black) women.[116] One such example is
contained in a fifth-century letter by Ennodius. Ennodius recommended
virginity by using a derogatory image of a "black girl":

> Thus, let your virginity stand firm within you in the age to come,
> neither let what the blessed life gave perish,
> thus do not let the limbs of a black girl (*nigrans puella*)
>   blemish (*maculare*) you,
> nor lie near her infernal face (*Tartaream feciem*)[117]
> in order that you raise up your brother through
>   the scriptures with your words,
> so that the wave[118] flows from your springs to your brother.[119]

In this text Ennodius is using *nigrans puella* (lit. "a blackening girl") as a foil to
establish the importance of virginity (*virginitas*). In doing so he contrasts the
blessed life (*vita beata*) to the underworld. The verb *maculare*, which I have
translated as "blemish," could actually refer to the stain of sin – presumably the
sin of fornication.[120] The color symbolism of blackness in this text is used to
warn the reader about the threat of fornication.

Because of such oversights by Brown and other modern scholars of monastic
literature, I suggest that attention be given to exploring how perceptions about
ethnic and color difference, coupled with aesthetic values about women,
influenced the vituperative rhetorics about Ethiopian women in monastic
writings. In this section I focus on two examples in order to demonstrate how
the desert fathers used Ethiopian women to symbolize the appropriate responses
to the sexual temptations that challenged the monks. I also demonstrate how
the construction of Ethiopian women in these texts reflected and established
power relationships and gender disparities that existed in late antique Egypt.[121]

Peter Frost claimed that the Ethiopian aroused sentiments linked to aesthetic
values deeply embedded in Greco-Roman culture.[122] Accordingly, people

around the Mediterranean regarded light skin as a hallmark of femininity; in contrast, the Ethiopian was viewed as the very antithesis of female beauty.[123] One author described a couple's reunion after a separation of many years; one having become a monk, the other a nun: "she recognized her husband, but he could not recognize her; so much her beauty had disappeared to the point where she looked like an *Ethiopian woman*."[124]

In a text by Pachomius, a virgin woman, who was a nun, is described as good-looking and beautiful:

> Since I did not find anyone to make the journey with me, I walked absolutely alone. And all of a sudden, looking behind me I saw a nun. She was a *very good-looking and beautiful woman (pany eueidē kai hōraian)*, and she said to me, "Hello, Abba!" And I said to her, "Peace to you, Amma. Where are you going?" She answered, "I am a virgin from the monastery of the Tabennesiots, and I am going to my family according to the flesh." And with those words the thoughts of fornication (*hoi logismoi tēs porneias*) began to beset and disturb me. I was no longer able to stay the burning. I locked her down and stripped her naked; whereupon she gave me a slap, and I saw the whole place looking like fire. Then I arose, having ejaculated, but she had disappeared. And forthwith I heard in the air laughter and clapping, as if from a numerous crowd. A fever and a shivering immediately seized me and I stayed lying there from the third to the ninth hour.[125]

The late fourth-century desert traveler, Rufinus, provides another account of a demon taking the form of a pretty woman:

> One evening a demon took the shape of a *pretty woman* traveling in the desert. She came to the door of a monk's cave, pretending to be tired and exhausted from her journey. She fell at the monk's knees as if to beg him for mercy. "Night overtook me," she said, "while I was still wandering in the desert, and now I am frightened. Just let me rest in a corner of your cell so that I don't fall prey to the wild animals." The monk, feeling pity, received her inside the cave, asking her why she was traveling alone in the desert. She began to converse normally enough but bit by bit sweetened her words and played upon his sympathies. The sweetness of her speech gradually took possession of his mind until she had turned it entirely to thoughts of lust. She began to mix jokes and laughter with her speech, reaching up to touch his chin and beard as if in reverence, and then stroking his throat and neck. The monk began to burn with desire, but just as he was about to consummate his passion, the demon let out a terrible shriek in a hoarse voice, slipped away from his embrace, and departed, laughing filthily at his shame.[126]

In a pithy example from one of the anonymous *Sayings of the Desert Fathers* we find the following:

> A brother was severely tempted by the demon of lust. In fact, four demons, under the appearance of very beautiful women, spent forty days attacking him to bring him to the shame of intercourse. But he fought courageously and was not overcome, and seeing his successful warfare, God allowed him to experience no more the flames of sensuality.[127]

These examples indicate how "beautiful women" were used as objects of temptation within the monastic sources. In general, women were associated with fornication and other passions of the flesh. But Ethiopian women, as compared to other women in monastic writings, are described in lurid detail and represented as ugly, filthy, dirty, sensuous, and evil. In some instances (to be discussed below), the lingering bad smell or foul odor of the Ethiopian woman is emphasized. As mentioned above, when a woman lost her beauty she was compared to, or described as, an Ethiopian.

The following two examples depict the Ethiopian woman as the ultimate personification of lust and fornication to the desert fathers. Given the hyper-symbolic language about the Ethiopian woman's appearance, the desert fathers must have found her attractive and quite seductive. The ambivalence toward Ethiopian women permeates these examples and further indicates that it is extremely difficult to assess the literature of the desert tradition because of the many psycho-social factors that may have influenced the storytellers and authors of these texts. I am not concerned with explicating the obsessions and fantasies of the desert fathers. What is of more interest, and far more convincingly documented in the literature, are the vituperative rhetorics desert fathers developed about the Ethiopian woman because she was perceived as a sexual threat. The authors of these texts appealed to assumptions about ascetic practices, ethnic differences, and gender stereotypes in developing these stories.

Sources

Anonymous, Apophthegmata patrum 5.5

The *Sayings of the Desert Fathers* is one of the most significant texts from late antique monastic culture that provides evidence for the threat represented by Ethiopian women. The Latin version of the *Sayings*, known as the *Verba Seniorum*, includes this story under the rubric of fornication. In this text, the devil appears as an ugly, evil-smelling Ethiopian woman who distracts a young monk from his ascetic life:

> A certain man went into the desert of Scete to become a monk. He took with him his infant son. When the boy became a young man

the demons (*daemones*) began to wage their war against him. The young man told his father, "I must go into the world because I am not able to bear the *desire of lust (carnales concupiscentias)*." His father consoled him. But the young man said, "I do not want to bear this burden any longer. Allow me to return to the world." His father said to him, "Listen to me, son, take with you forty days' worth of bread and work one more time and spend forty days in the inner desert." The young man obeyed his father and lived a life of seclusion and hard work in the remote desert. Twenty days passed when, suddenly, he saw the work of the devil appear before him, and it stood before him in the form of an *Ethiopian woman (mulier Aethiopissa), smelly and disgusting in appearance (fetida et turpis aspectu)*, so much so that he could not bear her smell. She then said to him, "I am she who appears sweet (*dulcis*) in the hearts of men, but because of your obedience and your labor, God does not permit me to seduce you, but I have let you know my *foul odor (fetorem)*." [The Ethiopian woman] left him, and he thanked God. He came to his father and said: "Father, I no longer wish to go into the world, for I have seen the work of the *devil* [*diabolos*] and have smelled her foul odor." The young man's father replied, "if you had stayed another forty days deep in the desert, you would have seen a greater vision."[128]

The Ethiopian woman in this *Saying* is used as a polemical device to indicate the threat of fornication. The author highlights the threat by drawing attention to the woman's smelly and disgusting appearance (*fetida et turpis aspectu*). These aesthetic features are symbolic of the multifaceted threats that plagued the desert monks.

Appeals to olfactory symbolism are not unusual in Greco-Roman writings.[129] For example, Martial describes Thais, a woman who had apparently rubbed him the wrong way, as follows:

> Thais smells worse than a grasping fuller's long-used crack [a pot filled with urine], and that, too, just smashed in the middle of the street; than a he-goat fresh from his amours; than the breath of a lion; than a hide dragged from a dog beyond Tiber; than a chicken when it rots in an abortive egg; than a two-eared jar poisoned by putrid fish-sauce.[130]

Older women and prostitutes were also associated with bad smells.[131] Again, Martial describes a bony, wrinkled old woman as having the odor of a goat.[132] Juvenal describes a promiscuous woman as carrying home with her "all the odors of the stews."[133] These examples reveal how olfactory symbolism was used to pass value judgments on different groups of people, especially women, in antiquity.[134]

Similarly, Christian authors also used olfactory symbolism to communicate certain values and beliefs. Paul claims, "we are the aroma of Christ to God among those who are being saved" (2 Cor 2:15). Susan Ashbrook Harvey has done extensive research on the function of aroma in Christian writings, especially sources discussing the practices of Simeon Stylites.[135]

The desert fathers often linked fornication to foul odors or stench (*dysōdia*). For example, John Climacus (579–649 CE) describes how the stench of fornication destroys the purity of the body:

> The Lord, being incorruptible and incorporeal, rejoices in the purity and incorruptibility of our body. But nothing gives such joy to the demons, some say, as the stench (*dysōdia*) of fornication; and no other passion so gladdens them as the defilement of the body.[136]

In one of the *Sayings* about fornication, passions are associated with bad odors:

> Against the same thought, another old man said, "Be like him who passes through the market place in front of an inn and breathes the smell of cooking and roasting. If he enjoys it, he goes inside to eat some of it; if not, he only inhales the smell in passing and goes on his way. It is the same for you: *avoid the bad smell* [emphasis mine]. Wake up and pray, saying, 'Son of God, help me.' Do this for other temptations also. For we do not have to uproot the passions, but resist them."[137]

Another *Saying* also makes the connection between a bad odor, a beautiful woman, and sexual desire:

> A brother at Scetis was a good fighter. The enemy suggested the remembrance of a very beautiful woman to him and he was much afflicted by it. Providentially, another brother who went to Scetis from Egypt said to him, while they were speaking together, "The wife of so and so is dead." Now it was the woman about whom the ascetic had experienced the conflict. When he heard this, he took his cloak and went to open her tomb by night; he soaked the cloak in the decomposing body. Then he returned to his cell bringing this bad smell with him, and he strove against his thoughts, saying, "Here is the desire you are seeking – you have it – be satisfied." And he chastised himself by means of that bad smell until the warfare in him ceased.[138]

These examples indicate that the connection between foul odor and fornication is understood as a common motif in monastic texts. But when the foul odor is associated with an ethnic other, such as the Ethiopian woman in

99

the *Saying* under review, it is possible that the authors are trying to communicate the importance of maintaining boundaries, or keeping a safe distance from those who would present a threat within the desert.

Scholars have begun to show how smell carries symbolic value that creates and enforces boundaries: "the odor of the other is not so much a real scent as a feeling of dislike transposed into the olfactory domain. In either case, smell provides a potent symbolic means for creating and enforcing class and ethnic boundaries."[139] For monastic writers, the smell associated with ethnic others (e.g., Ethiopian women) was an ideal symbol for isolating not only the threat of fornication, but also the need for clear boundaries between the monks and the "others" who dwelled in the desert.

In the *Apophthegmata patrum* 5.5, the author assigns to the Ethiopian woman a few lines that indicate the threat she represented to the male ascetics: "I am she who appears sweet (*dulcis*) in the hearts of men, but because of your obedience and your labor, God does not permit me to seduce (*seducere*) you, but I have let you know my foul odor (*fetorem*)." Here, the Ethiopian woman, who is described as ugly (*turpis*) earlier in the text, now appears "sweet in the hearts of men." She becomes the perfect personification of temptation and lust – sweet and attractive. She further establishes that her mission, which was to seduce (*seducere*) the monk, was interrupted by God. All that is left is her foul odor, which in this text, operates symbolically as a reminder of the importance of maintaining boundaries through the renunciation of sexual passions and other threats in the desert.

Evidence about the experiences of Ethiopian women within the desert is sparse – virtually nonexistent. Clearly, these women must have been considered attractive and seductive to the monks. This extreme attraction, coupled with a sense of danger and fear, led to a sense of ambivalence evident throughout the stories that depict Ethiopian women. The ethno-political rhetorics about Ethiopian women are focused on physical descriptions that effectively turned the presumably attractive and sexually seductive Ethiopian woman into a repugnant and invisible object. Iris Young offers a heuristic framework for identifying the cultural imperialism evident in such discourses.[140] The body of the Ethiopian woman is defined by the editor of *Apophthegmata patrum* 5.5 as "ugly" and "smelly" – someone to be avoided.

Palladius, Historia Lausiaca 23.4–5

The *Historia Lausiaca* (*The Lausiac History*), written around 420 CE by Palladius, contains another story about an Ethiopian woman (*Aithiopissan korēn*).[141] Throughout the *Historia Lausiaca*, Palladius includes a series of biographical sketches of holy men and women who fell from virtue because of excessive pride and failure to control their passions. This collection, along with the *Historia monachorum in Aegypto* by Rufinus, provides one of the best pictures of Egyptian monasticism at the beginning of the fifth century.[142] Courtès included this text in his section on sexuality in patristic literature, but summarized the text by saying, "a hermit is tempted by a pretty, black, peasant woman."[143] Peter Frost used this text as an example of how Ethiopian women were used to epitomize undesirablity in the literature left by the monks of the Egyptian desert.[144] Neither scholar provided detailed interpretive analysis of the text. The following discussion offers some insights about the rhetorical function of the Ethiopian maiden.

In chapter 23 of this text the fifth-century biographer Palladius provided a story of a monk called Pachon who lived in Scete. Palladius was troubled by his passions and sought counsel from Pachon. Pachon shared with Palladius about how he conquered the demon who attacked him. Because the demon had tormented him for twelve years, he resigned to live in a cave, hoping to be devoured by wild beasts.

In paragraph 4 of chapter 23 the author labels the beasts that tormented Pachon male (*arsēn*) and female (*thēleia*). The beasts smelled and licked Pachon, but did not devour him. Thinking that he was spared, he went back to his cell, but the demon (*ho daimōn*) returned and troubled him more.

> Evening came, and as Sacred Scripture says: *Thou hast appointed darkness, and it is night, in it shall all the beasts of the woods go about.*[145] The beasts, male and female, came out. They smelled me and licked me all over from head to foot. Just when I was expecting to be eaten, they left me. I lay there all night, but they did not devour me. Thinking that God had spared me, I went back to my cell. The demon waited for an opportunity for a few days and then again assailed me even more earnestly than before, so that I was on the verge of blasphemy.[146]

Palladius does not simply continue the story about the male and female beasts or the demon who had assailed Pachon. In paragraph 5 Palladius gives the demon an ethnic identity. The demon is transformed into an Ethiopian maiden:

> [The demon] took on the form of an *Ethiopian maiden* (*Aithiopissan korēn*) whom I had once seen in my youth gathering reeds, and sat on my knees. Filled with anger, I gave her a box on the ear and she disappeared. Then for two years, I could not bear the *evil smell* (*dysōdēs*) on my hand! Faint of heart and in despair, I went away into the Great Desert. I found a small snake, picked it up, and put it to myself, so that I might die being bitten in this fashion. Then I ground the head of the serpent into myself as being responsible for my temptation; but I was not bitten.[147]

The female (*thēleia*) reappears in this text and sits on Pachon's knees. Pachon became angry and hit the woman on her ear. This caused her to disappear, but the encounter left Pachon reeking with an evil smell (*dysōdēs*) that stayed with him for two years.

Palladius dedicated this work to Lausus, a royal chamberlain of Emperor Theodosius II. He wanted to demonstrate to Lausus and other Christians that the building of character through asceticism was more important than the construction of elaborate religious edifices.[148] The fact that he is a great story-teller and biographer is evident in his writings.[149] But the way Palladius employs the Ethiopian maiden in the story about Pachon has gone largely unexplored.

One possible interpretation of the Ethiopian maiden (*Aithiopissan korēn*) in this story calls attention to the polemical strategy of Palladius. He uses the Ethiopian maiden to signify both the political and religious threats that challenged the desert monks. As Joan Wallach Scott observes, gendered identities within narratives draw attention to political realities.[150] Once again, the bad smell (*dysōdēs*) of the Ethiopian woman is emphasized. The woman is made to disappear or become invisible after Pachon struck her on the ear. This physical encounter, however, left an odor with him that lasted for two years. The odor served as an ever-present reminder not only of sexual dangers, but also of political dangers, in the desert.

Summary

The Ethiopian woman was used in monastic sources to indicate the threat of sexual dangers in the desert. The monks in the examples above cultivated the attributes related to the virtuous life (*askēsis*) at the expense of the Ethiopian woman. They triumphed in their quest for *askēsis* by overcoming the seductive traps of the Ethiopian woman. The detailed vituperative physical descriptions of the Ethiopian women in these texts that ultimately emphasize their foul odor served as a constant reminder that the threat (*dysōdia*) of fornication (*porneia*) was always lurking. By avoiding the Ethiopian woman and keeping her in her place,[151] the male ascetics could attain the ideal form of sexual renunciation.

The Ethiopian woman was also used as a polemical device in the stories about the ascetic monks to indicate conditions that, as Maurice Godelier says, "have nothing to do with sexuality."[152] The depiction of Ethiopian women in these texts raises questions about the socio-political background that shaped the compilers and editors of the stories of the desert monks.

CONCLUSION: ETHNO-POLITICAL RHETORICS DEFINING SEXUAL THREATS

Ethiopians, symbolizing the sexual vices that distracted the desert monks, were used in monastic literature to emphasize the importance of overcoming the threat of fornication. They symbolized how the pleasures of the flesh can result in falling away from a life devoted to God. The body was viewed as a problem to be controlled and mastered by the desert monks, for whom "the act of intercourse was one of the many aspects of their lives that they could bring under control through good sense and breeding."[153]

In this chapter, I have provided several examples of how writers from late antique Egypt used Ethiopians and Blacks in their discourses about sexual vices. The Ethiopian woman, often associated with foul odor, was a compelling ethnic trope throughout the literature of the desert tradition. The use of Ethiopians as symbolic of sexual vices points to the political, military, and ideological threats that this ethnic group represented to Egyptians during the rise of monasticism. The vituperative depictions of Ethiopians not only signified social and political turmoil, but also religious challenges that could ultimately cause apostasy. The heresiologist Epiphanius summarized the overall contempt toward Ethiopians discussed throughout this chapter. According to Epiphanius, Origen's defense of the Black Bride in the Song of Solomon seems to have led him into a dilemma. The Roman authorities arrested him and offered him the following choice: either commit apostasy or have sexual intercourse with an *Ethiopian*:

> On account of his remarkable holiness and erudition he incurred the greatest jealousy and this stirred up even more those who were magistrates and prefects at that particular time. With devilish ingenuity the evildoers contrived to bring disgrace upon the man and, what is more, to mark out this sort of vengeance: that they would procure an *Ethiopian* for the purpose of causing defilement to his body. In response to this, Origen, not tolerating that deceptive plan of the devil proclaimed that of the two propositions set before him he preferred to offer sacrifice.[154]

5

"BEYOND THE RIVERS OF ETHIOPIA": ETHNO-POLITICAL RHETORICS DEFINING INSIDERS AND OUTSIDERS

The blackness of the soul, the dragon's poison and his dark color – the color of sin and vice – can disappear as soon as the teachers of false doctrines are left in the rivers of Ethiopia.

(Jerome, *In Soph.* 3.10–13)

INTRODUCTION

In the previous two chapters, I explored ethno-political rhetorics about Egyptians/Egypt, Ethiopians/Ethiopia, and Blacks/blackness that associated these groups with sinful activities and sexual vices. These ethnic groups, geographical locations, and color symbols were also associated with groups deemed heretical within early Christianity, and were used to symbolize the virtuous or ideal model for early Christians. In this chapter, I examine examples representing both streams of these traditions.

Beginning with the New Testament, and continuing through monastic literature of late antique Egypt, a pattern emerged whereby Christian writers defined the theological and ideological boundaries of the church (*ekklēsia*) by developing ethno-political rhetorics about Egyptians/Egypt, Ethiopians/ Ethiopia, and Blacks/blackness. In the first section below I will examine a mid-fifth-century story about Melania the Younger, who is depicted as having a conversation with a representative of Nestorius appearing in the form of a young black man (*melana neaniskon*).[1] In the second section, I will analyze two models of "virtue" within early Christianity: the Ethiopian eunuch in Acts 8:26–40 and the desert monk Ethiopian Moses.

There are at least two opposing ways in which Ethiopians or Blacks are used for defining insiders and outsiders in ancient Christian literature. In one, an "Ethiopian" or "Black One" is made to represent the ideal Christian because of his extraordinary virtuous qualities. The ways in which these figures are used in the literature raises questions about the intentions of the authors with regard to advancing a particular understanding of Christianity.[2] The Ethiopian eunuch in Acts 8:26–40 and the desert father Ethiopian Moses are two examples of the "virtuous" Ethiopian in Christian literature. The Ethiopian eunuch was used by Luke to indicate that salvation could extend even to Ethiopians and Blacks. The desert father Ethiopian Moses was used in the *Apophthegmata patrum* to demonstrate that even a Black man could achieve the virtue of ascetic humility. Why did Luke appeal to the Ethiopian eunuch in this baptism story? Why was it necessary for the editor of the *Apophthegmata patrum* to emphasize so strategically the color symbolism associated with Ethiopian Moses? These questions will be explored in this chapter.

At the opposing extreme, Ethiopians/Ethiopia and Blacks/blackness represent "heretical" movements.[3] The fourth-century church father Jerome identified Marcionites as a heretical group beyond the rivers of Ethiopia.[4] The church father Ambrose claims that Arianism and Manichaeism were the heresies that made the church "black" and threatened its orthodox existence.[5] Egyptians/Egypt were also used as polemical devices for designating insiders and outsiders, and for discussing orthodoxy and heresy. In a letter to Mark, a priest at Chalcis, Jerome associates Egypt with heretical tendencies:

> I am called a heretic for preaching that the Trinity is consubstantial. I am accused of the Sabellian heresy for proclaiming with unwearied voice that there are three subsistent persons, true, undiminished, and perfect. If I am accused by Arians, it is deserved. If by the orthodox, who criticize a faith of this kind, they have ceased to be orthodox. Or, if they please, let them condemn me as a heretic with the West, a heretic with *Egypt*, that is to say, with Damasus and Peter.[6]

This symbolic, discursive use of Egyptians/Egypt, Ethiopians/Ethiopia, and Blacks/blackness to represent heresies served as an effective strategy for establishing the ideological boundaries of the church (*ekklēsia*).[7] The rhetoric about the "ethnic other," so evident in the literature, reflects the theological controversies and religious hostilities that existed among different segments of Christian communities. Many of the conflicts among Christians were debated and sometimes resolved violently during church councils.[8] These intra-Christian controversies are buried in the polemical arguments of various early Christian writings. But before I begin a review of specific examples, a brief summary of the development of "orthodoxy" and "heresy" within ancient Christianity is in order. This background information will help establish how dominant voices within different communities came to shape early Christian understandings of insiders and outsiders.

"ORTHODOXY" AND "HERESY" IN EARLY CHRISTIANITY

Introduction

The magnum opus of Walter Bauer, entitled *Orthodoxy and Heresy in Earliest Christianity*, provides a useful interpretive opening for examining "orthodoxy" and "heresy" in early Christianity.[9] Bauer argues that in many geographical areas of antiquity, such as Egypt, Asia Minor, and Rome, "heresy" actually preceded "orthodoxy" as the original manifestation of Christianity. Bauer contends that "orthodoxy" was a later development and "represented the form of Christianity supported by the majority in Rome."[10] Rome was one of the major centers and chief sources of power for the "orthodox" movement within Christianity. Thomas A. Robinson sums up the matter best: "Orthodoxy" is "merely a word that describes what comes out of the Rome-dominated drive towards theological uniformity in the second and third centuries; its application to the church of the first century is misplaced and reflects theological and polemical concerns, not historical reality."[11] Bauer challenges the traditional view or major assumption advocated by church historians that heresy was a later development that evolved from orthodoxy. For example, Tertullian (160–225 CE) wrote that truth came before falsehood and that all heresy is a recent (or late) innovation.[12] But, according to Bauer, heresy did not spring forth from orthodoxy. Rather, heresy – that is, the specific form of indigenous or geographical manifestations of Christianity – already existed; orthodoxy triumphed over these earlier forms, which only thereafter came to be regarded as "heretical."[13]

Bauer's focus on geographical areas offers a much-needed departure from a monolithic understanding of early Christianity. He identifies the multiplicity of competing statements of faith and offers a useful analysis of the development of Christianity in major geographical regions.[14] I argue that a discursive strategy of othering is operative in writings that discuss heresies in early Christianity. This strategy reflects an awareness of ethnic and color differences in the ancient world. In the next section, I review a text that uses a young black man (*melana neaniskon*) to shape a certain response to the so-called heresy of Nestorianism.

Vita Melaniae Junioris 54

An example of the symbolic use of *melas* with respect to heretical sects can be found in the *Vita Melaniae Junioris* (ca. 452/453 CE).[15] This mid-fifth-century text was written by Gerontius during the time when Theodosius was bishop of Jerusalem. Commentators have debated whether this *Vita* was originally written in Greek or Latin.[16] In the Greek version of the story, Melania the Younger (385–439 CE) is depicted as having a conversation with the devil (*ho diabolos*) – a representative of Nestorius – who took on the form of a young black man (*melana neaniskon*). The Greek version of the story follows:

Just then the Devil threw the souls of simple people into great trouble through the *polluted doctrine of Nestorius*. Therefore many of the wives of senators and some of the men illustrious in learning came to our holy mother in order to investigate the orthodox faith with her. And she, who had the Holy Spirit indwelling, did not cease talking theology from dawn to dusk. She turned many who had been deceived to the orthodox faith and sustained others who doubted; quite simply, she benefited all those who risked coming to her divinely-inspired teaching. Thus the Devil, the enemy of truth, was very jealous both on account of those who came to her for edification and on account of her uncle's salvation. He changed into a *young black man (melana neaniskon)* and came to her, and said the following: "For how long do you destroy my hopes through your words? Know, then, that if I am strong enough to harden the hearts of Lausus and the emperors . . . if not, I inflict on your body such tortures that you will fear even for your life, so that you may be kept silent by necessity." After she had made him disappear by calling on our Lord Jesus Christ, she sent for my most humble self to tell me *the threats of the Black One (tas tou melanos apeilas)*. And she had not yet finished speaking to me when she began to feel a pain in her hip. Suddenly her suffering was so strong that she remained mute for three hours. After we had made an offering on her behalf, she scarcely recovered herself. She spent six days in that unspeakable suffering, feeling far greater pain at that hour than when she had seen *the Black One (ton melana)*.[17]

In this text, Gerontius seeks to demonstrate that the polluted (*miaros*) teachings of Nestorius (ca. 381–451) were leading many astray.[18] He depicts Melania as a strong defender of the orthodox faith (*orthodoxos pistis*) who instructed many wives of senators and learned men. According to Elizabeth Clark, Gerontius has represented Melania in this story in "shades of high orthodoxy."[19] Melania is depicted as a staunch defender of the faith. She is not linked with any of the heretical movements of the fourth and fifth centuries, even though there is strong evidence that the historical Melania was associated with many of the so-called heresies of her time.[20] Gerontius has more than likely manipulated the story about Melania's stay in Constantinople to advance his particular doctrinal loyalties.[21] Clark's insightful commentary of this text makes many important points about the ways that competing theological and doctrinal views influenced stories about orthodoxy and heresy. But I would add that Gerontius's use of *ton melana* also calls attention to movements that were considered heretical. He goes to great lengths to distance Melania from Nestorianism in this text.

In the Latin version of this story, the specific reference to Nestorianism is omitted.[22] But the editor apparently translates *melana neaniskon* (a young black man) as *adulescentis Aethyopis et horrido* (a horrible-looking Ethiopian young man). In her review of the Latin differences from the Greek text, Clark claims "such additions and subtractions in the Latin text suggest that its editor wished to remove Melania from any association with Monophysite tendencies and to maximize her *Romaninity*, presenting her as a model of orthodoxy suitable for emulation by Westerners."[23] I agree with Clark's reading of the editor's changes to the text. The Monophysite movement was a major challenge among Christians during the fourth and fifth centuries. It was not uncommon for so-called orthodox Christian writers to minimize any possible connections with this understanding of the faith.[24] Yet Clark does not comment on the "horrible-looking Ethiopian" in this text. I would suggest that the Ethiopian (black man) was used as a polemical device for shaping an orthodox understanding of Melania and her teachings. The author was able to use this ethnic reference as a symbolic trope within the narrative to appeal to the imaginations of the recipients of this text. The colorful language of *melana neaniskon* in Gerontius's text and the ethnic adaptation of the trope by the Latin editor functioned to inspire its audiences to remain steadfast in the orthodox faith (*orthodoxos pistis*).

Summary

One way that ancient Christian authors discussed heresies was to associate them with Blacks and Ethiopians. We have no way of knowing whether Melania encountered Blacks or Ethiopians in her day-to-day activities. But it is clear that the author of the stories about Melania knew of the symbolic power of appealing to such individuals (or images) in their descriptions of Melania's struggles to ward off the temptations and threats that vied for her attention. Thus "Blacks" or Ethiopians were used to represent polluted doctrines and developments in early Christianity that needed to be avoided. But Ethiopians and Blacks were used not only as models of "heresy." They also appeared in many sources as models of virtue. The next section will examine two examples of such use.

MODELS OF "VIRTUE"

Introduction

Ancient Christian writers developed an intricate form of ethnographic polemic about Ethiopians in some of their stories about conversion to early Christianity. Within these stories, Ethiopians were used to symbolize the ideal model or virtuous figure that could penetrate the boundaries of the early Christian community. In the words of Frank Snowden, "the early Christians used the Ethiopian as a prime motif in the language of conversion and as a means to emphasize their conviction that Christianity was to include all mankind."[25] In these conversion stories, the ethnicity and color of the Ethiopian served as an important literary feature that enabled the authors to establish certain virtuous characteristics within the Christian community.[26] In this section, I will examine the story of the Ethiopian eunuch in Acts 8:26–40 and the story of Ethiopian Moses as preserved in the *Sayings of the Desert Fathers*.

Sources

Acts 8:26–40 (Ethiopian Eunuch)

When Luke described the Ethiopian eunuch and his urgent request for baptism in Acts 8:26–40, it appeared that the Christian movement extended to the ends of the earth (*eschatou tēs gēs*).[27] Commentators have offered various interpretations of this passage by focusing upon the historical, literary, political, social-scientific, racial, and economic concerns of the text.[28] Many dissertations have also explored its ethnographic considerations, patristic readings, and text-critical issues.[29] The ethnic or racial identity of the eunuch has generally led scholars to conclude that race was inconsequential for early Christians. For example, Ernst Haenchen claimed that Acts 8:26–40 does not reflect any significant racial difficulties.[30] Frank Snowden also argued that race or color was inconsequential for early Christians.[31] In his brief analysis of the Ethiopian eunuch in Acts 8:26–40, Snowden concluded that considerations of race and external conditions were of no significance in determining membership in early Christian communities.[32] Nicholas Gier claimed that the conversion and baptism of the Ethiopian eunuch in Acts 8:26–40 is the prooftext of early Christians that Christianity was open to every person, whether male or female, Greek or Jew, circumcised or uncircumcised, barbarian, Scythian, slave, or free.[33] Robert Hood claimed that this text was included by Luke to indicate the fulfillment of the prophecy in Psalm 68:31 that "Ethiopia will soon stretch out her hands to God."[34]

This view of the Ethiopian as the symbol of universal salvation within early Christianity had been the standard interpretation of Acts 8:26–40. But New Testament scholars such as Cain Hope Felder and Clarice J. Martin have raised an important challenge to interpreters of this text that calls for an ethnographic and socio-political reading of Luke's narrative.[35] To Felder, Luke's narrative about the Ethiopian eunuch is one of the best illustrations of a process of "secularization" in the New Testament.[36] He argues that through the process of secularization, socio-political realities dilute the New Testament vision of racial inclusiveness and universalism.[37] In his analysis of Acts 8:26–40, Felder concludes that Luke participated in a process of secularization that was influenced by Roman socio-political realities and Hellenistic language and culture.[38] Felder focuses on the political environment of Rome at the end of the first century that influenced Luke's writing of Acts. For Luke and other New Testament authors, Rome, not Jerusalem, was the center of the inhabited world, which led to the exclusion of certain races of people: "The immediate significance of this New Testament tendency to focus on Rome instead of Jerusalem is that the darker races outside the Roman orbit are for the most part overlooked by New Testament authors."[39] Thus Felder argues that Luke emphasizes the baptism of the Roman centurion Cornelius (Acts 10:44–48) instead of the baptism of the Ethiopian eunuch who was returning from worship in Jerusalem.[40] According to Felder, given the importance of the "Holy Spirit" as a theological motif throughout Acts, Luke may have unwittingly called attention to the baptism of the Roman centurion as more legitimate than the baptism of the Ethiopian eunuch.[41] But Felder does not include in his analysis of this material Luke's use of spirit (*pneuma*) within Acts 8:26–40. He does not comment on how the spirit (*to pneuma*) led Philip to the eunuch (v. 29), or how the spirit of the Lord (*pneuma kyriou*) snatched Philip away after the baptism (v. 39). The process of secularization that Felder identifies does not adequately explain the many different functions of the Ethiopian eunuch in this text.

Clarice Martin's ethnographic reading of Acts 8:26–40 challenges many interpretations of this text that argue that the eunuch's nationality is of little or no significance.[42] Martin's basic premise is that the ethnic identity of the eunuch is virtually ignored in modern scholarship.[43] She identifies three leading approaches used in dealing with the Ethiopian's identity,[44] yet departs from these views by arguing that nationality *is* of great significance in the text. She then proceeds to develop an ethnographic framework for understanding Luke's literary intentions with respect to the eunuch by asking, "what is the significance for Luke of the inclusion of a story about a recognizably 'black African official?'"[45] She uses classical period evidence to support her claim that *Aithiops* is equivalent to Blacks in the ancient world,[46] and concludes that the eunuch provides a graphic illustration and symbol of the different persons who will constitute the church of the risen Christ.[47]

Martin suggests that Acts 8:26–40 provides a "symbolic – though partial – fulfillment of the commission in Acts 1:8c that the Christian mission would go "to the end of the earth."[48] She acknowledges scholars such as Theodor Zahn, H.J. Cadbury, Martin Hengel, and T.C.G. Thornton, who have also made the connection between Acts 1:8c and Acts 8:26–40, but Martin contends that their arguments suffer from a lack of specific detail and documentation, especially as it relates to the geographical and historical background of the Ethiopian.[49] She provides this data and persuasively documents the classical tradition that more than likely informed Luke's understanding of the Ethiopian eunuch.[50]

Her laudable work, however, does not escape criticism. Martin neglects to consider how Luke may have also been influenced by certain cultural understandings of the "eunuch."[51] Martin focuses on the ethnographic origins of the Ethiopian without showing how *Aithiops* functioned in the text as a polemical device. She stays within the basic theological framework established by her predecessors and refers to the Ethiopian only as a marker of a geographical extreme. Another reading of Acts 8:26–40 that takes into consideration the rhetorical intentions of Luke may yield new insights for understanding the function of the Ethiopian eunuch. Embedded in the text are clues that indicate Luke's assumptions about Ethiopia and Ethiopians. But before turning to the story about the eunuch, I want to review some ethnic markers in Acts.

In the second chapter of Acts, Luke lists the different groups of Jews (*Ioudaioi*) who had come to Jerusalem for Pentecost (Acts 2:1–13). In this pericope his focus on nationalities is apparent: "Now there were staying in Jerusalem God-fearing Jews from every nation (*apo pantos ethnous*) under heaven."[52] Luke includes in this list the following nations of people: Parthians; Medes; Elamites; residents of Mesopotamia, Judea, Cappadocia, Pontus, Asia, Phrygia, Pamphylia, Egypt,[53] and parts of Libya near Cyrene; visitors from Rome; Cretans; and Arabs.[54] Luke does not mention Ethiopia in this list. But later in chapter 2, he includes a subtle reference to Ethiopians in verses 38–39. After Peter's sermon in Acts 2:14–36 the people respond in Acts 2:37 with the question "Brothers, what shall we do?"[55] At this point Peter replies in verses 38–39, "Repent, and be baptized every one of you in the name of Jesus Christ so that your sins may be forgiven; and you will receive the gift of the Holy Spirit. For the promise is for you, for your children, and for all who are *far away*, everyone whom the Lord our God calls to him."[56] The reference to "all who are *far away*" (*pasin tois eis makran*) is a precursor to the Ethiopian eunuch in Acts 8:26–40 whom Luke represents as the first Gentile convert to be baptized.[57]

Luke is the only New Testament author who uses the Greek term *makran*. This term was a well-known description of distant peoples and was often used in connection with Ethiopians in the ancient world. Both Homer and Herodotus used it to describe Ethiopians.[58] Given his sophisticated use of Greek and his knowledge of different types of Greek literature, Luke would have been aware of this description for Ethiopians.[59] He therefore appropriated this geographical marker in his narrative in Acts 2 in order to set the stage for the Ethiopian eunuch in Acts 8:26–40. In this conversion-baptismal story, it is reasonable to conclude that Luke is using the Ethiopian eunuch to fulfill his objective stated in Acts 1:8c: "you will be my witnesses . . . to the ends of the earth (*eschatou tēs gēs*)."[60] But the significance of this pericope is not merely geographical.

The Ethiopian eunuch also functioned as an ethno-political trope. As a court official or chamberlain (*dynastēs*) of Candace (queen of the Ethiopians),[61] this Ethiopian was in charge of her entire treasury (*gazēs*). The Ethiopian queens were in constant battle with the Romans and other nations, from the early days of the empire when the general Gaius Petronius had led a military campaign against Candace's army,[62] up through the time when Nero planned but never executed a military campaign against Meroë.[63] Although it is impossible to state with any degree of certainty which of the queens who bore the title or name Candace Luke may be referring to in this text,[64] it is plausible to suggest that Luke knew his audience would understand the mere mention of a *Kandakē* as a signal of a political threat. Luke may have been using the Ethiopian eunuch as an "ethno-political" trope to demonstrate to his audience that even those associated with *Kandakē* could be converted to Christianity. In this way Luke sought to present a view of Christianity that would undercut the power and danger imposed by the Ethiopians. Thus the Ethiopian eunuch was an ideal *symbolic* convert or model of "virtue" for Luke.[65] He is appealing to widely held assumptions about ethnic and cultural differences, as well as political and military realities in the first century, to demonstrate that Christianity could extend to cultural and political outsiders.

In addition to these political realities, Luke surely had other cultural assumptions influencing his construction of the story. Luke's use of *eunouchos* in combination with *Aithiops* is further proof that he had a greater purpose for constructing this narrative about the eunuch's baptism.[66] Eunuchs were perceived as "other" and represented with much antagonism by Greco-Roman authors.[67] For example, the second-century satirist Lucian of Samosata describes a eunuch who was in the running for an Athenian chair of philosophy. Despite his intellectual qualities, his presumed status as a eunuch led to questions about his fitness for the job. Lucian says that "such people ought to be excluded . . . not simply from all that but even from temples and holy-water bowls and all the places of public assembly."[68] Lucian further provides a physical description of a eunuch: "markedly smooth of jowl" (beardless) and "effeminate in voice." A eunuch was "an ambiguous sort of creature like a crow, which cannot be reckoned either with doves or with ravens, neither man nor woman but something composite, hybrid, and monstrous, alien to human nature."[69]

Within the Hebrew Scriptures reactions to eunuchs are expressed in the statement "no one whose testicles are crushed or whose penis is cut off shall be admitted to the assembly of the Lord."[70] Eunuchs were also classified among the blemished and ritually impure, unfit for priestly service.[71] Two important Jewish writers of the first century CE reinforced this prejudicial stance toward the eunuch: Josephus called eunuchs "monstrosities" who should be avoided because of their unnatural effeminacy and lack of generative capacity.[72] Philo, similarly, chastised eunuchs as "the men who belie their sex and are affected with effemination, who debase the currency of nature and violate it by assuming the passions and the outward form of licentious women."[73]

The obvious hostility towards the eunuch in Greco-Roman and Jewish antiquity makes the placement of such a figure in Acts 8:26–40 a significant rhetorical strategy by Luke.[74] He is setting up a figure who would have been perceived by his audience as a social and cultural outsider. This social and cultural outsider, *eunouchos*, combined with the ethnic outsider, *Aithiops*, became a powerful polemical device for Luke.[75] The following analysis of the text demonstrates an ethno-political rhetoric that defines a commonly understood "outsider" as an "insider" in Luke's Gospel.

Luke opens this pericope with a geographical marker:

> Then an angel of the Lord said to Philip, "Get up and go *toward the south* (*kata mesēmbrian*) to the road that goes down from Jerusalem to Gaza." (This is a wilderness [*erēmos*] road.) So he got up and went.[76]

The phrase *kata mesēmbrian* can mean either "about midday" or "toward the south." In the LXX the phrase appears as a reference to time,[77] but here Luke uses it as a geographical marker to indicate that the southern road led to Ethiopia.

In the next section Luke introduces the Ethiopian eunuch:

> Now there was *a man* (*anēr*), an *Ethiopian eunuch* (*Aithiops eunouchos*), a court official of the Candace, queen of the Ethiopians, who was in charge of her entire treasury. He had come to Jerusalem to worship and was returning home; seated in his chariot, he was reading the prophet Isaiah.[78]

The political and cultural implications of this figure have been discussed above. What is worth further notice is Luke's use of *anēr* (man) in connection with *Aithiops*. It was common for Luke to use *anēr* with a word indicating national or local origin.[79] In several passages throughout Acts, Luke uses the plural form of *anēr* in connection with nations and groups.[80] He also uses *anēr* to emphasize dominant characteristics of a person. For example, in Acts 10:22, Luke describes the Roman centurion Cornelius as a righteous and God-fearing man (*anēr dikaios kai phoboumenos*).[81] Luke does not go this far with the Ethiopian eunuch. His purpose for using *anēr* here is most likely to call attention to the eunuch's national origin rather than to his moral and spiritual attributes.

The next section (Acts 8:29–35) is crucial for understanding Luke's depiction of the Ethiopian eunuch as a model of "virtue".

> Then the Spirit said to Philip, "Go over to this chariot and join it."
> So Philip ran up to it and heard him reading the prophet Isaiah. He asked, "Do you understand what you are reading?" He replied, "How can I, unless someone guides me?" And he invited Philip to get in and sit beside him. Now the passage of the scripture that he was reading was this:
>> "*Like a sheep he was led to the slaughter, and like a lamb silent (aphōnos) before its shearer, so he does not open his mouth. In his humiliation (tapeinōsei) justice was denied him. Who can describe his generation? For his life is taken away from the earth.*"[82]
> The eunuch asked Philip, "About whom, may I ask you, does the prophet say this, about himself or about someone else?" Then Philip began to speak, and starting with this scripture, he proclaimed to him the good news about Jesus.

In this section Luke presents the eunuch as one who was unable to comprehend the scroll from Isaiah. Philip is given the opportunity, therefore, to explain the contents of the scroll and to proclaim the Good News of Jesus Christ. The content of this particular passage from Isaiah 53:7–8 is significant for

Luke's rhetorical strategy. This text emphasizes silence (*aphōnos*) and humility (*tapeinōsei*) – two important traits of ascetic virtue.[83]

Scholars generally do not emphasize the ascetic tendencies in this text.[84] Yet Luke may have been attempting to inform his audience of the importance of cultivating the attributes of silence and even humility by including Isaiah 53:7–8 in this story about the Ethiopian eunuch. In other parts of his two-part document addressed to Theophilus, Luke emphasizes silence and humility. One occurrence is in the story about the woman who had been bleeding for twelve years (Luke 8:47–48):

> When the woman saw that she could not remain hidden, she came trembling; and falling down before him, she declared in the presence of all the people why she had touched him, and how she had been immediately healed. He said to her, "Daughter, your faith has made you well; go in peace."

A second occurrence is in the story about the Pharisee and the tax collector (Luke 18:13–14):

> But the tax collector, standing far off, would not even look up to heaven, but was beating his breast and saying, "God, be merciful to me, a sinner!" I tell you, this man went down to his home justified rather than the other; for all who exalt themselves will be humbled, but all who humble themselves will be exalted.

Although the Ethiopian is reading aloud, Luke effectively renders him "silent" and "humbled" when Philip appears and interprets the text from Isaiah. After hearing of the good news of Jesus, the Ethiopian eunuch is immediately ready to be baptized (Acts 8:36–39):

> As they were going along the road, they came to some water; and the eunuch said, "Look, here is water! What is to prevent me from being baptized?" He commanded the chariot to stop, and both of them, Philip and the eunuch, went down into the water, and Philip baptized him. When they came up out of the water, the Spirit of the Lord snatched Philip away; the eunuch saw him no more, and went on his way rejoicing.

This story about the Ethiopian eunuch is an example of how one New Testament author employed an ethno-political rhetoric about an Ethiopian. Its significance can be understood only by comparing this passage to other parts of Luke's text. The Ethiopian eunuch appears to be the first Gentile outsider to receive inclusion into the new Christian movement. When this text is compared to the conversion story about Cornelius in Acts 10:1–48 its ethno-political discursive strategy becomes clear. Peter's speech about Cornelius's baptism emphasizes the impartiality of God: "I truly understand that God shows no partiality (*prosōpolēmptēs*), but in every nation (*en panti ethnei*) anyone who fears him and does what is right is acceptable to him."[85] That God shows no partiality is exemplified by Luke in his inclusion of a baptism story about an Ethiopian and a baptism story about a Roman. Yet Luke further establishes the Ethiopian eunuch as a model of virtue and employs subtle clues within the story to demonstrate to his audience that Christianity can extend to every nation – *even* Ethiopia.

This story would have been regarded as a radical transgression of prevailing socio-political and cultural boundaries.[86] In another story about an Ethiopian desert father, the same phenomenon occurs. Ethiopian Moses is venerated as a model of monastic virtue because of his conversion and subsequent adherence to the ascetic life. The next section will examine the rhetorical strategy used to present him as a penitent sinner who struggled with his color identity. His response to the negative treatment he experienced because of his skin color and ethnic identity rendered him a model of virtue.

Anonymous, Apophthegmata patrum *(Ethiopian Moses)*

The desert father Ethiopian Moses is another exemplar of "virtue" in ancient Christian literature.[87] According to the fifth-century church historian Sozomen, Ethiopian Moses was a slave, who had been driven out of his master's house because of his bad moral character.[88] He later became the leader of a group of robbers and committed many evil deeds and murders.[89] He appeared within a community of monks at Scete in order to demonstrate that ascetic virtue can reach even an ex-slave, reformed robber, convicted murderer, and big, black (*makros kai melanos*) imbecile.[90] Kathleen O'Brien Wicker has translated four extant Greek versions of this story: Palladius, *Historia Lausiaca* (fifth century); Sozomen, *Ecclesiastical History* (fifth century); *Apophthegmata patrum* (sixth century); and *The Life of St. Moses the Ethiopian* (tenth century).[91] All of these texts offer a view of Moses that emphasizes the otherness of his color or ethnic identity. Wicker concludes that the *Apophthegmata patrum* and the *Acta Sanct.* contain more explicit references to his color.[92] While some of the references to Moses' color are more benign than others, the story contained in the *Apophthegmata patrum* includes the most powerful connection between color symbolism and ascetic piety.[93] This text will be the basis for my review of Ethiopian Moses in this section, but the larger argument may apply in some degree to the other texts.

The color symbolism in the story about Ethiopian Moses has drawn considerable attention from biblical scholars, ancient historians, and classicists. Ancient historian and classicist Philip Mayerson asserts that the clearest instance of color prejudice against Ethiopian Moses occurs when the monks treat him with contempt and ask, "Why does this Ethiopian (*Aithiops*) come and go among us?"[94] Mayerson views the treatment of Moses as deliberate acts of humiliation because of the color of his skin. He further argues, "there can be no question but that the use of the word 'Ethiopian' in these contexts is strongly deprecatory and is the equivalent of the most offensive word used against Blacks in American society."[95] Classicist Lellia Cracco Ruggini argues that the story about Ethiopian Moses is an example of Christian humility, but apparently does not view the remarks as indicative of color prejudice.[96] Similarly, philosopher Nicholas Gier argues that there was color blindness in the ancient world. In his study of the philosophical origins of modern racism, Gier claims that "Aristotle, and all other ancients of whom we are aware, did not ever think of discriminating against people because of the color of their skin."[97] His study is a deliberate attempt to demonstrate ancient color blindness. To this end he provides several examples to prove his point: "demons and evil people in Christian art do not have Negroid features";[98] "Xenophanes compared the physical characteristics of Thracians and Ethiopians without a hint of racial discrimination";[99] and "Terence, a black writer from Carthage, was given the same recognition as the white Roman Horace."[100] Using New Testament texts such as Acts 8:26–40 and Colossians 3:11, Gier argues that Christianity was open to every person. But his broad generalization that "early Christian communities had the advantage of not only being nonracist but nonsexist as well" is clearly problematic.[101] Gier draws attention to the power of color symbolism in antiquity, but does not explore the reason for such symbolism in Christian writings.[102] His analysis indicates that the ancients were aware of the light/dark color symbolic language, in which "black [was] the color of sin, evil, and death; and white was the symbol of goodness, God and eternal life." Yet he does not link this light/dark dichotomy to skin color.[103]

According to classicist Lloyd Thompson, the story about Ethiopian Moses illustrates the Christian symbolic usage of *Aithiops* and *melas* as indicators of sin.[104] Thompson also argues that this story was influenced by conditions of contemporary society.[105] His reading of the text offers an important change of perspective in understanding this ascetic document that departs from the traditional focus on Christian humility.

Although church historian Robert Hood also finds significant meaning in the use of the Ethiopian's skin color in this story,[106] it is New Testament scholar Vincent L. Wimbush who offers one of the most sophisticated readings of the text to date. By identifying a possible connection between the "rhetorics of ascetic piety" and the "rhetorics of color difference" Wimbush argues that new insights can be gleaned from the stories about Ethiopian Moses. He challenges assumptions like those held by Frank Snowden, which view the story of Moses as an example of racial inclusiveness within early Christianity,[107] by offering a discursive entrée into the stories about Moses that explores the "heavy and thick" color symbolism found in several key passages. He says,

> not only is Black Moses *rare* among early Christian spiritual athletes
> and heroes as preserved in the oral and written legacies of ancient

Christianity, but the advancement of the attractiveness and superiority of the ascetic life is done at the expense of Moses, not just as individual, but as representative of Black peoples.[108]

He suggests that an examination of different rhetorical strategies may provide a helpful heuristic key for understanding the "Black African presence and influence in ancient Christianity, as well as fundamental questions about Christian self-definitions and orientations."[109] Wimbush raises some important questions about the "worldliness" of ascetic practices, and the "reprioritization of the world, complete with selected cultural and political assumptions and prejudices," but he does not carry his suggestions far enough.

I argue that the stories about Ethiopian Moses, especially in the *Apophthegmata patrum*, contain ethno-political rhetorics that are used to establish Moses as a model of virtue and an "insider" within a community of monks at Scete. The symbolizing of "virtue" comes at the expense of the Ethiopian's ethnic and color difference.

The first occurrence of color symbolism appears when some of the monks want to test Moses before his ordination.[110]

> Another time, a council was convoked in Scete. The Fathers wished to put Moses to the test. They treated him with contempt, saying "Why has this *Ethiopian* (*Aithiops*) come into our midst?" He, upon hearing this, kept silent (*esiōpēse*). After they were dismissed, they said to him, "Father, weren't you troubled (*etarachthēs*) just now?" He said to them, "I was troubled but I did not say anthing (*ouk elalēse*)."[111]

Apparently, the monks are trying to test his virtues of indifference (*adiaphoros*) and lack of passion (*apatheia*). His ability to restrain himself in the midst of verbal persecution is being put to the test. The Fathers' question "Why has this Ethiopian come into our midst?" implies that they constitute a group of non-Blacks. Moses's self-perceived silence (*esiōpēse*) becomes the litmus test for his inclusion into the group.[112] When later questioned about his ability to endure the insults in silence, Moses responded by alluding to Psalm 76:5 (LXX): "I am so troubled that I cannot speak." Douglas Burton-Christie suggests that silence was a virtue for the ascetic monks that reflected the spirit of long-suffering and patience, and served as a privileged means of communicating the essence of the spiritual life.[113]

The second occurrence of color symbolism occurs in the scene in which Moses is ordained a cleric:

> It was said of Father Moses that he became a cleric, and they laid the tunic upon him. And the archbishop said to him, "Behold, you have become completely white (*hololeukos*), Father Moses." The old man said to him, "Indeed, the outside, O Lord Father; would that the

inside were also white!" The archbishop, wishing to put him to the test, said to the clerics, "When Father Moses comes into the sanctuary, drive him out, and go along with him to hear what he says." So the old man came in and they rebuked him and drove him out, saying, "*Go away, Ethiopian (Hupage exō, Aithiops)*." He left and said to himself, "Rightly have they treated you, *ash skin, Black one (spododerme melane)*. As you are not a human, why should you come among humans?"[114]

Two observations about the color-symbolic language in this text are worth noting. First, the author appeals to white–black dualism to discuss the spiritual transformation that has apparently taken place. The same monk, described as black (*melas*), is now referred to as completely white (*hololeukos*). The symbolic meaning of the tunic (presumably *leukos*) placed on him after his ordination indicates that whiteness is the preferred marker for being set apart and prepared for the challenges of the ascetic life. *Leukos* in this case symbolizes purity, renunciation, and readiness. The author depicts Moses as one who recognizes that the outer garment of whiteness is not enough: "O Lord Father; would that the inside were also white!"

Second, the author combines an ethnic label with a color descriptor in order to emphasize the importance of the additional test that Moses had to endure. The archbishop suggests that the clerics drive him out from among them in order to observe his response: "When Father Moses comes into the sanctuary, drive him out, and go along with him to hear what he says." The clerics not only drove him out, but also rebuked him (*epetimēsan*) with an ethnic trope: "Go away, *Aithiops*." What is most compelling about this text is the way the editor depicts Moses in a self-denigrating manner. After being driven out of the community, Moses does not lash out at his antagonists. He turns inward and reprimands himself with color-symbolic language: "Rightly have they treated you, *ash skin, Black One (spododerme melane)*. As you are not a human, why should you come among humans?"

According to Lloyd Thompson, Moses's self-deprecation is a reflection of societal structures in the Roman world. Thompson claims that "in societies organized, like that of the ancient Romans, on the premise of inequality of 'estates' or 'orders' (*ordines*), there is often a tendency among the upper ranks to see the lower orders as 'non-men' or 'less than human'."[115] I agree with Thompson's class-based assessment of the references to humans in this text. But I do not agree with his claim that this class-based prejudice has nothing to do with race prejudice.[116] Thompson's complete disregard for the possibility that biases about ethnicity and color may have influenced the editor and later commentators of this text is a critical oversight. The editor of this text is appealing to attitudes about ethnic and color difference in order to shape an understanding of ascetic virtue. Self-humiliation became a standard for entry into this community of Egyptian monks.

Another example of denigration can be found in chapter 8 of *Apophthegmata patrum*. Here Ethiopian Moses, in order to avoid meeting with an official, attempts to divert the official by referring to himself as an imbecile (*salos*).

> "Because I heard about Father Moses, I came down to see him. And, lo, an old man on his way to Egypt met us, and we said to him, 'Where is the cell of Father Moses?' and he said to us, 'What do you want with him? He is an *imbecile* (*salos*).'" When the clerics heard this, they were distressed and said, "What sort of person was the man who said such things about the holy one?" They said, "An old man wearing old clothes. He was *big and black* (*makros kai melanos*)." They said to him, "That was Father Moses himself, and because he did not want to meet you, he said these things to you." The official was greatly edified and went away.[117]

In this story Moses is unable to avoid his pursuer because of his size and color, which apparently stood out among the other monks. The official was greatly edified by the denigrating descriptions about Moses. Why would this level of denigration become a strategy for emphasizing the virtue of Moses? What forces within the society allowed such discourses about color to become a part of the monastic tradition? Chapters 9 and 10 of this *Saying* help answer these questions. This section draws attention to barbarians who were present in the desert:

> Father Moses used to say in Scete, "If we observe the commands of our Fathers, I decree to you before God that *barbarians* (*barbaroi*) will not come here. But if we do not observe them, this very place will be made desolate." Once as the brothers were sitting before him, he said to them, "Behold, *barbarians* (*barbaroi*) are coming to Scete today. So rise and flee." They said to him, "Are you not going to flee, too, Father?" He said to them, "I have looked forward for many years to this day, so that the word of the Lord Christ might be fulfilled that says, 'All who take the sword will perish by the sword.'" They said to him, "Then we will not flee either, but we will die with you." He said to them, "This is not my affair. Let each person decide how he stands." They were seven brothers, and he said to them, "Lo, *the barbarians* (*hoi barbaroi*) are at the door." And coming in, they slew them. One of them fled and hid behind a pile of rope and saw seven crowns descending and crowning them.[118]

I contend that there was possibly some barbarian threat that motivated the ethnic and color-symbolic language about Moses. As discussed in chapter 4, Upper Egypt (particularly the region around Scetis) was under constant attack by military barbarian groups. The author of this text, similar to Palladius, was more than likely aware of the menacing threat of the barbarians.[119] The author also gives Moses an opportunity to provide commentary on the socio-political conditions in the desert. Moses himself could have been associated with "barbarian" groups before turning to the ascetic life. The editor of this text has chosen Moses as an exemplar of virtue. He develops ethno-political rhetorics about Moses' ethnic identity in order to show that even one who had been originally known for leading robbers and inciting trouble in the desert is no longer a threat. His silence, humility, and self-control become a model for all.

There were apparently many like Ethiopian Moses who were deemed exemplary in the desert. Rufinus (ca. 345–411 CE) gives some indication of this in his *History of the Monks in Egypt*: "We saw there a number of men of the Ethiopian race who lived with the monks and far outdid many of them in virtue and religious observance, so much so that in them the Scripture seemed fulfilled wherein it says that 'Ethiopia shall soon stretch out her hands to God.'"[120] Moses is depicted as a model of virtue as a result of his humility, which is exemplified by controlling his anger and negating his blackness. This leads him to avoid confrontations with his spiritual leaders and peers, which is one important value of *askēsis*. It causes the monks to attain a certain kind of spiritual perfection that allows them to forget about the oppressive conditions around them. The color-ful language about Moses is a type of ethno-political rhetoric that emphasizes some of the chief virtues of the ascetic life: self-control (*enkrateia*), indifference (*adiaphoros*), and lack of passions (*apatheia*).

Summary

The use of the Ethiopian as a model of "virtue" raises important questions about the complexities of ethnic polemic in ancient Christian writings. The examples in this section indicate that Ethiopians were not always the objects of vituperative rhetoric in early Christian writings. They were in fact subject to praise and exaltation because of their outstanding attributes as models of virtue. These portrayals of virtuous Ethiopians, however, should not be accepted uncritically.

The stories about the Ethiopian eunuch and Ethiopian Moses offer a view into some of the ways Christian writers established boundaries for inclusion into their respective communities. In the case of the first-century story about the Ethiopian eunuch (Acts 8:26–40), Luke was interested in demonstrating that Christianity could extend to the most culturally and ethnically different people. In other words, "outsiders" were not barred from inclusion into the Christian community. Luke may have also used the Ethiopian eunuch to emphasize the value of ascetic virtue within his community. In the case of the story about Ethiopian Moses, the anonymous editor of the *Apophthegmata patrum* was interested in shaping a view of ascetic virtue that could serve as a response to political threats within the desert. The rhetorical strategies used in both of these writings challenged the members of the respective communities, not only to emulate the models of "virtue," but also to avoid the military and political threats that these models represent.

CONCLUSION

The texts under review in this chapter isolate ethno-political rhetorics about Ethiopians and Blacks that represent them symbolically as heresies and models of virtue. The rhetorics work only if the authors assume that the audiences would respond to the conversion stories based on accepted perceptions about ethnic and color difference. That is, Ethiopians had to be perceived not only as other or foreign, but also as inferior from the perspective of the audiences addressed in the texts. In addition, assumptions about the importance of ascetic virtues were instrumental in shaping the stories about both the Ethiopian eunuch and Ethiopian Moses. The language of conversion in the stories about these models of "virtue" was shaped by ethno-political rhetorics that appealed to the physical traits and the remote geographical location of Ethiopians.[121] Both of these edifying stories[122] contain themes of humility and silence. Both stories were constructed with heavy editorializing that focused on the ethnic difference of the Ethiopians. Both stories indicate that within Christian communities ideological and cultural boundaries were drawn between insiders and outsiders.

The rhetorics identified in this chapter confirm that early Christianity was not a homogeneous belief system, but rather a variegated movement informed by cultural and other prejudices of the period.[123] Peter Frost claims that some of the many different understandings of early Christianity tended to minimize skin color differences, while others tended to magnify them.[124] The young black boy (*melas neaniskon*), the *Ethiopian* eunuch, and Moses the Black (*ho melas*) are examples of how early Christians used ethnic- and color-symbolic "others" in their writings to advance understandings of insiders and outsiders, which subsequently shaped and defined views about orthodoxy and heresy.

CONCLUSION

Another time, a council was convoked in Scete. The Fathers wished to
put Moses to the test. They treated him with contempt, saying, "Why
has this *Ethiopian* come into our midst?" He, upon hearing this, kept
silent. After they were dismissed, they said to him, "Father, weren't you
troubled just now?" He said to them, "I was troubled but I did not say
anything."

(Apophthegmata patrum, Ethiopian Moses, 3)

The story about Ethiopian Moses provides a fitting way to close this study of
ancient Christian ethno-political rhetorics. A council of desert fathers attempted
to put Moses to the test by raising the question "Why does this Ethiopian come
among us?"[1] The author emphasizes Moses' silence (*siōpē*) after some of the
fathers questioned him about his ethnic and color difference, assuming that
the derogatory remarks would have troubled him. Moses said "I was troubled
(*etarachthēn*), but I did not say anything."[2] The story does not end there, however.
While the real Moses may have remained silent as an act of humility, the Moses
within the narrative does speak – not only to himself, but also to the many
audiences that would subsequently hear and read this story. He speaks through
the ethno-political rhetoric of the author(s) who, through the use of ethnic and
color-symbolic language, painted a picture of the virtuous ascetic life.

In this book Moses and many other Ethiopians, Egyptians, and Blacks provide
subtle clues about the socio-political, religious, cultural, economic, and
ideological realities that shaped ancient Christian discourses. The words written
about and put into the mouths of these ethnic and color-coded symbolic tropes
came from Christian authors who were influenced by Greco-Roman forms of
political invective, rhetorical persuasion, and ethnic othering. The taxonomy
of early Christian ethno-political rhetorics generated in this book highlights
the range of challenges that faced early Christians. I hope that the taxonomy
will lead to an accounting of the socio-political, ideological, cultural, religious,
and economic forces that inspired some of the discursive representations of
Egyptians/Egypt, Ethiopians/Ethiopia, and Blacks/blackness.

CONCLUSION

Based upon the review of ethno-political rhetorics in this book, it is safe to conclude that assumptions about ethnic groups, geographical locations, and color differences in antiquity influenced the way early Christians shaped their stories about the theological, ecclesiological, and political developments in their communities. As a result, Egyptians/Egypt, Ethiopians/Ethiopia, and Blacks/blackness became associated with the threats and dangers that could potentially destroy the development of a certain "orthodox" brand of Christianity. In spite of the basic contention that Christianity was to extend to all peoples – even the remote Ethiopians – it is clear that certain groups of Christians were marginalized and rendered invisible and silent through ethnic and color-coded language. These Christians, I have argued, were *blackened by their sins*. They were not necessarily *blackened* because of the color of their skin or their ethnic identity; more than likely, they were *blackened* because of certain ideas and values held in early Christianity. Ethnic and color difference came to *symbolize* theological, ideological, and even political intra-Christian controversies and challenges.

The authors were not consistent in their use of the terms. This was due, in part, to the different historical, social, and political contexts represented in the Christian writings. The rhetorics range from a discussion of individuals, to activities, to specific content, or even interpretive processes. Also, we find that ethnic groups and geographical locations function interchangeably within ethno-political rhetorics. Moreover, the use of blacks and blackness indicated the influence of attitudes about light/dark color symbolism. In chapter 3 we saw how the patristic writers drew upon biblical traditions that mentioned Egyptians/Egypt and Ethiopians/Ethiopia. For example, Tertullian referred to Egypt and Ethiopia as places of sin and vice. In chapter 4 we saw how the monastic writers used Ethiopians as a type of human yardstick for measuring the inferiority or superiority of the Egyptian monks. In chapter 5 the Black One was used as a symbol for a so-called heretical movement. In addition, chapter 5 documented how Ethiopians and Blacks could be used to represent both insiders and outsiders within early Christian communities through the depiction of models of "virtue."

Many of the scholarly discussions about Egyptians/Egypt, Ethiopians/Ethiopia, and Blacks/blackness are laden with the authors' own ideological concerns that led to inconsistent and sometimes inaccurate translations of the Greek and Latin primary source documents. The cultural and racial politics of a given period of history strongly influences how academic discussions about these ethnic groups, geographical locations, and color symbols take shape. Thus many of the modern discussions about this material exhibit ethno-political rhetorics *within* ethno-political rhetorics. Similarly, within the ancient accounts, Egyptians, Ethiopians, and Blacks are also understood in terms of the language operative in the time and place in which the ancient author is writing. Thus some authors describe Ethiopians as an ethnic group ("Blacks"), or they make reference to the color of their skin ("black"). Some may speak in terms of

123

light/dark symbolism (blackness), while others simply use the generic label *ho melas* (the Black One).

The ethno-political rhetorics analyzed in this book call into question the so-called inclusive and universalist claims of early Christianity. No longer can one claim that the early Christians were oriented around a universalist worldview that extended its arms to the ends of the earth. No longer is it acceptable to dismiss the possibility that ethnic and color difference played a significant role in the Greco-Roman world, in general, and in early Christianity in particular. No longer is it possible to claim that the references to ethnic and color-coded language are sporadic and exceptional in ancient Christian literature. No longer can one examine the New Testament in isolation from the larger historical and rhetorical climate out of which it emerged.

The major contribution of this study is that it challenges the general reader and interpreter of ancient Christian sources to consider the power of symbolic language in shaping attitudes, values, worldviews, and practices of early Christians.[3] In addition, this book (1) identifies and classifies some of the diverse representations of Egyptians, Ethiopians, Blacks, and blackness through a *historical*[4] taxonomy of ethno-political rhetorics; (2) proposes a methodological framework based on rhetorical criticism, ethnocriticism, and feminist/womanist hermeneutics that overcomes some of the hermeneutical roadblocks that scholars generally face when dealing with texts about ethnic and color differences within the New Testament and other ancient Christian literature; (3) highlights the socio-political, cultural, and ideological realities that shaped ancient Christian literature; (4) examines how ancient Christian authors utilized discursive strategies for the purpose of defining socio-political, religious, and ideological boundaries for their communities; and (5) demonstrates the importance and need for an interdisciplinary approach for interpreting the New Testament and early Christianity.

I have discovered the different ways that Christian authors adopted and adjusted the rhetorical strategies about Egyptians/Egypt, Ethiopians/Ethiopia, and Blacks/blackness operative within Greco-Roman antiquity. There was no uniform strategy for developing or deploying the rhetorics. The depictions of these ethnic groups, geographical locations, and color symbols varied depending on the author, genre, location, and date of a given text.[5] Three general patterns, however, have been identified.

First, the Christian writers adopted fairly consistent patterns that were already established within antiquity. For example, the depictions of Ethiopia (both physically and as representing the ends of the earth) were similar to such depictions in Greco-Roman writings. Second, the writers adjusted the existing discourses to fit their own goals for meeting the challenges within their respective communities. For example, the caricature of Egyptians and Ethiopians found in many Roman writings was now included by church fathers, such as Jerome in his commentaries. Christians adopted in their discussions about sins and vices the color-symbolic association of "black" as evil found in many Greco-

Roman writings. Third, Christian writers invented their own particular ethno-political rhetoric based on the specific conditions within their respective communities. For example, the authors of monastic literature from late antique Egypt revealed a particular symbolic use of Ethiopians and Blacks. In this material Egyptians were no longer at the heart of the ethno-political rhetorics; they were now in fact advancing and shaping the rhetorics to help define an understanding of the virtues of asceticism. The special military and political conditions that were threatening the stability of the empire during late antiquity, along with the emergence of many so-called barbarian groups, contributed in some ways to this shift in the use of the rhetoric.[6]

Also within monastic literature we find a special type of ethno-political rhetoric about Ethiopian women. In several stories of temptation and triumph the symbolism of gender and ethnicity merge to draw attention to social and economic disparities in Roman Egypt, as well as possible military threats posed by the Queens of Ethiopia. This rhetoric also points to aesthetic values that governed the consciousness of the desert monks and the elite authors who collected and edited their *Sayings*. The Ethiopian women are represented as sexually attractive, as well as malodorous and demonic. A pattern of violence against Ethiopian women is discernible within the literature. This pattern does not necessarily reflect actual encounters with Ethiopian or Black women, but it certainly raises questions as to how such vituperative depictions could become a common source of Christian edifying discourse. These monastic sources would also be helpful in facilitating discussions about sexuality among contemporary Christians.[7] Generally, Christians are reluctant to talk about the body, sexuality, or attitudes that inform an understanding of sexual immorality. I hope that this examination of Ethiopian women in monastic sources might be a way of furthering the dialogue by demonstrating that stereotypes about Black women go back to ancient *Christian* authors and church leaders.

The taxonomy developed in Part 2 demonstrates how the most remote people ("beyond the rivers of Ethiopia") symbolized the moral and political extremes to which Christianity could extend. Ancient Christian authors used Egyptians/Egypt, Ethiopians/Ethiopians, and Blacks/blackness as polemical devices or symbolic tropes to respond to their intra-Christian opponents as well as external persecutors of their communities. These tropes became a handy pedagogical tool for early Christian self-definition. Through the study of ethno-political rhetorics we have begun to isolate some of the major threats that challenged the early Christians and, more importantly, we have begun to explore how Christian writers developed discourses that centered upon ethnic difference and color symbolism in order to respond to some imminent threats.

What made such ethno-political rhetorics possible? How and why did these rhetorics persist throughout the history and development of ancient Christianity? Michael Mann, in *The Sources of Social Power*, suggests that early Christians developed an ideological infrastructure that made it possible for ideas to be codified and then transmitted to different Christian communities.[8] Christian writers from the time of the New Testament through the growth of monastic literature were concerned about developing polemical responses to their various opponents – both internal and external – and about establishing the boundaries for inclusion within their communities. In this book I have demonstrated how references to Egyptians/Egypt, Ethiopians/Ethiopia, and Blacks/blackness became symbolic tropes within the ideological infrastructure of ancient Christian writings. These ethnic groups, geographical locations, and color symbols were used by Christian writers to signal the threats, challenges, and opponents in their respective communities. They call attention to intra-Christian debates and controversies, as well as the vast cultural diversity within early Christian communities that would have made such rhetorics possible.

New Testament passages, apocryphal writings, patristic commentaries, homilies, treatises, and desert sayings included ethno-political rhetorics about Egyptians/Egypt, Ethiopians/Ethiopia, and Blacks/blackness as forms of political invective and cultural signifiers that addressed the problems of sinful beliefs and practices, sexual temptations and bodily passions, and heretical movements within early Christianity. Such rhetorics developed as a response to the political situations, social conditions, and ethnic and gender differentiations in the ancient world. The rhetorics were based upon the perceived differences among ethnic groups within early Christianity. Based upon the evidence in this book, assumptions about ethnic and color differences influenced the way early Christians shaped their stories about the theological, ecclesiological, and political developments in their communities. As a result, Egyptians, Ethiopians, Blacks, and blackness invariably became associated with the threats and dangers that could potentially destroy the development of a certain orthodox manifestation of early Christianity.

It is important to realize that ethno-political rhetorics are not limited to ancient literary sources. Unfortunately, the world today is still strongly influenced by ideas about ethnic and color difference.[9] In the United States the "problem of the color line" has caused major divisions within many mainline Protestant denominations.[10] Christian documents have often been used to support and justify the unfair practices that stem from the exploitation of certain ethnic groups.

This book has some contemporary implications for understanding the rhetorics about "Blacks" and other ethnic groups in American society – contemporary ethno-political rhetorics. One striking example of how ethno-political rhetorics operate in American society can be seen in the story of a young woman by the name of Susan Smith who committed an unimaginable crime. In November 1994 she killed her two children by setting up her car to drive off of a boat ramp into a lake, carrying her two sons who were strapped in car seats. For nine days she lied about the tragic situation by claiming "a black gunman" had stolen her car and abducted her children. She provided a vivid description of this phantom black person and a hypothetical picture of him was posted on national TV and in newspapers and magazines across the country. This story captivated the media and the American public.[11] Smith apparently knew that her story would be plausible in a society that has certain negative perceptions of "Blacks." The entire country was shocked when Smith later confessed that she in fact had released the emergency brakes and watched as her car, along with the two boys strapped down in car seats, rolled down a boat ramp into the dark, murky waters of the John D. Long Lake.

Such incidents of "blaming the black man" are not uncommon.[12] This incident represents what historian of religion Charles Long would call "signifying."[13] According to Long, the language of signification is often created by those who have power in order to keep the "signified" group in its place.[14] In many respects early Christian authors "signified" on that which was considered most extreme in their culture: Egyptians, Ethiopians, and Blacks. This discursive strategy is evident within ancient Christian writings through what I call ethno-political rhetorics. Christian authors adapted existing discursive patterns and even advanced their own rhetorical and ideological stories as a way of keeping certain groups, perspectives, and activities in their place – silenced or marginalized.

Long calls attention to the way "Blacks" have been defined by the majority culture. He says:

> For the majority culture of this country, Blacks have always been signified. By this I mean that they have always been a part of a cultural code whose euphemisms and stereotypes have indicated their meaning within the larger framework of American cultural languages. The cultural reality of Blacks in the United States has been created by those who have the power of cultural signification – and the range of this power in the language of political, social, and cultural reality is enormous.[15]

In this book I have examined the ways in which Egyptians, Ethiopians, Blacks, and blackness have been signified by way of ethno-political rhetorics within a representative sample of ancient Christian literature. The rhetorics that have been identified call attention to the power of language to create the religious, political, social, and cultural reality of ancient Christians. The power of the rhetorics is in their cumulative effect. No one text tells the whole story, but all of the texts indicate that there was a consistent pattern of world-making among early Christians that was based upon assumptions about extreme forms of difference as manifested in Egyptians/Egypt, Ethiopians/Ethiopia, and Blacks/blackness. This book is a study of how symbolic language about ethnic groups, geographical locations, and color differences both reflects and defines certain perceptions about religious, social, and political realities.

The rhetorics also draw attention to gender disparities in early Christianity and provide a means for utilizing womanist readings of ancient Christian sources. According to Clarice Martin, womanist hermeneutics moves beyond the feminist critique of patriarchy and challenges all ideologies of dominance and subordination in the biblical writers and the theoretical models underlying contemporary biblical and theological interpretations.[16] Its chief concern is "to amplify the voices of *all* persons who are marginalized in the text."[17] Because of their emphasis on canonical texts, womanist interpreters have generally overlooked the multiple depictions of Ethiopian women in ancient Christian writings. This book attempts to amplify the marginalized voices of Ethiopian women within ancient Christian literature. Ethiopian women symbolized gender disparities, political insecurities, aesthetic sensibilities, and socio-economic realities in early Christianity. The way that Christian writers (especially the monastic authors) included Ethiopian (and Black) women in their ethno-political rhetorics has implications for understanding how Black women are used within contemporary discussions about politics and morality.[18]

The numerous ambiguous, enigmatic references to Egyptians, Ethiopians, and Blacks in the New Testament, apocryphal acts, patristic commentaries, homilies, theological treatises, and monastic hagiographical literature warrant a method for understanding their purposes and functions in these texts. A taxonomy of ethno-political rhetorics enables the reader to assess the use of ethnic tropes within ancient Christian writings. These tropes symbolize movements and voices around the Mediterranean that have been largely ignored or rendered silent by New Testament scholars and historians of early Christianity. New Testament scholar Vincent L. Wimbush draws attention to these submerged voices and movements by challenging interpreters to pay more attention to the character of the language of opposition.[19]

> To interpret the New Testament and early Christianity without reference to voices and movements not fully or directly represented is not simply to fail to be inclusive and comprehensive; it is to fail to be self-critical and intellectually honest about what the whole enterprise of interpretation, including the historical work that is Christian origins, is really all about.[20]

The submerged voices within early Christian communities were not necessarily ethnic, but rather ideological, theological, and political. This book is a study of how symbolic language both reflects and defines certain perceptions about religious, social, and political realities. My purpose has simply been to analyze how the language about ethnic and color differences in early Christian texts served to shape certain ideas and values in different Christian communities. I have included a diverse range of representations in order to classify and analyze some of the ancient Christian discourses related to Egyptians/Egypt, Ethiopians/Ethiopia, and Blacks/blackness and to isolate some of the socio-political, religious, cultural, and economic forces that influenced how and why these ethnic groups, geographical locations, and color symbols were included in the writings of ancient Christian authors. This book, I hope, will at least invite others to raise questions about the diverse cultural background of early Christianity and to analyze how ethno-political rhetorics functioned in the discursive strategies of ancient Christian writers – "Why does *the Ethiopian* come among us?"

NOTES

INTRODUCTION

1 Ethiopian (*Aithiops*) was the term used by Greeks to refer to a person with a black or sunburned face. Ethiopia (*Aithiopia*) is the region commonly known as Nubia in the ancient world (modern Sudan). In this study I will use the designation "Ethiopia" to refer to the land south of Egypt in the ancient world. For a useful discussion of the complexities related to determining the boundaries of Ethiopia (i.e., Nubia) in the ancient world, see William Y. Adams, "The Invention of Nubia," in *Hommages à Jean Leclant* (2: Nubie, Soudan, Ethiopie; ed. C. Berger et al.; BdE 106/2; Cairo: IFAO, 1994), 17–22; W.Y. Adams, *Nubia: Corridor to Africa* (Princeton: Princeton University Press, 1977); and David O'Connor, "Understanding Ancient Nubia," in *Ancient Nubia: Egypt's Rival in Africa* (Philadelphia: University Museum of Archaeology and Anthropology, 1993), 1–8.

2 Black (Gk. *melas*, Lat. *niger*) carried many different meanings within Greco-Roman writings. Throughout this study, I have attempted to distinguish the uses of *melas* or *niger* in terms of ethnic identity (upper-case "Black") and color symbolism (lower-case "black"); although in some instances the meanings overlap. As an ethnic designation, *melas* was often equated with *Aithiops* to indicate the "burnt-skinned" people who dwelled south of Egypt (Herodotus 2.22). As a color referent, it was used to support dualistic conceptions of good and evil. As a name or title designation it functioned as a proper noun to designate a particular person such as *Symeōn ho kaloumenos* Niger (Acts 13:1) or as a nickname in the case of Apollonius *ho melas* (*Amherst Papyri* 62, 6–7). Among Christian authors, there was no consistent use of *melas* or *niger*. For example, Antony's encounter with the black boy (*melas pais*) is quite different from the black-robed women (*tōn gynaikōn tōn ta melana himatia endedymenōn*) discussed in the *Shepherd of Hermas*. Origen's interpretation of the black bride of Solomon, who says, "I am black and beautiful" (*melaina eimi kai kalē*), is quite different from Jerome's discussion of Ethiopians being blackened by their sins (*peccata nos nigros fecerant*). There were also allusions to darkness (*skotos*) that coincided with many references to black or blackness in Christian writings (cf. *Epist. Barn.* 14.6). For a basic introduction to "the Black One" in early Christian writings, see S. Vernon McCasland, "The Black One," in *Early Christian Origins* (ed. Allen Wikgren; Chicago: Quadrangle, 1961), 77–80.

3 Tropes are literary devices that generate a certain thought or response from the reader. According to Hayden White, tropes are "deviations from literal, conventional, or 'proper' language use, swerves in locution sanctioned neither by custom nor logic. Tropes generate figures of speech or thought by their variation from what is 'normally' expected, and by the associations they establish between

concepts normally felt not to be related or to be related in ways different from that suggested in the trope used." See Hayden White, *Tropics of Discourse: Essays in Cultural Criticism* (Baltimore: Johns Hopkins University Press, 1978), 2. Cf. Arnaldo Momigliano's critique of White's method in "The Rhetoric of History and the History of Rhetoric: On Hayden White's Tropes," in *Comparative Criticism: A Year Book* (ed. E.S. Shaffer; Cambridge: Cambridge University Press, 1981), 3:259–68. For a discussion on the theoretical foundation for the use of tropes, see James W. Fernandez, *Beyond Metaphor: The Theory of Tropes in Anthropology* (Stanford: Stanford University Press, 1991); and *Persuasions and Performances: The Play of Tropes in Culture* (Bloomington: Indiana University Press, 1986).

4　Edward Said, "An Ideology of Difference," in *"Race," Writing, and Difference* (ed. Henry Louis Gates, Jr.; Chicago: University of Chicago Press, 1986), 38–58.

5　Taxonomy refers to the science or technique of classification. For examples of taxonomies within religious and biblical studies, see Richard J. Mouw, "The Bible in Twentieth-Century Protestantism: A Preliminary Taxonomy," in *The Bible in America: Essays in Cultural History* (ed. Nathan O. Hatch and Mark A. Noll; New York: Oxford University Press, 1982), 139–62; Daniel P. Sheridan, "Discerning Difference: A Taxonomy of Culture, Spirituality, and Religion," *JR* 66 (1986): 37–45; and Urban T. Holmes, "Taxonomy of Contemporary Spirituality," in *Christians at Prayer* (ed. John Gallen; Notre Dame, Ind.: University of Notre Dame Press, 1977), 26–45.

6　Bart Ehrman, describing the diversity of early Christianity, refers to a "proto-orthodox" group of early Christians who eventually came to represent the dominant form of Christianity that emerged in late antiquity. See Bart Ehrman, *The New Testament: A Historical Introduction to the Early Christian Writings* (2nd ed.; New York: Oxford University Press, 2000), 6–7.

7　For a useful discussion about the literary traditions related to political invective, see Jacqueline Long, *Claudian's In Eutropium: Or, How, When, and Why to Slander a Eunuch* (Chapel Hill: University of North Carolina Press, 1996), esp. ch. 3, "Literary Traditions of Political Invective," 65–105. See also, Severin Koster, *Die Invektive in der griechischen und römischen Literatur* (Beiträge zur Klassischen Philologie 99; Meisenheim am Glan: A. Hain, 1980); and Ilona Opelt, *Die Polemik in der christlichen lateinischen Literatur von Tertullian bis Augustin* (Heidelberg: C. Winter – Universitätsverlag, 1980).

8　For a useful definition of ethnicity, which will be used throughout this study, see Werner Sollors, "Ethnicity," in *Critical Terms for Literary Study* (ed. Frank Lentricchia and Thomas McLaughlin; Chicago: University of Chicago Press, 1990), 288–305. See also, J.M. Yinger, "Ethnicity," *Annual Review of Sociology* 11 (1985): 151–80.

9　The Greek word ἔθνος (*ethnos*), from which the English terms "ethnic" and "ethnicity" are derived, contains an ambivalence between the inclusive meaning, "people in general," and the dissociative sense, "other people." See Sollars, "Ethnicity," 288.

10　See Jonathan Z. Smith, "What a Difference a Difference Makes," in *"To See Ourselves as Others See Us": Christians, Jews, "Others" in Late Antiquity* (ed. J. Neusner and E.S. Frerichs; Chico, Calif.: Scholars Press, 1985), 3–48; and Sze-Kar Wan, "Collection for the Saints as Anticolonial Act: Implications of Paul's Ethnic Reconstruction," in *Paul and Politics* (ed. Richard A. Horsley; Harrisburg, Pa.: Trinity Press International, 2000), 191–215, esp. 192.

11　Mark G. Brett, "Interpreting Ethnicity: Method, Hermeneutics, Ethics," in *Ethnicity and the Bible* (ed. Mark G. Brett; Leiden: E.J. Brill, 1996), 3–22, esp. 10. See also, Fredrik Barth, "Ethnic and Group Boundaries," in *Theories of Ethnicity* (ed. Werner Sollors; New York: New York University Press, 1996), 294–324; and

Philip F. Esler, "Group Boundaries and Intergroup Conflict in Galatians: A New Reading of Galatians 5:13–6:10," in Brett, *Ethnicity and the Bible*, 215–40.

12 For a useful discussion on how the "other" functioned in ancient Christian writings, see Adela Yarbro Collins, "Vilification and Self-Definition in the Book of Revelation," *HTR* 79:1–3 (1986): 308–20; and Sean Freyne, "Vilifying the Other and Defining the Self: Matthew's and John's Anti-Jewish Polemic in Focus," in Neusner and Frerichs, *"To See Ourselves as Others See Us,"* 117–43.

13 See Hans Windisch, "βάρβαρος," *TDNT* (Grand Rapids: Eerdmans, 1964), 1:546–53.

14 See, for example, Helen H. Bacon, *Barbarians in Greek Tragedy* (New Haven: Yale University Press, 1961); Edith Hall, *Inventing the Barbarian: Greek Self-Definition through Tragedy* (Oxford: Oxford University Press, 1989); Timothy Long, *Barbarians in Greek Comedy* (Carbondale: Southern Illinois University Press, 1986); Richard F. Thomas, *Lands and Peoples in Roman Poetry: The Ethnographic Tradition* (Cambridge Philological Society Suppl. 7; Cambridge: Cambridge University Press, 1982); James B. Rives, trans. and ed., *Germania* (New York: Oxford University Press, 1999); Peter Schäfer, *Judeophobia: Attitudes Toward the Jews in the Ancient World* (Cambridge, Mass.: Harvard University Press, 1997); and Gerhart B. Ladner, "On Roman Attitudes Toward Barbarians in Late Antiquity," *Viator* 7 (1976): 1–26.

15 Richard Fletcher, *The Barbarian Conversion: From Paganism to Christianity* (Berkeley: University of California Press, 1997), 1–33; E.A. Thompson, "Barbarians, Collaborators, and Christians," in *Romans and Barbarians: The Decline of the Western Empire*, 230–51; J.H. Waszink, "Some Observations on the Appreciation of the 'Philosophy of the Barbarians' in Early Christian Literature," in *Mélanges Christine Mohrmann* (Utrecht: Anvers, Spectrum, 1963), 41–56; and Amy L. Wordelman, "The Gods Have Come Down: Images of Historical Lycaonia and the Literary Construction of Acts 14" (Ph.D. diss., Princeton University, 1994).

16 Some scholars have gone as far as to claim that this text reflects an ancient form of racism. See, for example, Wolfgang Stegemann, "Anti-Semitic and Racist Prejudices in Titus 1:10–16," in *Ethnicity and the Bible* (ed. Mark Brett; Leiden: E.J. Brill, 1996), 271–94, esp. 293. Stegemann claims that the xenophobic prejudices against Jews and Cretans by the author of the letter to Titus can be placed within the framework of "negative labelling" of a heterodox Christian group. He calls the opponents a "deviant Christian group."

17 Luke T. Johnson, "The New Testament's Anti-Jewish Slander and the Conventions of Ancient Polemic," *JBL* 108, no. 3 (1989): 419–41.

18 See, for example, Jonathan M. Hall, *Ethnic Identity in Greek Antiquity* (Cambridge: Cambridge University Press, 1997), esp. chap. 3, "The Discursive Dimension of Ethnic Identity," 34–66; and the collection of essays in Brett, *Ethnicity and the Bible*. These and other related ethnocritical studies will be discussed in chapter 1.

19 Tertullian, *De spectaculis* 3: "*cum Aegypto et Aethiopiae exitium comminatur, utique in omnem gentem peccatricem praeiudicat.*" Text and translation in *De spectaculis* (trans. T.R. Glover; LCL; Cambridge: Harvard University Press, 1977), 240–41.

20 *Acts of Peter* 22: "*et ante turbam magnam, et mulierem quendam turpissimam, in aspectu Aethiopissimam, neque Aegyptiam, sed totam nigram sordibus, pannis inuolutam.*" Text in *Acta Apostolorum Apocrypha* (2 vols.; ed. Ricardus A. Lipsius and Maximilianus Bonnet; Hildesheim: G. Olms, 1959), 1:69–70. English translation in *New Testament Apocrypha* (2 vols.; trans. E. Hennecke and W. Schneemelcher; Louisville: Westminster/John Knox, 1991–2), 2:305.

21 See John A. Wilson, *The Culture of Ancient Egypt* (Chicago: University of Chicago Press, 1951), 305. Wilson concludes that many of the inconsistencies occur as a result of the confusion among the ancient authors themselves. See also Franz

Joseph Dölger, *Die Sonne der Gerechtigkeit und der Schwarze: Eine religions-geschichtliche Studie zum Taufgelöbnis* (Liturgiewissenschaftliche Quellen und Forschungen 14; 2nd ed.; Münster: Aschendorff, 1971), 52–53.

22 Jean Marie Courtès "The Theme of 'Ethiopia' and 'Ethiopians' in Patristic Literature," in *The Image of the Black in Western Art* (2/1; ed. Jean Devisse; New York: W. Morrow, 1979), 30. Courtès inaccurately translates *Aegyptius* (Egyptian) as "Ethiopian" (cf. *Passio Perpetuae* 10.6).

23 Courtès, "'Ethiopians' in Patristic Literature," 30; Jerome, *Commentary on Isaiah* 7.18.2.

24 Lloyd A. Thompson identifies this problem. He concludes that the Roman concept of *Aethiops* as a label for a distinct somatic type and the significance of that concept with regard to Roman social ideology should be clarified. See Lloyd A. Thompson, *Romans and Blacks* (Norman: University of Oklahoma Press, 1989), 54.

25 Frank M. Snowden, Jr., "Bernal's 'Blacks' and the Afrocentrists," in *Black Athena Revisited* (ed. Mary R. Lefkowitz and Guy MacLean Rogers; Chapel Hill: University of North Carolina Press, 1996), 113.

26 Herodotus, 2.104.

27 See, for example, classicists such as Grace H. Beardsley, *The Negro in Greek and Roman Civilization: A Study of the Ethiopian Type* (New York: Russell & Russell, 1967 [1929]); Frank M. Snowden, Jr., *Before Color Prejudice: The Ancient View of Blacks* (Cambridge, Mass.: Harvard University Press, 1983); and *Blacks in Antiquity: Ethiopians in the Greco-Roman Experience* (Cambridge, Mass.: Harvard University Press, 1970); Mary R. Lefkowitz, *Not Out of Africa: How Afrocentrism Became an Excuse to Teach Myth and History* (New York: Basic, 1996); and Lefkowitz and Rogers, *Black Athena Revisited*; Afrocentrists such as Cheikh Anta Diop, *The African Origin of Civilization: Myth or Reality* (trans. Mercer Cook; Chicago: Lawrence Hill, 1974); and *Civilization or Barbarism: An Authentic Anthropology* (trans Y.M. Ngemi; Chicago: Lawrence Hill, 1991 [1981]); Molefi K. Asante, *The Afrocentric Idea* (Philadelphia: Temple University Press, 1987); *Afrocentricity* (Trenton, N.J.: Africa World, 1988); *Kemet, Afrocentricity, and Knowledge* (Trenton, N.J.: Africa World, 1990); and *The Painful Demise of Eurocentrism: An Afrocentric Response to Critics* (Trenton, N.J.: Africa World, 1999). While Asante is the premiere Afrocentrist scholar who coined the term "Afrocentric," it was W.E.B. DuBois who first attempted to set forth the contributions of Africans in the development of Western civilization. See W.E.B. DuBois, *The Negro* (London: Oxford University Press, 1970 [1915]); anthropologists St. Clair Drake, *Black Folk Here and There: An Essay in History and Anthropology* (2 vols; Los Angeles: Center for Afro-American Studies, University of California, 1987–90); Roger Bastide, "Color, Racism, and Christianity," in *Color and Race* (ed. John Hope Franklin; Boston: Houghton Mifflin, 1968), 34–49; and Peter Frost, "Attitudes toward Blacks in the Early Christian Era," *SecCent* 8, no. 1 (1991): 1–11. See also, Egyptologists such as Pierre Montet, *Egypt and the Bible* (trans. Leslie R. Keylock; Philadelphia: Fortress, 1968); J. Gwyn Griffiths, "Was Damaris an Egyptian? (Acts 17:34)," *BZ* 8 (1964): 293–95; and George D. Kilpatrick, "The Land of Egypt in the New Testament," *JTS* 17 (1966): 70; Nicolas Grimal, *A History of Ancient Egypt* (Oxford: Basil Blackwell, 1992); Nubiologists such as W.Y. Adams, *Nubia: Corridor to Africa* (Princeton: Princeton University Press, 1977); and "The Invention of Nubia"; Nadeau, "Ethiopians Again and Again," *Mnemosyne* 30 (1977): 75–78; and "Ethiopians," *CQ* 20, no. 2 (1970): 339–49; Edward Ullendorff, *Ethiopia and the Bible* (London: Oxford University Press, 1968); and Jacob A. Dyer, *The Ethiopian in the Bible* (New York: Vantage, 1974); and ancient historians such as Stanley M. Burstein, *Graeco-Africana: Studies in the History of Greek Relations with Egypt and Nubia* (New Rochelle, N.Y.: A.D. Caratzas, 1995);

and Alan K. Bowman, *Egypt after the Pharaohs: 332 BC – AD 642 from Alexander to the Arab Conquest* (Berkeley: University of California Press, 1989).

28 Afrocentrists, for example, generally consider Egyptians as Blacks, while classicists understand Ethiopians as Blacks. Egyptologists tend to stay away from making distinctions about ethnic and color difference in their writings. Egyptologist Ann Macy Roth, concerned about the way that most Egyptologists have generally dismissed the conclusions of Afrocentric scholars, offers an important challenge to her colleagues: "The Afrocentric movement has a great potential to advance or to damage our field. Which of these directions it takes will depend upon the degree to which traditionally-trained American Egyptologists can come to understand and adapt to its existence." See Ann Macy Roth, "Building Bridges to Afrocentrism: A Letter to my Egyptological Colleagues: Part 1," *American Research Center in Egypt Newsletter* 167 (1995): 1, 14–17, esp. 1. Roth challenges her colleagues to recognize the European bias inherent in Egyptology: "Egyptology is a Eurocentric profession. It was founded by European and American scholars whose primary interest was in confirming the Classical sources and in confirming and explicating the Old and New Testaments for the furtherance of Christianity." See Ann Macy Roth, "Building Bridges to Afrocentrism: A Letter to my Egyptological Colleagues: Part 2," *American Research Center in Egypt Newsletter* 168 (1995): 1, 12–15, esp. 14.

29 The debate surrounding Martin Bernal's provocative and controversial book *Black Athena: The Afroasiatic Roots of Classical Civilization* (2 vols.; New Brunswick, N.J.: Rutgers University Press, 1987–91) is a perfect example of this point. See Glen Bowersock, "Rescuing the Greeks: A Classicist Defends the Traditional Version of Greek Cultural Achievement" (review of *Not Out of Africa*, by Mary R. Lefkowitz and *Black Athena Revisited*, ed. Mary R. Lefkowitz and Guy M. Rogers), *New York Times Book Review*, February 25, 1996, 6–7. Bowersock contends that Mary Lefkowitz "unsystematically demolishes Afrocentric contentions about ancient history." He further claims that her "impassioned defense of the Greeks arises from the racial politics of our time." For an excellent assessment of Bernal's argument and the ensuing debate and its consequences, see Jacques Berlinerblau, *Heresy in the University: The Black Athena Controversy and the Responsibilities of American Intellectuals* (New Brunswick, N.J.: Rutgers University Press, 1999).

30 See Snowden, *Blacks in Antiquity* and *Before Color Prejudice*.

31 See Snowden, "Early Christian Attitude toward Ethiopians – Creed and Conversion," chap. 9 in *Blacks in Antiquity*, 196–215, and *Before Color Prejudice*, 99–108.

32 Snowden, *Blacks in Antiquity*, 206.

33 Snowden, *Blacks in Antiquity*, 196. For Snowden, the Ethiopian's conversion symbolizes how there is no distinction in the church on account of race or color because God is no respecter of persons (Acts 10:34).

34 For other useful studies, see, for example, Engelbert Mveng, ed., *Les sources grecques de l'histoire negro-africaine: depuis Homère jusqu'à Strabon* (Paris: Présence Africaine, 1972); Joseph E. Harris, ed., *Africa and Africans as Seen by Classical Writers: The William Leo Hansberry African History Notebook* (vol. 2; Washington, D.C.: Howard University Press, 1977); and Lloyd A. Thompson, *Romans and Blacks* (Norman: University of Oklahoma Press, 1989).

35 See, for example, Morton Smith, "Book Review of *Blacks in Antiquity*," *AHR* 76 (1971): 139–40. Smith emphasizes how Snowden neglected to include in his study the many uses of "apotropaic or grotesque Negroid figures" found throughout Greco-Roman antiquity. Smith also draws attention to the methodological deficiencies in Snowden's work and contends that Snowden used ancient Christian writings as prooftexts. See also, Thompson, *Romans and Blacks*. Thompson claims

that Snowden should have focused more on both the positive and negative references to Blacks. See also, Philip Mayerson, "Anti-Black Sentiment in the *Vitae Patrum*," *HTR* 71 (1978): 304–11. For an example of the complimentary reviews of Snowden's work, see B.H. Warmington, "Book Review of *Blacks in Antiquity*," *African Historical Studies* 4, no. 2 (1971): 383–86.

36 See, for example, D.B. Saddington, "Race Relations in the Early Roman Empire," in *ANRW* 112–37; and Lellia Cracco Ruggini, "Il negro buono e il negro malvagio nel mondo classico," in *Conoscenze etniche e rapporti* (ed. Marta Sordi; Milan: Università Cattolica del Sacro Cuore, 1979), 6:108–35, esp. 118. For earlier studies about race relations in the ancient world, see Aubrey Diller, *Race Mixture Among the Greeks Before Alexander* (Urbana: University of Illinois Press, 1937); Simon Davis, *Race-Relations in Ancient Egypt: Greek, Egyptian, Hebrew, Roman* (London: Methuen, 1951); and A.N. Sherwin-White, *Racial Prejudice in Imperial Rome* (Cambridge: Cambridge University Press, 1967).

37 Joseph E. Harris, ed., *Africa and Africans as Seen by Classical Writers: The William Leo Hansberry African History Notebook* (vol. 2; Washington, D.C.: Howard University Press, 1977).

38 Harris, *Africa and Africans*, xii.

39 Harris, *Africa and Africans*, xx.

40 These negative or vituperative discourses are characterized by abusive or slanderous language that vilifies a person or group of people. See Sean Freyne, "Vilifying the Other and Defining the Self: Matthew's and John's Anti-Jewish Polemic in Focus," in Neusner and Frerichs, *"To See Ourselves as Others See Us"*, 117–43. See especially section 2 of this essay, "The Rhetoric of Vituperation and Community Building," 129–40.

41 *Apophthegmata patrum* (PG 65.281–9); Palladius, *Historia Lausiaca* 19; Sozomen, *Historia ecclesiastica* 6.29; "Vita S. Moyse Aethiope," in *Acta Sanct.*, Augusti Tomus Sextus (ed. Joannes Bollandus et al.; Paris: V. Palme, 1868). For English translations of these texts, see Kathleen O. Wicker, "Ethiopian Moses (Collected Sources)," in *Ascetic Behavior in Greco-Roman Antiquity: A Source Book* (ed. Vincent L. Wimbush; Minneapolis: Fortress, 1990), 329–48.

42 See, for example, Clarice J. Martin, "The Function of Acts 8:26–40 within the Narrative Structure of the Book of Acts: The Significance of the Eunuch's Provenance for Acts 1:8c" (Ph.D. diss., Duke University, 1985); and "A Chamberlain's Journey and the Challenge of Interpretation for Liberation," *Semeia* 47 (1989): 105–35; F. Scott Spencer, "The Ethiopian Eunuch and His Bible: A Social-Science Analysis," *BTB* 22, no. 4 (1992): 155–65; Abraham Smith, "'Do You Understand What You are Reading?': A Literary Critical Reading of the Ethiopian (Kushite) Episode (Acts 8:26–40)," *Journal of the Interdenominational Theological Center* 22, no. 1 (1994): 48–70; and "A Second Step in African Biblical Interpretation: A Generic Reading Analysis of Acts 8:26–40," in *Reading from this Place: Social Location and Biblical Interpretation in the United States* (2 vols.; ed. Fernando Segovia and Mary Ann Tolbert; Minneapolis: Fortress, 1995), 1: 213–28; Cottrel R. Carson, "'Do You Understand What You are Reading?': A Reading of the Ethiopian Eunuch Story (Acts 8:26–40) from a Site of Cultural Marronage" (Ph.D. diss., Union Theological Seminary, 1999); and William Frank Lawrence, Jr., "The History of the Interpretation of Acts 8:26–40 by the Church Fathers Prior to the Fall of Rome" (Ph.D. diss., Union Theological Seminary, 1984).

43 See, for example, Robert A. Bennett, Jr., "Africa and the Biblical Period," *HTR* 64 (1971): 483–500; and "The Black Experience and the Bible," *ThTo* 27 (1971): 422–33; Latta R. Thomas, *Biblical Faith and the Black American* (Valley Forge, Pa.: Judson, 1976); Cain Hope Felder, *Troubling Biblical Waters: Race, Class, and Family*

(Maryknoll, N.Y.: Orbis, 1989); Cain Hope Felder, ed., *Stony the Road We Trod: African American Biblical Interpretation* (Minneapolis: Fortress, 1991); Walter M. McCray, *The Black Presence in the Bible* (Chicago: Black Light Fellowship, 1990); and Alvin A. Jackson, *Examining the Record: An Exegetical and Homiletical Study of Blacks in the Bible* (New York: P. Lang, 1994).

44 Vincent L. Wimbush, "Ascetic Behavior and Color-ful Language: Stories about Ethiopian Moses," *Semeia* 58 (1992): 81–92, esp. 89.

45 Wimbush, "Ascetic Behavior and Color-ful Language," 89.

46 Wimbush, "Ascetic Behavior and Color-ful Language," 90.

47 Charles B. Copher, "Three Thousand Years of Biblical Interpretation with Reference to Black Peoples," *Journal of the Interdenominational Theological Center* 13 (1986): 225–46; repr. in *Black Biblical Studies: An Anthology of Charles B. Copher* (Chicago: Black Light Fellowship, 1993), 95–120.

48 Copher, "Three Thousand Years," 231.

49 Charles B. Copher, "Egypt and Ethiopia in the Old Testament," *Journal of African Civilizations* 6, no. 2 (1984): 163–78; repr. in *Black Biblical Studies*, 45–65.

50 Copher, "Egypt and Ethiopia," 46.

51 Copher, "Egypt and Ethiopia," 46.

52 Copher, "Egypt and Ethiopia," 64.

53 See Randall C. Bailey and Jacquelyn Grant, eds., *The Recovery of Black Presence: An Interdisciplinary Exploration. Essays in Honor of Charles B. Copher* (Nashville: Abingdon, 1995).

54 For a more recent study of Africans in the Bible, see David T. Adamo, "The African and Africans in the Old Testament and its Environment" (Ph.D. diss., Baylor University, 1986); later published as *Africa and the Africans in the Old Testament* (San Francisco: International Scholars, 1998). See also, Randall C. Bailey, "Beyond Identification: The Use of Africans in Old Testament Poetry and Narratives," in *Stony the Road We Trod*, 165–84; and Alfred G. Dunston, Jr., *The Black Man in the Old Testament and its World* (Trenton, N.J.: Africa World, 1992).

55 Cf. Matt 2:13ff; 27:26; Mark 15:21; Luke 23:26; Acts 2:5–10; 6:9; 7:2–37; 13: 1, 16ff; Heb 3:16; 8:9; 11:20ff; Rev 7:9–10; 14:6ff. See Charles B. Copher, "The Bible and the African Experience: The Biblical Period," *Journal of the Interdenominational Theological Center* 16, nos. 1 and 2 (1988–89): 32–50; repr. in *Black Biblical Studies*, 133–48.

56 Robert Hood, *Begrimed and Black: Christian Traditions on Blacks and Blackness* (Minneapolis: Fortress, 1994). Hood was trained as a theologian and social ethicist. His review of the Greco-Roman and ancient Christian material does not provide evidence of his direct engagement with the sources in their original languages. At the time of Hood's sudden death in 1994, he was Professor of Religious Studies and Director of the Center for African-American Studies at Adelphi University, Garden City, New York. He had been Professor of Church and Society at General Theological Seminary in New York City.

57 For references to Blacks in the apocryphal sources, patristic literature, and writings from late antiquity, see Robert E. Hood, "Blackness as Evil and Sex in Early Christian Thought," chap. 3 in *Begrimed and Black*, 73–90.

58 Hood, *Begrimed and Black*, 90.

59 See especially his evaluations of color symbolism in the ancient world. Hood, "Africa and the Christian Tradition," chap. 2 in *Begrimed and Black*, 45–71. Cf. Rudolf Bultmann, "Zur Geschichte der Lichtsymbolik im Altertum," *Phil* 97 (part 1/2, 1948): 1–36; Christopher Rowe, "Conceptions of Colour and Colour Symbolism in the Ancient World," in *Die Welt der Farben le Monde des Couleurs* (ed. A. Portmann and R. Ritsema; Leiden: E.J. Brill. 1974), 327–64; and Eleanor Irwin, *Colour Terms in Greek Poetry* (Toronto: Hakkert, 1974).

60 Hood, *Begrimed and Black*, "Egypt and Ethiopia and the Christian Tradition," 53–65.

61 Although Hood identifies many Ethiopian women in this study, he does not analyze the rhetorical significance of the detailed descriptions and graphic representations of Ethiopian women, nor does he explore how assumptions about gender relate to assumptions about ethnicity. See, for example, his discussion of Scybale in *Begrimed and Black*, 42.

62 Generally, studies on women in the ancient world do not examine Ethiopian or Black women. See, for example, Sarah B. Pomeroy, *Goddesses, Whores, Wives, and Slaves: Women in Classical Antiquity* (New York: Schocken, 1975); Elaine Fantham et al., *Women in the Classical World: Image and Text* (New York: Oxford University Press, 1994); and Ross S. Kraemer, ed., *Maenads, Martyrs, Matrons, Monastics: A Sourcebook on Women's Religions in the Greco-Roman World* (Philadelphia: Fortress, 1988). The one study that focuses on Black women in antiquity provides a collection of general essays about Egyptian and Ethiopian queens. See Ivan van Sertima, ed., *Black Women in Antiquity* (New Brunswick, N.J.: Transaction, 1989). For useful studies on women in ancient Egypt, see Sarah B. Pomeroy, *Women in Hellenistic Egypt: From Alexander to Cleopatra* (Detroit: Wayne State University Press, 1990); Gay Robbins, *Women in Ancient Egypt* (Cambridge, Mass.: Harvard University Press, 1993); and Jane Rowlandson, ed., *Women and Society in Greek and Roman Egypt: A Sourcebook* (Cambridge: Cambridge University Press, 1998).

63 Vincent Wimbush discusses the ways that African Americans have engaged and interpreted the Bible. His understanding of "reading Scriptures" as "reading darkness" captures the impetus for my engagement with this project: "Almost from the beginning of their engagement with it, African Americans interpreted the Bible differently from those who introduced them to it, ironically and audaciously seeing in it – the most powerful of the ideological weapons used to legitimize their enslavement and disenfranchisement – a mirroring of themselves and their experiences, seeing in it the privileging of all those who like themselves are the humiliated, the outcasts and powerless. It was seen as a sort of rhetorical paint brushing of their existences and a virtual manifesto for their redemption and triumph. So for African Americans to read Scriptures is to read darkness. By referring here to darkness . . . I mean here simply that African Americans' engagement of the Bible points to the Bible as that which both reflects and draws unto itself and engages and problematizes a certain complex order of existence associated with marginality, liminality, exile, pain, trauma." See Vincent L. Wimbush, "Introduction: Reading Darkness, Reading Scriptures," in *African Americans and the Bible: Sacred Texts and Social Textures* (ed. Vincent L. Wimbush; New York: Continuum, 2000), 1–43, esp. 17. See also, Fernando Segovia, "Racial and Ethnic Minorities in Biblical Studies," in *Ethnicity and the Bible* (ed. Mark G. Brett; Leiden: E.J. Brill, 1996), 469–92.

64 For some important studies that attempt to classify the references to Egyptians, Ethiopians, and Blacks in Greco-Roman (including Christian) literature, see Jean-Jacques Aubert, "Du Noir en noir et blanc: eloge de la dispersion," *MH* 56 (1999): 159–82; E. Oréal, "'Noir parfait': un jeu de mot de l'égyptien au grec," *REG* 111 (1998): 551–65; Courtès, "'Ethiopians' in Patristic Literature"; and Saddington, "Race Relations in the Early Roman Empire," 115–19.

65 Averil Cameron, *Christianity and the Rhetoric of Empire: The Development of Christian Discourse* (Sather Classical Lectures 55; Berkeley: University of California Press, 1991).

66 My use of gender analysis and womanist hermeneutics will be explained in chapter 1. For definitions of "gender" and "womanist," see Joan Wallach Scott,

"Gender: A Useful Category of Historical Analysis," in *Feminism and History* (ed. Joan Wallach Scott; Oxford: Oxford University Press, 1996), 152–80; and Clarice J. Martin, "Womanist Interpretations of the New Testament: The Quest for Holistic and Inclusive Translation and Interpretation," *JFSR* 6, no. 2 (1990): 41–61.

67 Pierre Bourdieu, *Language and Symbolic Power* (trans. Gino Raymond and Matthew Adamson; Cambridge, Mass.: Harvard University Press, 1991).

68 See, for example, Burton Mack, *Rhetoric and the New Testament* (Minneapolis: Fortress, 1989); and Brian K. Blount, *Cultural Interpretation: Reorienting New Testament Criticism* (Minneapolis: Fortress, 1995); and "A Social-Rhetorical Analysis of Simon of Cyrene: Mark 15:21 and Its Parallels," *Semeia* 64 (1993): 171–98. One scholar has attempted to look at the rhetorical significance of Egypt in the book of Revelation. See Edwin Earl Reynolds, "The Sodom/Egypt/Babylon Motif in the Book of Revelation" (Ph.D. diss., Andrews University, 1994).

69 Because of the focus on identifying and classifying the rhetorics, the historical background was developed around the themes generated by the taxonomy. Given the complex nature of the rhetorics, a mere diachronic analysis starting in the first century CE and proceeding through late antiquity could not be achieved; the ethno-political rhetorics overlap different time periods.

70 Most of the evidence in this study is literary; artistic and iconographical sources have been omitted. For useful studies on the representations of Blacks in ancient art, see Beardsley, *Negro in Greek and Roman Civilization*; Snowden, *Blacks in Antiquity*; Jehan Desanges, "The Iconography of the Black in Ancient North Africa," in *From the Pharaohs to the Fall of the Roman Empire* (vol. 1 of *The Image of the Black in Western Art*, ed. Ladislas Bugner; New York: W. Morrow, 1976), 246–68, 308–12; Theodore Calenko, ed., *Egypt in Africa* (Indianapolis: Indiana University Press, 1997); Marilyn Heldman et al., *African Zion: The Sacred Art of Ethiopia* (New Haven: Yale University Press, 1993); and Fritz Hintze, ed., *Africa in Antiquity: The Arts of Ancient Nubia and the Sudan* (vol. 1; New York: Brooklyn Museum, 1978).

71 Averil Cameron, ed., *History as Text: The Writing of Ancient History* (Chapel Hill: University of North Carolina Press, 1989), 1–10.

72 Jerome, *Homily 18 on Psalm 86*.

1 INTERPRETING ETHNIC AND COLOR DIFFERENCES IN EARLY CHRISTIAN WRITINGS

1 *Acts of Peter* 22. Text in *Acta Apostolorum Apocrypha* (2 vols.; ed. Ricardus A. Lipsius and Maximilianus Bonnet; Hildesheim: G. Olms, 1959), 1:69–70. English translation in *New Testament Apocrypha* (2 vols.; trans. E. Hennecke and W. Schneemelcher; Louisville: Westminster/John Knox, 1991–2), 2:305.

2 See, for example, *The Apocryphal Acts of Peter: Magic, Miracles and Gnosticism* (ed. Jan N. Bremmer; Leuven: Peeters, 1998); and *The Apocryphal Acts of the Apostles* (ed. François Bovon et al.; Cambridge, Mass.: Harvard University Press, 1999).

3 See, for example, George A. Kennedy, "Christianity and Classical Rhetoric," chap. 12 in *A New History of Classical Rhetoric* (Princeton: Princeton University Press, 1994); *New Testament Interpretation Through Rhetorical Criticism* (Chapel Hill: University of North Carolina Press, 1984); and Mack, *Rhetoric and the New Testament*. Discussions about ethnocriticsim are scattered in a variety of sources, which will be reviewed later in this chapter. I am not aware of a comprehensive theoretical introduction of the subject for biblical interpretation. For a useful

starting point, see Brett, *Ethnicity and the Bible*. For more recent studies, see Gerd Baumann, *The Multicultural Riddle: Rethinking National, Ethnic, and Religious Identities* (New York: Routledge, 1999); Shaye J.D. Cohen, *The Beginnings of Jewishness: Boundaries, Varieties, Uncertainties* (Berkeley: University of California Press, 1999); and Hall, *Ethnic Identity in Greek Antiquity*. For a useful guide to gender criticism and early Christian writings, see Kraemer and D'Angelo, Women and Christian Origins. See also, Elizabeth A. Castelli, ed., *Women, Gender, Religion: A Reader* (New York: Palgrave, 2001).

4 See, for example, Vernon K. Robbins, *The Tapestry of Early Christian Discourse: Rhetoric, Society and Ideology* (London: Routledge, 1996); and Blount, "A Social-Rhetorical Analysis," 171–98; and J. David Hester Amador, *Academic Constraints in Rhetorical Criticism of the New Testament: An Introduction to a Rhetoric of Power* (JSNT 174; Sheffield: Sheffield Academic Press, 1999).

5 Cameron, *Christianity and the Rhetoric of Empire*, 14.

6 Cameron, *Christianity and the Rhetoric of Empire*, 13, 16, 20.

7 Cameron, *Christianity and the Rhetoric of Empire*, 28–29.

8 Elisabeth Schüssler Fiorenza, "The Rhetoricity of Historical Knowledge: Pauline Discourse and its Contextualizations," in *Religious Propaganda and Missionary Competition in the New Testament World: Essays Honoring Dieter Georgi* (ed. Lukas Bormann et al.; Leiden: E.J. Brill, 1994), 443–69.

9 Schüssler Fiorenza, "Rhetoricity of Historical Knowledge," 466. For more discussion on the process of vilification and idealization, see Adela Yarbro Collins, "Insiders and Outsiders in the Book of Revelation and Its Social Context," in Neusner and Frerichs, *"To See Ourselves as Others See Us,"* 187–218.

10 Luke T. Johnson, "Anti-Jewish Slander," 419–41, esp. 421; See also John Gager, *The Origins of Anti-Semitism: Attitudes Toward Judaism in Pagan and Christian Antiquity* (New York: Oxford University Press, 1983); Rosemary Radford Ruether, *Faith and Fratricide: The Theological Roots of Anti-Semitism* (New York: Seabury, 1974); Peter Schäfer, *Judeophobia*; and Norman R. Petersen, *The Gospel of John and the Sociology of Light: Language and Characterization in the Fourth Gospel* (Valley Forge, Pa.: Trinity Press International, 1993).

11 Robert L. Wilken, *John Chrysostom and the Jews: Rhetoric and Reality in the Late 4th Century* (Berkeley: University of California Press, 1983).

12 See Wilken, "Fourth-Century Preaching and the Rhetoric of Abuse," chap. 4 in *John Chrysostom*, 95–127.

13 John Chrysostom, *Jud.* 1.2; 845. Quoted in Wilken, *John Chrysostom*, 123.

14 Wilken, *John Chrysostom*, 115. Wilken includes a passage from Gregory Nazianzus who attacks an Arian bishop: "There was a monster from Cappadocia, born on our farthest confines, of low birth, and lower mind, whose blood was not perfectly free, but mongrel, as we know that of mules to be . . . he fled without any of his belongings, and after passing, as exiles do, from country to country and city to city, finally, in an evil hour for the Christian community, *like one of the plagues of Egypt* [emphasis mine], he reached Alexandria. There, he ceased his wanderings, and he began his villainy. Good for nothing in all other respects, without culture, without fluency in conversation, without even the form of pretence of reverence, his skill in working villainy and confusion was unequalled" (*Or.* 21.16).

15 Wilken, *John Chrysostom*, 112–16; 126.

16 For a general survey of the many approaches to understanding ethnicity, see Werner Sollors, ed., *Theories of Ethnicity: A Classical Reader* (New York: New York University Press, 1996).

17 For ethnocritical studies related to the Hebrew Bible, see Hugh Rowland Page, "Ethnological Criticism: An Apologia and Application," in *Exploring New*

Paradigms in Biblical and Cognate Studies (Macon: Mellen Biblical Press, 1996), 84–107; Kenton L. Sparks, *Ethnicity and Identity in Ancient Israel: Prolegomena to the Study of Ethnic Sentiments and Their Expression in the Hebrew Bible* (Winona Lake, Ind.: Eisenbrauns, 1999); Christian Sigrist und Rainer Neu, *Ethnologische Texte zum Alten Testament* (vol. 1; Neukirchen-Vluyn: Neukirchener Verlag, 1989); and Timothy K. Beal, *The Book of Hiding: Gender, Ethnicity, Annihilation, and Esther* (London: Routledge, 1997).

18 See, for example, Denise Kimber Buell, "Rethinking the Relevance of Race for Early Christian Self-Definition," *HTR* 94, no. 1 (2001): 449–76; Wan, "Collection for the Saints," 191–215.

19 Hall, *Ethnic Identity in Greek Antiquity*; Roger S. Bagnall, "Greeks and Egyptians: Ethnicity, Status, and Culture," in *Cleopatra's Egypt: The Age of the Ptolemies 305–30 BCE* (Brooklyn: Brooklyn Museum in association with Verlag P. von Zabern, 1988), 21–27; John and Jean Comaroff, *Ethnography and the Historical Imagination* (Boulder, Colo.: Westview, 1992); and Arnold Krupat, *Ethnocriticism: Ethnography, History, Literature* (Berkeley: University of California Press, 1992). See also Gregory E. Sterling, *Historiography and Self-Definition: Josephos, Luke-Acts and Apologetic Historiography* (Leiden: E.J. Brill, 1992). This study provides a description of Greek ethnography found in the writings of Hekataius of Miletus, Herodotus, Hekataius of Abdera, and Megasthenes.

20 Tessa Rajak, "The Location of Cultures in Second Temple Palestine: The Evidence of Josephus," in *The Book of Acts in Its Palestinian Setting* (ed. Richard Bauckham; Grand Rapids: Eerdmans, 1995), 1–14.

21 James C. Walters, *Ethnic Issues in Paul's Letter to the Romans: Changing Self-Definitions in Earliest Roman Christianity* (Valley Forge, Pa.: Trinity Press International, 1993).

22 David M. Olster, "Classical Ethnography and Early Christianity," in *The Formulation of Christianity by Conflict Through the Ages* (ed. Katherine B. Free; Lewiston: Edwin Mellen, 1995), 9–31. See also, Adolf Harnack, *The Expansion of Christianity in the First Three Centuries* (2 vols.; trans. and ed. J. Moffatt; New York: G.P. Putnam's Sons, 1904), 1:336–52.

23 Olster, "Classical Ethnography," 1.

24 Olster, "Classical Ethnography," 10.

25 Olster cites two examples of scholarship that rely on a fundamental dichotomy of religion and culture in late antiquity: Robert L. Wilken, *The Christians as the Romans Saw Them* (New Haven: Yale University Press, 1984); and Robin Lane Fox, *Pagans and Christians* (New York: HarperCollins, 1986).

26 Olster, "Classical Ethnography," 12.

27 Olster, "Classical Ethnography," 11.

28 Olster, "Classical Ethnography," 13–14. Olster uses in this essay Paul's letters, *Epistle of Barnabas*, and the *Apology of Aristides*.

29 Olster, "Classical Ethnography," 14.

30 Olster, "Classical Ethnography," 28–30.

31 Olster discussed the polemical attacks between Apion and Josephus. Apion asserted that the Jews were merely leprous Egyptians who were led into exile by a renegade Egyptian priest named Moses. Olster rightly claims that Greek ethnography had a long tradition of ridiculing Egyptian customs, but does not address the reasons for this commonly held assumption. See Olster, "Classical Ethnography," 15–16.

32 For example, in his discussion about the ethnographic invective in the *Epistle of Barnabas*, Olster says that the invective "comes right out of the 'Egyptian' ethnographic tradition; indeed, it is a common *topos* within that tradition" (29). The Egyptian ethnographic tradition merits further exploration.

33 Olster, "Classical Ethnography," 15, 25.

34 Olster, "Classical Ethnography," 30.

35 Olster, "Classical Ethnography," 11. For a more recent interpretation of the meaning of "third race," see Andrew McGowan, "'A Third Race' or Not: The Rhetoric of Ethnic Self-Definition in the Christian Apologists" (paper delivered at the North American Patristic Society Annual Meeting, Chicago, May 26, 2001).

36 Bagnall, "Greeks and Egyptians," 21.

37 For an important assessment of the ideological implications of ancient references to Blacks and blackness, see Thompson, *Romans and Blacks*.

38 Koen Goudriaan, "Ethnical Strategies in Graeco-Roman Egypt," in *Ethnicity in Hellenistic Egypt* (ed. P. Bilde, Troels Engberg-Pedersen, Lise Hannestad, and Jan Zahle; Aarhus: Aarhus University Press, 1992), 74–99, esp. 75–76.

39 Goudriaan, "Ethnical Strategies," 76.

40 Goudriaan, "Ethnical Strategies," 75–76.

41 Goudriaan, "Ethnical Strategies," 76.

42 D.B. Saddington says the most common ethnic term for Black people in antiquity was *Aithiops*. See Saddington, "Race Relations in the Early Roman Empire," 119. See also Snowden, *Blacks in Antiquity*, 2–7. For useful studies on ethnicity and ethnic diversity in ancient Egypt, see Anthony Leahy, "Ethnic Diversity in Ancient Egypt," in *Civilizations of the Ancient Near East* (4 vols.; ed. Jack M. Sasson; New York: Scribner, 1995), 1:225–34; Bilde et al., *Ethnicity in Hellenistic Egypt*; and Herbert J. Foster, "The Ethnicity of the Ancient Egyptians," *Journal of Black Studies* 5 (1974): 175–91. The issues raised in these studies are still being debated among scholars. Ultimately, my argument does not rest upon the historical findings proposed in these studies; I am more concerned with identifying and examining the discursive strategies associated with the use of Egyptians, Ethiopians, and Blacks in early Christian writings.

43 Henry Louis Gates, Jr., "'What's in a Name?' Some Meanings of Blackness," in *Loose Canons: Notes on the Culture Wars* (New York: Oxford University Press, 1992), 131–51.

44 bell hooks, "Postmodern Blackness," in *Yearnings: Race, Gender, and Cultural Politics* (Boston: South End, 1990), 23–31.

45 hooks, "Postmodern Blackness," 23.

46 Hood, *Begrimed and Black*; Frost, "Attitudes toward Blacks," 1–11; and Nicholas F. Gier, "The Color of Sin/The Color of Skin: Ancient Color Blindness and the Philosophical Origins of Modern Racism," *JRT* 46, no. 1 (1989–90): 42–52.

47 See Fernandez, *Beyond Metaphor*; and *Persuasions and Performances*.

48 Henry Louis Gates, Jr., *The Signifying Monkey: A Theory of Afro-American Literary Criticism* (New York: Oxford University Press, 1988); and Charles H. Long, *Significations: Signs, Symbols, and Images in the Interpretation of Religion* (Philadelphia: Fortress, 1986).

49 See, for example, Renita J. Weems, *Battered Love: Marriage, Sex, and Violence in the Hebrew Prophets* (Minneapolis: Fortress, 1995); and Phyllis Trible, *Texts of Terror: Literary-Feminist Readings of Biblical Narratives* (Philadelphia: Fortress, 1984).

50 Castelli, *Women, Gender*.

51 See, for example, Ellen Greene, *The Erotics of Domination: Male Desire and the Mistress in Latin Love Poetry* (Baltimore: Johns Hopkins University Press, 1998); Catharine Edwards, *The Politics of Immorality in Ancient Rome* (Cambridge: Cambridge University Press, 1993); Shelley P. Haley, "Black Feminist Thought and Classics: Re-membering, Re-claiming, Re-empowering," in *Feminist Theory and the Classics* (ed. Nancy Sorkin Rabinowitz and Amy Richlin; New York: Routledge, 1993), 23–43; Caroline Walker Bynum, *Jesus as Mother: Studies in the Spirituality of the High Middle Ages* (Berkeley: University of California Press,

1982); Caroline Walker Bynum et al., eds. "Introduction," in *Religion and Gender: Essays on the Complexity of Symbols* (Boston: Beacon Press, 1987); Miriam B. Peskowitz, *Spinning Fantasies: Rabbis, Gender, and History* (Berkeley: University of California Press, 1997); Iris Marion Young, *Justice and the Politics of Difference* (Princeton: Princeton University Press, 1990); Ross S. Kraemer and Mary Rose D'Angelo, eds. *Women and Christian Origins* (New York: Oxford University Press, 1999); Virginia Burrus, "Word and Flesh: The Bodies and Sexuality of Ascetic Women in Christian Antiquity," *JFSR* 10, no. 1 (1990): 27–51; Athalya Brenner, *The Intercourse of Knowledge: On Gendering Desire and 'Sexuality' in the Hebrew Bible* (Biblical Interpretation Series 26; Leiden: E.J. Brill, 1997); Weems, *Battered Love*; and *Just a Sister Away: A Womanist Vision of Women's Relationships in the Bible* (San Diego: LuraMedia, 1988); Martin, "Womanist Interpretations of the New Testament," 41–61; Amy-Jill Levine, ed., *"Women Like This": New Perspectives on Jewish Women in the Greco-Roman World* (Atlanta: Scholars Press, 1991); Elisabeth Schüssler Fiorenza, *In Memory of Her: A Feminist Theological Reconstruction of Christian Origins* (New York: Crossroad, 1983); Ross S. Kraemer, *Her Share of the Blessings: Women's Religions Among Pagans, Jews, and Christians in the Greco-Roman World* (New York: Oxford University Press, 1992); and Elizabeth A. Castelli, "'I Will Make Mary Male': Pieties of the Body and Gender Transformation of Christian Women in Late Antiquity," in *Body Guards: The Cultural Politics of Gender Ambiguity* (ed. Julia Epstein and Kristina Straub; New York: Routledge, 1991), 29–49.

52 For a study of Roman attitudes about sexual roles and practices related to Blacks in antiquity, see Bernard Braxton, "The Influence of Black Sexuality," chap. 3 in *Women, Sex, and Race*, 60–78, esp. 62–63. Braxton discusses how Romans were fascinated with the sexual prowess of Blacks, especially Black women. He says, "Black women were bought at high prices from traders along the shores of the Mediterranean, or from generals returning from the wars." Furthermore, he asserts, "large sums were spent in the notion that black women possessed some unique sexual attributes. Exotic black females were installed in beautiful homes and provided with many luxuries." Braxton's sweeping generalizations about the Romans' understanding of black sexuality are not adequately documented. He mentions primary sources, but does not include bibliographic information.

53 Edwards, *Politics of Immorality*, 63–97. Edwards identifies a useful theoretical framework for examining the vituperative rhetorics about Ethiopian women within monastic literature. In her chapter dealing with *mollitia* (effeminacy), Edwards examines Roman discourses about sexual behavior and how these discourses were deployed in the pursuit of nonsexual (as well as sexual) ends.

54 Joan Wallach Scott, "Gender: A Useful Category of Historical Analysis," in *Feminism and History* (ed. Joan Wallach Scott; Oxford: Oxford University Press, 1996), 152–80.

55 Scott, "Gender," 167.

56 Scott lists as examples Eve and Mary as symbols of woman, myths of light and dark, purification and pollution, innocence and corruption.

57 Scott, "Gender," 167–69.

58 Scott, "Gender," 169.

59 Maurice Godelier, "The Origins of Male Domination," *New Left Review* 127 (1981): 17; quoted in Scott, "Gender," 170.

60 Scott, "Gender," 169–70.

61 Scott, "Gender," 171.

62 Young, *Justice and the Politics of Difference*, 123.

63 Peskowitz, *Spinning Fantasies*, 7.

64 Peskowitz, *Spinning Fantasies*, 7

65 For a useful summary of feminist and womanist criticism, see Bible and Culture Collective, *The Postmodern Bible* (New Haven: Yale University Press, 1995), 225–71.

66 Martin, "Womanist Interpretations," 41–61, esp. 42–43; repr. in *Black Theology* (2 vols.; ed. James H. Cone and Gayraud Wilmore; Maryknoll, N.Y.: Orbis, 1993), 2:225–44.

67 Martin, "Womanist Interpretations," 60. One major limitation of womanist biblical hermeneutics is its lack of a comprehensive interpretive framework. Martin's extensive knowledge of New Testament rhetorical criticism would have been useful in developing the theoretical framework for her womanist hermeneutic. See Clarice J. Martin, "The Rhetorical Function of Commercial Language in Paul's Letter to Philemon (verse 18)," in *Persuasive Artistry: Studies in New Testament Rhetoric in Honor of George A. Kennedy* (ed. Duane F. Watson; Sheffield: Sheffield University Press, 1991), 321–37.

68 Martin, "Womanist Interpretations," 53.

69 Clarice J. Martin, "Womanist Biblical Interpretation," in *Dictionary of Biblical Interpretation* (2 vols.; ed. John H. Hayes; Nashville: Abingdon, 1999), 2:655–58.

70 Martin, "Womanist Biblical Interpretation," 656.

71 Martin, "Womanist Biblical Interpretation," 656. See, for example, Ex 1:1–15; 1 Kgs 10:1–10, 13; Jer 38:7–13; Luke 4:16–20; 8:40–48; Acts 8:26–40.

72 Martin, "Womanist Biblical Interpretation," 656–57.

73 Martin, "Womanist Biblical Interpretation," 657.

74 Martin, "Womanist Biblical Interpretation," 657.

75 Renita J. Weems, "The Hebrew Women Are Not Like the Egyptian Women: The Ideology of Race, Gender, and Sexual Reproduction in Exodus 1," *Semeia* 59 (1992): 25–34.

76 Weems, "Hebrew Women," 32.

77 Renita J. Weems, "Reading Her Way through the Struggle: African American Women and the Bible," in *Stony the Road We Trod: African American Biblical Interpretation* (ed. Cain Hope Felder; Minneapolis: Fortress, 1991), 57–77; and *Just a Sister Away*.

78 Weems, *Battered Love*.

79 See, for example, Ann Holmes Redding, "Together, Not Equal: The Rhetoric of Unity and Headship in the Letter to the Ephesians" (Ph.D. diss., Union Theological Seminary, 1999).

80 For some important studies that attempt to classify the references to Egyptians, Ethiopians, and Blacks in Greco-Roman (including Christian) literature, see Jean-Jacques Aubert, "Du Noir en noir et blanc: eloge de la dispersion," *MH* 56 (1999): 159–82; E. Oréal, "'Noir parfait': un jeu de mot de l'égyptien au grec," *REG* 111 (1998): 551–65; Courtès, "'Ethiopians' in Patristic Literature"; and Saddington, "Race Relations in the Early Roman Empire," 115–19.

2 EGYPTIANS, ETHIOPIANS, BLACKS, AND BLACKNESS IN GRECO-ROMAN LITERATURE

1 See, for example Snowden, Jr., *Blacks in Antiquity*; Courtès, "'Ethiopians' in Patristic Literature," 9–32; Raoul Lonis, "Les trois approches de l'Ethiopien par l'opinion gréco-romaine," *Ktema* 6 (1981): 69–87; Adams, "The Invention of Nubia," 17–22; Thompson, *Romans and Blacks*, 57–85; Harris, *Africa and Africans*; Mveng, *Les sources grecques*; Peter Habermehl, *Perpetua und der Aegypter oder Bilder des Bösen im Frühen Afrikanischen Christentum: Ein Versuch zur "Passio*

Sanctarum Perpetuae et Felicitatis" (TUGAL 140; Berlin: Akademie, 1992), 130–60; and "'Noir parfait,'" 551–65.

2 Cameron, *Christianity and the Rhetoric of Empire.*

3 Cameron, *Christianity and the Rhetoric of Empire*, 5.

4 Koster, *Invektive*; and Opelt, *Polemik.*

5 It would be impractical to include all of the references to Egyptians/Egypt, Ethiopians/Ethiopia, and Blacks/blackness mentioned throughout Greco-Roman literature in this chapter. Electronic resources have been utilized for searching and selecting data for this project. For Greek sources, see *Thesaurus Linguae Graecae* CD-ROM (Data Bank, Version D; University of California at Irvine). See also Luci Berkowitz and K.A. Squitier, *Thesaurus Linguae Graecae: Canon of Greek Authors and Works* (3rd ed.; New York: Oxford University Press, 1990). For Latin non-Christian sources, see *Thesaurus Linguae Latinae*; for Latin Christian sources, see *CETEDOC Library of Christian Latin Texts* (CLCLT-3; Universitas Catholica Lovaniensis; Turnhout: Brepols, 1996). The rhetorical categories identified in this chapter reflect some of the more representative examples (or patterns) that occur in Greco-Roman literature.

6 James S. Romm, *The Edges of the Earth in Ancient Thought: Geography, Exploration, and Fiction* (Princeton: Princeton University Press, 1992), 3–8.

7 For a general introduction on the geographical significance of Egypt and its role in economic and cultural relations in the Mediterranean, see Jean Leclant, "Egypt, Land of Africa, in the Greco-Roman World," in *The Image of the Black in Western Art* (2 vols.; gen. ed. Jean Devisse; New York: W. Morrow, 1976), 1:269–85.

8 Plutarch, *De Iside et Osiride* 10 (354E). See text in Plutarch, *De Iside et Osiride* (trans. F.C. Babbitt; LCL; Cambridge, Mass.: Harvard University Press, 1969), 5:25.

9 For an important discussion on the use of Egypt in the writings of classical geographers, see John Ball, *Egypt in the Classical Geographers* (Cairo: Government Press, Bulaq, 1942).

10 Ball, *Egypt*, 10.

11 Ball, *Egypt*, 46.

12 See Victoria Ann Foertmeyer, "Tourism in Graeco-Roman Egypt" (Ph.D. diss., Princeton University, 1989). Foertmeyer examines "all discernible travel patterns and motives of tourists in Egypt, from the time of Alexander's conquest 332 B.C.E. to the destruction of the Serapeum at Alexandria in 392 A.D." She demonstrates that the motives of travelers for visiting sites in Egypt were usually cultural or religious and not recreational. Her definition of tourism encompasses "rulers on formal tours, savants seeking after the wisdom of priests, and peasants travelling to the capital of their nome for the festival of an indigenous god or goddess" (1–2).

13 Romm, *Edges of the Earth*, 45–60.

14 Strabo, *Geography* (8 vols.; trans. Horace Leonard Jones; LCL; Cambridge, Mass.: Harvard University Press, 1967–83) 1.2.27–28; 2.2.2. For a useful discussion about the remote geographical location of Ethiopia, see Romm, *Edges of the Earth*, 49–60.

15 Ethiopians were described as the most remote people (*eschatoi andrōn*). See Homer, *Odyssey* 1.22–24. Cf. Herodotus 3.17ff and 3.25ff.

16 Homer, *Odyssey* 1.23–24; cf. Herodotus 3.94, 7.70 and Strabo, *Geography* 1.2.25, 27.

17 See Nadeau, "Ethiopians," 339–49. Nadeau's article documents the widespread confusion among the ancients in their understanding of the different geographical references to ancient Ethiopians. Nadeau provides examples from Homer, Herodotus, Strabo, et al., who wrote about southern, eastern, and western

Ethiopians. See also Snowden, *Blacks in Antiquity*, vii–viii and 11 for a similar discussion about the complexities of understanding southern and eastern (Asiatic) Ethiopians. This book focuses on southern Ethiopians. Eastern Ethiopians (those in India) and western Ethiopians (those in Mauretania) are beyond the scope of this project. For more information about eastern Ethiopians, see U.P. Arora, "India vis-à-vis Egypt-Ethiopia in Classical Accounts," *Graeco-Arabica* (1982): 131–40; and A. Dihle, *The Conception of India in Hellenistic and Roman Literature*, Proceedings of the Cambridge Philological Association (CXC, 1964).

18 Herodotus 7.70.

19 Philostratus, *The Life of Apollonius of Tyana* 6.1. See text in *The Life of Apollonius of Tyana* (2 vols.; trans. F.C. Conybeare; LCL; Cambridge, Mass.: Harvard University Press, 1969).

20 For useful studies on the mythical tradition of the Ethiopians, see Albin Lesky, "Aithiopika," *Hermes* 87 (1957): 27–38; Moses Hadas, "Utopian Sources in Herodotus," *CP* 30 (1935): 113–21; L. Kakosy, "Nubien als mythisches Land im Altertum," in *Annales Universitatis Scientiarum Budapestinensis de Rolando Eötvös nominatae* (Sectio Historica 8; Budapest: Universitatis Scientiarum Budapestinensis, 1966), 3–10; Snowden, "Ethiopians in Classical Mythology," chap. 6 of *Blacks in Antiquity*, 144–55; and Joseph E. Harris, "A Tradition of Myths and Stereotypes," chap. 1 of *Africans and their History* (rev. ed.; New York: Penguin, 1987 [1972]), 13–28. Afrocentrists emphasize in their studies the mythical depictions of Egyptians and Ethiopians. See, for example, Asante, *Afrocentricity*; and Diop, *African Origin*, 12–16; and "Origin of the Ancient Egyptians," *Journal of African Civilizations* 4, no. 2 (1982): 9–37.

21 Homer, *Iliad* 1.423–24. See Homer, *The Iliad* (2 vols.; trans. A.T. Murray, rev. William F. Wyatt; LCL; Cambridge, Mass.: Harvard University Press, 1999); cf. Diodorus Siculus, *History* 1.97.8–9. Zeus and Hera visited the Ethiopians for twelve days.

22 Homer, *Odyssey* 4.231. See Homer, *The Odyssey* (2 vols.; trans. A.T. Murray; LCL; Cambridge, Mass.: Harvard University Press, 1976–80).

23 Herodotus 3.17.

24 Herodotus 3.20.

25 See Herodotus 2.35–92.

26 Herodotus 2.2. For an insightful discussion about Herodotus's literary representations of Egyptians and other ethnic groups, see François Hartog, *The Mirror of Herodotus: The Representation of the Other in the Writing of History* (Berkeley: University of California Press, 1988).

27 Diodorus Siculus, *History* 1.10. See text in *Diodorus Siculus* (trans. C.H. Oldfather; LCL; Cambridge, Mass.: Harvard University Press, 1968), 1: 34–7.

28 Cicero, *De senectute* 6; in *De senectute* (vol. 20; trans. William Armistead Falconer; LCL; Cambridge, Mass.: Harvard University Press, 1979); and Juvenal, *Satires* 2.23, in *Juvenal and Persius* (trans. G.G. Ramsey; LCL; Cambridge, Mass.: Harvard University Press, 1979), 18–19.

29 Pliny the Elder, *Naturalis historia* 2.80.189. See text in *Naturalis historia* (10 vols.; trans. H. Rackham; LCL; Cambridge, Mass.: Harvard University Press, 1979).

30 Pliny the Elder, *Naturalis historia* 6.3.194, 195.

31 Snowden, *Blacks in Antiquity*, 175–77.

32 Scythia is a land of *eremia*, a zone of *eschatia*, a deserted place and a frontier: one of the ends of the earth. It represents the northern boundary at the edges of the ancient world. Aeschylus describes Scythia as follows: "Here we are on the soil of a distant land," declares Power, "journeying in the Scythian country, in a desert empty of human beings." See Aeschylus, *Prometheus Bound* 1–2; 416–17. For more information about the Scythians, see Gareth D. Williams, *Banished Voices: Readings*

in Ovid's Exile Poetry (Cambridge: Cambridge University Press, 1994), 8ff. See also Hartog, *Mirror of Herodotus*, 12–33; Thomas, *Lands and Peoples*; Snowden, *Blacks in Antiquity*.

33 Snowden, *Blacks in Antiquity*, 177.

34 Menander, Frag. 612. See text and translation in *Menander: The Principal Fragments* (trans. Francis G. Allinson; LCL; Cambridge, Mass.: Harvard University Press, 1951 [1930]), 480–81. Cited in Snowden, *Blacks in Antiquity*, 176.

35 Snowden, *Blacks in Antiquity*, 177.

36 Aristotle, *Politica* 7.7.2 (1327b). Aristotle relied on the environmental theory for establishing the superiority of the Hellenic race over the races of Asia and Europe.

37 Aristotle, *De generatione animalium* 5.3.782b(33)–783a. See Aristotle, *De generatione animalium* (trans. A. L. Peck; LCL; Cambridge, Mass.: Harvard University Press, 1979), 8: 516–19.

38 Claude Nicolet, "The *Res Gestae* of Augustus: Announcing the Conquest of the World," chap. 1 in *Space, Geography, and Politics in the Early Roman Empire* (Ann Arbor: University of Michigan Press, 1991), 15–27; Eleanor G. Huzar, "Augustus, Heir of the Ptolemies," in *ANRW* 10.1, 343–82. See also, Erik Iversen, "Egypt in Classical Antiquity: A Résumé," in *Hommages à Jean Leclant* (Études Isiaques Bd. 106/3; ed. Berger et al.; Cairo: IFAO, 1994), 305.

39 Augustus, *Res gestae divi Augusti* 26.5–27.1. Augustus restored peace to the provinces of the Empire and divided them into two classes: (1) some remained under the direct control of the Senate, and (2) some – those where the danger of armed invasion or revolt was greatest – were under the direct supervision of Augustus himself. See Latin text and English translation in Augustus, *Res gestae divi Augusti: The Achievements of the Divine Augustus* (introduction and commentary by P.A. Brunt and J.M. Moore; Oxford: Oxford University Press, 1967), 32–33.

40 Peter Garnsey, Keith Hopkins, and C.R. Whittaker, eds., *Trade in the Ancient Economy* (Berkeley: University of California Press, 1983).

41 Cassius Dio, 51.17; 55.26.2–3. Cf. G.E. Rickman, "The Grain Trade under the Roman Empire," in *The Seaborne Commerce of Ancient Rome* (MAAR 36; ed. J.H. D'Arms and E.C. Kopff; Rome: American Academy in Rome, 1980), 264; and S.L. Wallace, *Taxation in Egypt from Augustus to Diocletian* (Princeton University Studies in Papyrology 2; Princeton: Princeton University Press, 1938).

42 Huzar, "Augustus," 352–53. Known as the *praefectus Aegypti* Gallus was possibly the most powerful governor in the Roman provinces, responsible for the full military, judicial, economic, and religious controls of the province.

43 Kandakē, Queen of Ethiopia, is described by Strabo as "a masculine sort of woman and blind in one eye". See Strabo, *Geography* 17.1.54.

44 Huzar, "Augustus," 364.

45 Cassius Dio, 54.5.4–6. See text and translation in *Dio's Roman History* (trans. Earnest Cary; LCL; London: W. Heinemann, 1917), 6: 292–95.

46 Roger S. Bagnall, "Greeks and Egyptians," 21.

47 Pliny, *Naturalis historia* 10.6; Cassius Dio, 51.17.1–3.

48 Pliny the Younger, *Epistulae* 10.6.1–2. Latin text and English translation in *Letters and Panegyricus* (2 vols.; trans. Betty Radice; LCL; Cambridge, Mass.: Harvard University Press, 1972–75), 1:175.

49 For a succint summary of the complex system of citizenship of the Romans, see Roger S. Bagnall, "The Fayum and its People," in *Ancient Faces: Mummy Portraits from Roman Egypt* (ed. Susan Walker and Morris Bierbrier; London: British Museum, 1997), 17–20, esp. 19. See also Diana Delia, *Alexandrian Citizenship during the Roman Principate* (Atlanta: Scholars Press, 1991).

50 Pindar, *Fragment Incert.* 225.1–2.

51 Aristotle, *Physiognomics* 6, 812b. See Aristotle, *Minor Works* (trans. W.S. Hett; LCL; Cambridge, Mass.: Harvard University Press, 1963). In this example, Aristotle establishes symmetry between those who are excessively white (*leukoi*) and those who are excessively black (*melanes*). He is using color symbolism to demonstrate that courage appears in those who are neither too black (i.e., Egyptians and Ethiopians) nor too white (i.e., women). N.b. *leukos* is sometimes used as a mark of effeminacy, see LSJ, 470.

52 Plutarch, *Moralia* 12E.

53 Strabo, *Geography* 17.1.12.

54 Philo, *Flaccus* 78. Cf. Goudriaan, "Ethnical Strategies," 88.

55 Josephus, *Against Apion* 2.28–30. Greek text and English translation in *The Life, Against Apion* (trans. H. St. J. Thackeray; LCL; Cambridge, Mass.: Harvard University Press, 1976), 302–303.

56 Josephus, *Against Apion* 2.31. See *The Life, Against Apion*, 302–305.

57 Pseudo-Callisthenes, *Historia Alexandri Magni*, 3.18.6 (ed. W. Kroll; Berlin, 1926), 1.116. Cited in St. Clair Drake, *Black Folk Here and There, An Essay in History and Anthropology* (2 vols; Los Angeles: Center for Afro-American Studies, University of California, 1987–1990) 1:305–307; and Snowden, *Blacks in Antiquity*, 177–78.

58 See text in Étienne Bernand, *Inscriptions métriques de l'Égypte gréco-romaine* (Annales Littéraires de l'Université de Besançon vol. 98; Paris: Les Belles Lettres, 1969), no. 26.5–10. Cited in Thompson, *Romans and Blacks*, 41.

59 Ausonius, *Parentalia* 5.3–6. See text in Ausonius, *Parentalia* (trans. Hugh G. Evelyn White; LCL; Cambridge, Mass.: Harvard University Press, 1977), 67.

60 For more background information on this topic, see Rowe, "Conceptions of Colour and Colour," 327–64; Irwin, *Colour Terms*, 1–36. For two brief studies on the use of *melas* and *leukos* in ancient sources, see Alan Cameron, "Black and White: A Note on Ancient Nicknames," *AJP* 110 (1998): 113–17; and A.M. Devine, "Blacks in Antiquity? (The Case of Apollonios ὁ μέλας)," *Ancient History Bulletin* 2, no. 1 (1988): 9.

61 Jeffrey Burton Russell has provided the most comprehensive survey of the image of the devil within Greco-Roman antiquity and the early Christian tradition. See Jeffrey Burton Russell, *The Devil: Perceptions of Evil from Antiquity to Primitive Christianity* (Ithaca: Cornell University Press, 1977); and *Satan: The Early Christian Tradition.* (Ithaca: Cornell University Press, 1981). See also Pierre du Bourget, "La couleur noire de la peau du démon dans l'iconographie chrétienne a-t-elle une origine précise?" in *Actas del VIII Congreso Internacional de Arqueologia Cristiana – Barcelona 5–11 Octubre 1969* (Barcelona: Città del Vaticano, 1972), 271–72. For specific references to blackness, see Russell, *The Devil*, 62, 64–66, 68, 76, 78, 141–42, 217, 246–47, 253.

62 See definition of *daimōn* in *TDNT* 2:1–19. See also D. Felton, *Haunted Greece and Rome: Ghost Stories from Classical Antiquity* (Austin: University of Texas Press, 1999), 14–15, 84.

63 Suetonius, *Life of Caligula* 57.4. See Suetonius, *Life of Caligula* (vol. 1; trans. J.C. Rolfe; LCL; Cambridge, Mass.: Harvard University Press, 1979).

64 Lucian, *Philopatris* 31. See Lucian, *Philopatris* (vol. 8; trans. M.D. MacLeod; LCL; Cambridge, Mass.: Harvard University Press, 1979).

65 Cassius Dio, 67.9.

66 Martial, *Epigrams* 115. Latin text and English translation in Martial, *Epigrams* (ed. and trans. D.R. Shackleton Bailey; LCL; Cambridge, Mass.: Harvard University Press, 1993), 1.129.

67 Juvenal, *Satires* 6.594–601. See text and translation in Juvenal, *Satires* (trans. G.G. Ramsay; LCL; Cambridge, Mass.: Harvard University Press, 1979) 131–33. Cf.

Pliny, *Naturalis historia* 7.51. Cited in Hood, *Begrimed and Black*, 41; J.P.V.D. Balsdon, *Romans and Aliens* (London: Duckworth, 1979), 218.

68 Cited in Braxton, *Women, Sex, and Race*, 63.

69 Braxton, *Women, Sex, and Race*, 63.

70 Frank Snowden provides a useful summary of the physical characteristics of Ethiopians. See Snowden, "The Physical Characteristics of Ethiopians – The Textual Evidence," chap. 1 of *Blacks in Antiquity*, 1–14.

71 Homer, *Odyssey* 19.246–47.

72 Philostratus, *Life of Apollonius of Tyana* 6.1.

73 Sextus Empiricus, *Adversus mathematicos* 43. See text in *Adversus mathematicos* (trans. R.G. Bury; LCL; Cambridge, Mass.: Harvard University Press, 1968).

74 Herodotus 3.20; cf. Diogenes Laertius, *Lives of Eminent Philosophers* 7.1.

75 Philostratus, *Imagines* 1.5. Text and English translation in Philostratus, *Imagines* (trans. Arthur Fairbanks; LCL; Cambridge, Mass.: Harvard University Press, 1960). Cf. Homer, *Iliad* 3.6 (*andrasi Pygmaioisi*).

76 Frank Snowden claims that this text "provides the most complete, single anthropological portrait of a Negro in classical literature." See Snowden, *Blacks in Antiquity*, 9. According to Robert Hood, Virgil summarized the aesthetic and exotic view of Blacks in his world when he described this black woman. See Hood, *Begrimed and Black*, 42. See also Thompson, *Romans and Blacks*, 30–31.

77 *Moretum*, 31–35. See text in *Poeta Latini Minores* (ed. Aemilius Baehrens; Appendix Vergiliana rev. by F. Vollmer and W. Morel; Bibliotheca Scriptorum Graecorum et Romanorum Teubneriana; New York: Garland, 1979).

78 This list of physical characteristics is attributed to Galen by Mas 'udi, a tenth-century Arab scholar. It is cited in Drake, *Black Folk Here and There*, 2:56–57. Drake copied the list from the Arabist Bernard Lewis, *Race and Color in Islam* (New York: Harper & Row, 1971), 34. Frank Snowden raises doubts about the attribution of these ideas to Galen. See Snowden, *Before Color Prejudice*, 114–15. Snowden states that he has not found this passage in any extant work of Galen or any other author of the Greco-Roman period. Like Snowden, I have not been able to find this list in my review of Galen's writings, but I have chosen to include it because many of these characteristics, especially "smelly skin," are used to describe Ethiopians by other Greco-Roman writers (including early Christians).

79 Drake, *Black Folk Here and There*, 2:57

80 Drake, *Black Folk Here and There*, 2:56–57. Drake admits that his assertions about Galen's influence on early Christian theologians may be invalid, if Snowden's conclusions about the authorship of the list are correct (325, n. 139).

81 Herodotus, 2.57.

82 Herodotus, 2.104.

83 Ammianus Marcellinus, 22.16.23. See text in *Ammianus Marcellinus* (3 vols.; trans. John C. Rolfe; LCL; Cambridge, Mass.: Harvard University Press, 1972), 309.

84 Lucian, *The Ship or the Wishes*, paras. 2 and 3. Greek text and English translation in Lucian, *The Ship or the Wishes (Navigium)* (vol. 6; trans. K. Kilburn; LCL; Cambridge, Mass.: Harvard University Press, 1968).

85 See text in *Amherst Papyri*, no. 62, lines 6–7.

86 Devine, "Blacks in Antiquity? (The Case of Apollonios ὁ μέλας)," *The Ancient History Bulletin* 2, no. 1 (1988): 9. Devine's conclusions are in direct opposition to the findings of Snowden in *Blacks in Antiquity*, 18–19; 268, n. 94. Snowden argues that *melas* in this context is the equivalent of *Aithiops* or Negro. Devine, on the other hand, asserts that (1) there is little hard evidence to suggest that general color terms like *melas* by themselves carried any specific racial connotation in antiquity, (2) color-referent nicknames are particularly common in communities

of men or boys, and (3) there is an exact parallel to the Apollonii attested in Diodorus and Athenaeus (12.539c): Cleitus *ho melas* and Cleitus *ho leukos*. In regard to Cleitus *ho melas*, Devine says that he was "a celebrated figure of impeccable Macedonian antecedents and connexions . . . of Caucasoid race."

87 Cameron, "Black and White," 113–17. I want to thank Professor James Rives for leading me to this article. Rives also suggests that C. Pescennius Niger (proclaimed emperor in 193 CE, but defeated by Septimius Severus) is an example of a Latin cognomen.

88 Cameron cites Snowden, author of *Blacks in Antiquity*; and Thompson, author of *Romans and Blacks*. See Cameron, "Black and White," 113.

89 Cameron, "Black and White," 113.

90 See example of Aemilia Corinthia Maura above.

91 See text in Étienne Bernand, *Inscriptions métriques*, no. 26.5–10. Cited in Thompson, *Romans and Blacks*, 41.

92 Foster, "Ethnicity," 175–91; Goudriaan, "Ethnical Strategies," 74–99; Frank M. Snowden, Jr., "Ethiopians and the Graeco-Roman World," in *The African Diaspora: Interpretive Essays* (ed. Martin L. Kilson and Robert I. Rotberg; Cambridge, Mass.: Harvard University Press, 1976), 11–36; Iversen, "Egypt in Classical Antiquity," 3:295–305.

93 Burton Mack, *Who Wrote the New Testament? The Making of the Christian Myth* (San Francisco: HarperCollins, 1995), 27. Mack discusses the challenges related to the mix of people, cultures, and politics that came together during the Greco-Roman period. He argues that ethnicity was a common basis for stereotyping. The first thing someone wanted to learn about a stranger was where he or she was from and of what ethnic extraction.

94 Cf. Tacitus, *Germania* (LCL; Cambridge:Harvard University Press, 1970); and Josephus, *Against Apion* (trans. H. St. J. Thackeray; LCL; Cambridge, Mass.: Harvard University Press, 1976).

95 See, for example, Stegemann, "Anti-Semitic and Racist Prejudices," 271–94; Walters, *Ethnic Issues*; and Johnson, "Anti-Jewish Slander," 419–41.

96 Col 3:11.

97 Gal 3:26–29. Cf. 1 Cor 12:13 (For by one Spirit we were all baptized into one body – Jews or Greeks, slaves or free – and we were made to drink of one Spirit.)

98 Song 1:5–6 (LXX).

99 Origen, *Homiliae in Canticum Canticorum* 1.6 (GCS 8:36).

100 Gregory of Elvira, *In Canticum Canticorum* 1.23–30 (CCL 69.176–79).

101 Num 12:1–16; *Commentarium in Canticum Canticorum* 2.362, 2.366–67 (GCS 8:115, 117–18).

102 Robert Hood discusses this topic and provides several examples in *Begrimed and Black*, 73–90.

103 Tertullian, *De spectaculis* 3.

104 Origen, *Homiliae in Canticum Canticorum* 1.6 (GCS 8:36)

105 Jerome, *Homily 18 on Psalm 86*. Text in *St. Jerome: Homilies on the Psalms* (Ancient Christian Writers 48; trans. M.L. Ewald; Westminster, Md.: Newman, 1964), 140.

106 Herm. *Sim.* 9.15.3. Text and English translation in *Apostolic Fathers* (trans. Kirsopp Lake; LCL; Cambridge, Mass.: Harvard University Press, 1976–85), 2:258–61.

107 Herm. *Sim.* 9.19.1. English Translation in *Apostolic Fathers*, 2:268–9.

108 *Epist. Barn.* 4.9.

109 *Epist. Barn.* 20.1.

110 *Acts of Peter*, 22.

111 *Acts of Peter*, 4.
112 R. Reitzenstein, *Poimandres: Studien zur griechischägyptischen und früchristlichen Literatur* (Leipzig: Teubner, 1904), 293.
113 See, for example, Castelli, "'I Will Make Mary Male', 29–49; and Margaret R. Miles, "'Becoming Male': Women Martyrs and Ascetics," chap. 2 of *Carnal Knowing: Female Nakedness and Religious Meaning in the Christian West* (Boston: Beacon, 1989), 53–77.
114 Both Maureen Tilley and Joyce Salisbury have made cursory attempts at discussing the meaning of the Egyptian in this text. Tilley, in her analysis of this text, claims that "Perpetua's identification of the Egyptian with the devil raises the question of ethnic and racial prejudice." See Maureen A. Tilley, "The Passion of Perpetua and Felicity," in *Searching the Scriptures* (2 vols.; ed. Elisabeth Schüssler Fiorenza; New York: Crossroad, 1994), 2:845. Salisbury claims that Perpetua's "mind's selection of an Egyptian as opponent would have been a natural image to oppose her Christianity . . . In sum, the gigantic Egyptian embodied many levels of evil for Perpetua." See Joyce E. Salisbury, *Perpetua's Passion: The Death and Memory of a Young Roman Woman* (New York: Routledge, 1997), 110. Neither of these readings addresses the discursive and ideological strategies at work in this text.
115 Cf. *Passio S. Perpetuae* 10.8–14. Latin text and English translation in Perpetua and Felicity, *Passio Sanctarum Perpetuae et Felicitatis* (ed. Cornelius Ioannes Maria and Ioseph van Beek; Nijmegen: Dekker & Van De Vegt, 1936).
116 For a recent assessment of Ethiopian demons in monastic writings, see David B. Brakke, "Ethiopian Demons: Male Sexuality, the Black-Skinned Other, and the Monastic Self." *Journal of the History of Sexuality* 10.3/4 (2001): 501–35.
117 Athanasius, *Vita Antonii* 6.
118 PG 34.1137; PL 73.1155.
119 PG 65.284. English translation in Wicker, "Ethiopian Moses," 340.
120 Wimbush, "Ascetic Behavior and Color-ful Language," 81–92; and Wicker, "Ethiopian Moses."
121 Ambrose, *Expositio Psalmi* 118, 19.26–27 (CSEL 62.435); cf. Courtès, "'Ethiopians' in Patristic Literature," 18.
122 *Vie de Sainte Mélanie* (ed. Denys Gorce; SC 90; Paris: Cerf, 1962). English translation in *Life of Melania the Younger* (trans. Elizabeth A. Clark; New York: Edwin Mellen, 1984).
123 Palladius, "Of Fornication," in *Apophthegmata Patrum*, 579.
124 Cassian, *On Impurity* 1.67, in *Les sentences des pères du désert* (ed. L. Regnault; Sarthe: Solesmes, 1966).
125 Anonymous, *Apophthegmata Patrum* 5.5 (PL 73, col. 879).
126 Palladius, *Historia Lausiaca* 23. English translation in *Palladius: Historia Lausiaca* (Ancient Christian Writers 34; trans. Robert T. Meyer; New York: Newman, 1965), 81–83.
127 Anonymous, *Apophthegmata Patrum*, in *Les sentences des pères du désert: nouveau recueil* (ed. L. Regnault; 2nd ed.; Sarthe: Solesmes, 1985), 184.
128 Rufinus, *Historia monachorum in Aegypto* 1.2. English translation in *The Lives of the Desert Fathers* (trans. Norman Russell, intro. Benedicta Ward; London: Mowbray, 1980), 52.
129 Palladius, *Dialogue on the Life of St. John Chrysostom* 20 (Ancient Christian Writers 45; trans. Robert T. Meyer; New York: Newman, 1985), 132.
130 English translation in Palladius, *Historia Lausiaca*, 94–95; Greek text in Butler, *Lausiac History*, 2:95.
131 Cf. Hos 11:1: "When Israel was a child, I loved him, and out of Egypt I called my son."

132 Matt 2:13–15.

133 Egypt or Egyptian(s) appears thirteen times in Acts 7.

134 Acts 7:22.

135 Jude 5.

136 *Vita S. Mariae Aegyptiae* 13 (PG 87 (3), cols. 3693–726, esp. 3709). Benedicta Ward, trans., *Harlots of the Desert: A Study of Repentance in Early Monastic Sources* (Kalamazoo, Mich.: Cistercian, 1987).

137 Augustine, *Enarrationes in Psalmos* 71.12 (CC 39.980).

138 Acts 13:1. *Symeōn ho kaloumenos Niger*. Cain Hope Felder concludes that "the Latinism *Niger* probably reinforces the idea that Symeon was a dark-skinned person, probably an African": *Troubling Biblical Waters*, 47–48.

139 Acts 21:37–39.

140 Some commentators view Luke's use of "the Egyptian" as an ethnic slur. See, for example, John Clayton Lentz, *Luke's Portrait of Paul* (Cambridge: Cambridge University Press, 1993).

141 Luke may have followed Josephus's description of militant groups in this description of the Egyptian. See Josephus, *Jewish War* 2.261–65; *Jewish Antiquities* 20.169–72. Cf. Acts 5:36–37.

142 *Epist. Barn.* 4.9; 20.1.

143 See Kathleen O'Brien Wicker, "Ethiopian Moses (Collected Sources)," in *Ascetic Behaviour in Greco-Roman Antiquity: A Sourcebook* (ed. Vincent L. Wimbush; Minneapolis: Fortress Press, 1990), 328–29.

144 Jude 4. "For certain intruders have stolen in among you, people who long ago were designated for this condemnation as ungodly, who pervert the grace of our God into licentiousness and deny our only Master and Lord, Jesus Christ."

145 Jude 6, 13. Cf. Rom 1:21. See also in Jude 12 a related verse that refers to the intruders as "blemishes" (*spilades*). "These are blemishes on your love-feasts, while they feast with you without fear, feeding themselves." *Spilades* is used symbolically in this text. Bauer suggests two possible meanings: (1) a rock washed by the sea, or (2) spot, stain, blemish. See BAGD, 762. The second meaning is most likely intended. The author may be calling attention to dangers and threats that this intra-Christian group represented.

146 Ephraem Syrus, *The Pearl, or Seven Rhythms on the Faith* 3.2–3 (Library of the Fathers 41; ed. and trans. J.B. Morris; Oxford: J.H. Parker, 1847), 92–93. English translation in Courtès, " 'Ethiopians' in Patristic Literature," 29.

147 See, for example, *Pachomian Koinonia* 2.117.

148 Anonymous, *Apophthegmata patrum* 1596, 10 in *Les sentences des pères du désert: nouveau recueil.* (ed. and trans. L. Regnault; Sarthe: Solesmes, 1985), 241.

149 With all due respect to Professor Frank Snowden and others who have been persuaded by his research on Blacks (or Ethiopians) in antiquity, it is clear from the taxonomy developed in this chapter that the ancients were well aware of ethnic and color differences and displayed their understandings (sometimes negative and sometimes positive) in various forms of symbolic representations of Egyptians/Egypt, Ethiopians/Ethiopia, and Blacks/blackness.

3 "WE WERE ETHIOPIANS IN OUR VICES AND SINS": ETHNO-POLITICAL RHETORICS DEFINING VICES AND SINS

1 Ps 86(87):4.

2 Ps 67(68):32.

3 Isa 1:16.

4 Ps 50:9.

5 Jerome, *De Psalmo* 86:137–57 (CC 78:114). For English translation see, Jerome, *Homily 18 on Psalm 86*, 140–41. I follow Ewald's translation with minor modifications.

6 Ewald translates *"populus Aethiopum"* as "Ethiopia."

7 Snowden, *Before Color Prejudice*, 100. According to Snowden, those who have been "whitened" by God can gain spiritual purity and wholeness. *Candor* had many meanings in Greco-Roman antiquity. In addition to "whiteness" it could also mean bright light, brightness, snow, fairness of complexion, moral purity, and lucidity. See *Oxford Latin Dictionary* (ed. P.G.W. Glare; New York: Oxford University Press, 1982), 1:265.

8 Jerome, *De Psalmo* 86 (CC 78.114).

9 Jerome, based mostly in Rome, used rhetorical patterns related to Ethiopians and Blacks similar to those of the Alexandrian exegete Origen and the North African patristic writers Tertullian and Augustine.

10 Jean-Remy Palanque, "St. Jerome and the Barbarians," in *A Monument to Saint Jerome: Essays on Some Aspects of His Life, Works and Influence* (ed. Francis X. Murphy; New York: Sheed & Ward, 1952), 173–99, esp. 196.

11 Jerome, *Letters* 60.17 (CSEL 54.572). English translation in J.H.D. Scourfield, *Consoling Heliodorus: A Commentary on Jerome, Letter 60* (New York: Oxford University Press, 1993), 71.

12 Scourfield, *Consoling Heliodorus*, 28.

13 Jerome is not unique in this view. There is a long biblical and patristic tradition that understands vices and sins as the result of political and military downturns. See Elizabeth Allo Isichei, *Political Thinking and Social Experience: Some Christian Interpretations of the Roman Empire from Tertullian to Salvian* (Canterbury: University of Canterbury, 1964).

14 See, for example, Courtès, "'Ethiopians' in Patristic Literature," 9–32. Courtès discusses how "Scriptures use the name *Ethiopian* for those who are deeply sunken in vice." See also, Hood, *Begrimed and Black*, 85–90.

15 See Frost, "Attitudes toward Blacks," 1–11, esp. 3–4. Frost cites the following sources: Origen, *Commentary on the Song of Songs* 2.1–2.2; Jerome, *Homily 18 on Psalm 86*; and Paulinus of Nola, *Carmen* 28.241. Frost argues that color prejudice is exemplified in these writings through metaphors of sin. See also Gier, "The Color of Sin/The Color of Skin," 42–52. Gier does not see color prejudice in ancient Christian writings that contain metaphors of sin. Gier does not seem to be aware of Frost's pertinent study on Blacks.

16 Egypt also served as an image for the sinful world in Christian writings (cf. Rev 11:8; 18:4). For research on this subject, see Reynolds, "Sodom/Egypt/Babylon Motif."

17 The term "apostolic" was coined in the seventeenth century and used to designate those fathers of the age immediately succeeding the New Testament period whose works in whole or in part have survived. These fathers include Clement of Rome; Ignatius, bishop of Antioch; Polycarp, bishop of Smyrna; Papias; and the anonymous authors of the *Shepherd of Hermas, Letter to Diognetus*, the *Didache*, the *Epistle of Barnabas*, and 2 Clement. For more background information, see "Apostolic Fathers," in *The Oxford Dictionary of the Christian Church* (3rd ed. ed. F.L. Cross and E.A. Livingstone; New York: Oxford University Press, 1997), 90–91; Carolyn Osiek, "Apostolic Fathers," in *The Early Christian World* (ed. P. Esler; London: Routledge, 2000), 1:503–24; and *The Apostolic Fathers: Greek Texts and English Translations of Their Writings* (trans. J.B. Lightfoot and J.R. Harmer; ed. and rev. Michael W. Holmes; Grand Rapids: Baker, 1992), 1.

18 See Claudia Setzer, *Jewish Responses to Early Christians: History and Polemics 30–150 CE* (Minneapolis: Fortress, 1994).
19 Holmes, *Apostolic Fathers*, 10–12.
20 See Maureen A. Tilley, *The Bible in Christian North Africa: The Donatist World* (Minneapolis: Fortress, 1997), 26.
21 Manlio Simonetti, *Biblical Interpretation in the Early Church: An Historical Introduction to Patristic Exegesis* (trans. John A. Hughes; Edinburgh: T&T Clark, 1994), 100.
22 Simonetti, *Biblical Interpretation*, 99.
23 Jerome cites Plautus, Terence, Cicero, et al.; cf. Simonetti, *Biblical Interpretation*, 99.
24 Simonetti, *Biblical Interpretation*, 99.
25 Simonetti, *Biblical Interpretation*, 102.
26 Adalbert Hamman, "The Turnabout of the Fourth Century: A Political, Geographical, Social, Ecclesiastical, and Doctrinal Framework of the Century," in *Patrology* (4 vols.; ed. Johannes Quasten; Westminster, Md.: Christian Classics, 1994), 4.18.
27 Drake, "Color Evaluation and Early Christianity," in *Black Folk Here and There*, 2:44–70.
28 Gal 3:27–28; cf. Col 3:11.
29 Snowden, *Blacks in Antiquity*, 196–215; Snowden, *Before Color Prejudice*, 101.
30 *Epist. Barn.* 4.9 (Translation mine). Greek text in *The Apostolic Fathers* 1:350–53.
31 Cf. *Epist. Barn.* 2.10.
32 *Did.* 16.1–2. See Greek text and English translation in *Apostolic Fathers*, 1.332–33. For a brief discussion on the eschatological intent of *Epist. Barn.*, see Brian E. Daley, *The Hope of the Early Church: A Handbook of Patristic Eschatology* (Cambridge: Cambridge University Press, 1991), 11.
33 *Epist. Barn.* 4.3–5 and 16.3–4.
34 *Epist. Barn.* 21.3.
35 *Epist. Barn.* 5.7.
36 *Epist. Barn.* 9.4.
37 See, for example, F.X. Gokey, *The Terminology for the Devil and Evil Spirits in the Apostolic Fathers* (Washington, D.C.: Catholic University of America Press, 1961), 101–102, 112–13; McCasland, "Black One," 77–80; Courtès, "'Ethiopians' in Patristic Literature," 19; Hood, *Begrimed and Black*, 76; Russell, *Satan*, 38–41; Gier, "The Color of Sin/The Color of Skin," 45; and Dölger, *Die Sonne der Gerechtigkeit*, 49–83, esp. 62. See also, Elaine Pagels, *The Origin of Satan* (New York: Random House, 1995), 154–55, 158. Pagels identifies how Gospel writers and other Christian authors used Satan to represent their enemies. In her brief discussion about the *Epistle of Barnabas* she does not raise any questions about the use of *ho melas* as a part of the demonizing strategy of the author. Russell, *Satan*, says, "the equation of evil, darkness, and blackness, a source of later racial stereotypes" in Christian literature occurs for the first time in the *Epistle of Barnabas* (40).
38 *Epist. Barn.* 2.10.
39 *Epist. Barn.* 20.1–2. This English translation is based on Kirsopp Lake's translation in *Apostolic Fathers*, with minor changes. Greek text in *Apostolic Fathers*, 1:406.
40 For a discussion about virtue and vice lists in Greco-Roman literature, see Abraham J. Malherbe, ed., *Moral Exhortation: A Greco-Roman Sourcebook* (Philadelphia: Westminster, 1986), 138–41. Cf. 1 Tim 1:9–10; 6:3–5; 2 Tim 3:2–5.
41 *Epist. Barn.* 19.1–12.
42 *Epist. Barn.* 18.1–2.
43 Cf. Gal 5:19–23.

44 Cf. 2 Pet 1:5–7.
45 Cf. Herm. *Mand.* 2–5.
46 *Did.* 5.1.
47 Cf. Homer, *Iliad* 2.834; 11.332; 16.350, and Homer, *Odyssey* 12.92; 17.326.
48 Cf. *Epist. Barn.* 14.6: "For it is written that the Father enjoins on him that he should redeem us from darkness (*skotous*) and prepare a holy people for himself."
49 *Epist. Barn.* 18.1–2.
50 *Epist. Barn.* 19.1–12 discusses the way of light.
51 *Did.* 1.1.
52 *Did.* 5.1–2.
53 Cf. Petersen, *Gospel of John*; Wayne A. Meeks, "The Social Functions of Apocalyptic Language in Pauline Christianity," in *Apocalypticism in the Mediterranean World and the Near East* (Proceedings of the International Colloquium on Apocalypticism – Uppsala, August 12–17, 1979; ed. David Hellholm; Tübingen: J.C.B. Mohr, 1983), 687–705.
54 See James Carleton Paget, *The Epistle of Barnabas: Outlook and Background* (Tübingen: J.C.B. Mohr, 1994), 32–35. Scholars have challenged this proposal for an Alexandrian provenance, leading to suggestions that the letter originated in Syria-Palestine and Asia Minor.
55 Cf. Clement, *Strom.* 2.20.116: "And how we say that the powers of the devil, and the unclean spirits sow into the sinner's soul, requires no more words from me, on adducing as a witness the apostolic Barnabas who speaks these words."
56 Snowden, *Blacks in Antiquity*, 132–36.
57 See Snowden, *Blacks in Antiquity*, 28, 185–86. Snowden relies on iconographical evidence to support this claim. He cites "Negro terra cottas in the museum at Alexandria" that depict various roles in which Ethiopians may have participated (see Figs. 40a–b, 68–69). This evidence is inconclusive. I have not found any other studies that discuss the presence of Ethiopians within Alexandrian society.
58 Paget, *Epistle of Barnabas*, 42–45.
59 In *Epist. Barn.* 4.6b; 9.6; 12.10 the author appears to be quoting opponents.
60 For the basic form of an ancient letter, see Jerome Murphy-O'Connor, *Paul the Letter-Writer: His World, His Options, His Skills* (Collegeville: Liturgical Press, 1995).
61 The greeting (1.1) is terse – addressed to both men and women (*huioi kai thygateres*).
62 *Epist. Barn.* 2.1.
63 *Epist. Barn.* 21.9.
64 Paget, *Epistle of Barnabas*, 186.
65 *Epist. Barn.* 1.5; 4.3.
66 Paget, *Epistle of Barnabas*, 7–9. Paget discusses the debate about the ethnic origins of the author of *Barnabas*. Those in favor of a Jewish origin argue their case on the basis of the Jewish character of the epistle. See, for example, the presence of rabbinic traditions (chaps. 7–8), similarities to Jewish apocalypses (4.3–5 cf. *4 Ezra* 11–12 and *Sib. Or.* 5.403–33), a future hope expressed in terms of the Jewish idioms of land (6.8–19) and temple (4.11; 6.15; 16.7ff), the "Two Ways" material, which is considered of Palestinian origin, and the great concern for the law expressed in the letter (10.12). Those who oppose the Jewish origin for the author point to the scathing attack on Jewish customs, the apparent ignorance of rabbinic traditions, the comparison of the temple to a pagan place of worship, and the assumption of a former state of unbelief (14.5; 16.7). Paget is unable to draw a definitive conclusion on this matter: "Any conclusion on this matter must therefore be guarded. The epistle is strongly Jewish in character, but this observation does not allow us to state that the author himself was Jewish. Greater

certainty can probably be established with regard to the identity of some of the recipients. Given the prominence of the issue of circumcision (ch. 9), and such verses as 3:6 and 13:7, a gentile origin for them seems more likely." See Paget, *Epistle of Barnabas*, 9.

67 *Epist. Barn.* 20.1.

68 Trajan is referred to as the "evil one" in the Jerusalem Talmud. See Jerusalem Talmud, *Sukkah* 5.1, 55B. "In the time of Trogianos [Trajan], *the evil one* [emphasis mine], a son was born to him on the ninth of Av, and [the Israelites] were fasting. His daughter died on Hanukkah, and [the Israelites] lit candles. His wife sent a message to him, saying: 'Instead of going out to conquer the barbarians, come and conquer the Jews, who have rebelled against you.'" This text is cited in Joseph Mélèze Modrzejewski, *The Jews of Egypt: From Rameses II to Emperor Hadrian* (Princeton: Princeton University Press, 1997), 209.

69 Paget, *Epistle of Barnabas*, 181–82.

70 Olster, "Classical Ethnography," 28.

71 Olster, "Classical Ethnography," 29.

72 Josephus, *The Life, Against Apion*. For an insightful discussion on this text, see Jan Assmann, *Moses the Egyptian: The Memory of Egypt in Western Monotheism* (Cambridge, Mass.: Harvard University Press, 1997), 30–33, 37–38.

73 Olster translates *ho laos* as "race." See Olster, "Classical Ethnography," 29.

74 *Epist. Barn.* 9.6.

75 Olster, "Classical Ethnography," 16. Olster claims that Josephus was concerned with establishing the "historical and racial legitimacy of the Jews" in *Against Apion*. Cf. Josephus, *The Life, Against Apion*.

76 Olster, "Classical Ethnography," 30.

77 Carolyn Osiek, "The Second Century through the Eyes of Hermas: Continuity and Change," *BTB* 20 (1990): 116–22; L.W. Barnard, "The Shepherd of Hermas in Recent Study," *HeyJ* 9 (1968): 29–36.

78 Carolyn Osiek, *Rich and Poor in the Shepherd of Hermas: An Exegetical-Social Investigation* (CBQMS 15; Washington, D.C.: Catholic Biblical Association of America, 1983), 6–7.

79 See, for example, Carolyn Osiek, *Shepherd of Hermas: A Commentary* (Hermeneia Series; Minneapolis: Fortress, 1999); Osiek, *Rich and Poor*; J.C. White, "The Interaction of Language and World in the 'Shepherd of Hermas'" (Ph.D. diss., Temple University, 1973); L. Pernveden, *The Concept of the Church in the Shepherd of Hermas* (Studia Theologica Lundensia 27; Lund: Gleerup, 1966); J. Reiling, *Hermas and Christian Prophecy: A Study of the Eleventh Mandate* (NovTSup 37; Leiden: E.J. Brill, 1973). For a useful survey of the scholarship, see Osiek, *Rich and Poor*, 3–6.

80 See discussions in *Der Hirt des Hermas* (trans. Molly Whittaker; GCS 48; Die Apostolischen Väter 1; Berlin: Akademie, 1967), xiii; G. Snyder, *The Shepherd of Hermas* (Apostolic Fathers 6; ed. Robert Grant; Camden, N.J.: T. Nelson, 1968), 3–4.

81 Herm. *Vis.* 2.

82 The fifth vision, referred to as *apokalypsis*, is intended as an introduction to the Mandates.

83 Herm. *Vis.* 5.5–6.

84 Herm. *Vis.* 3.8.9. For discussions about the eschatological content of the *Shepherd of Hermas*, see Carolyn Osiek, "The Genre and Function of the *Shepherd of Hermas*," *Semeia* 36 (1986): 113–21; Daley, *Hope of the Early Church*, 16–17.

85 Herm. *Vis.* 3.3.5. For Greek text, see Whittaker, *Der Hirt des Hermas*. For another Greek text and English translation, see *Shepherd of Hermas* in *Apostolic Fathers* (vol. 2; trans. Kirsopp Lake; LCL; Cambridge, Mass.: Harvard University Press, 1976). For a more recent translation, see Osiek, *Shepherd of Hermas*. All English

translations of the *Shepherd of Hermas* in this section come from Lake's LCL edition (modified slightly).

86 Herm. *Vis.* 4.2.5.

87 Herm. *Vis.* 4.1.10.

88 Herm. *Vis.* 4.3.2.

89 Herm. *Vis.* 4.3.5.

90 Osiek, "Genre and Function," 116–17. Cf. Adela Y. Collins, "The Early Christian Apocalypses," *Semeia* 14 (1979): 61–121.

91 Paul D. Hanson argues that apocalyptic literature such as the *Shepherd of Hermas* functions to sustain a community in its present reality. See Paul D. Hanson, *The Dawn of the Apocalyptic: The Historical and Sociological Roots of Jewish Apocalyptic Eschatology* (Philadelphia: Fortress, 1975). Adela Y. Collins argues that there has to be a perceived crisis that has to do with the social identity of Christians in response to Nero's persecutions and the destruction of Jerusalem. See Adela Y. Collins, *Crisis and Catharsis: The Power of the Apocalypse* (Philadelphia: Westminster, 1984), 84–110.

92 Osiek, "Genre and Function," 116.

93 Herm. *Sim.* 9.19–29.

94 Herm. *Sim.* 9.1.5.

95 Herm. *Sim.* 9.19.1.

96 Herm. *Sim.* 9.29.1–2.

97 Herm. *Sim.* 9.13.1. The tower (*pyrgos*) that is being built is the church (*ekklēsia*).

98 Herm. *Vis.* 3.3.3; 5.5; 8.9; 9.5.

99 The last leaf of the Greek text is missing. The Latin text which follows is that of L(1). The few verses in Greek are from P(am). See *Shepherd of Hermas* LCL, 290.

100 Herm. *Sim.* 9.30.1–3.

101 Herm. *Sim.* 9.33.1.

102 Herm. *Sim.* 32.1.

103 Many editors and translators translate *genos* as race. This is one possible meaning of the term, but there are also several other definitions for the term. *Genos* (γένος) can denote posterity or family (see Acts 17:29; Rev 22:16), or it can be understood in the sense of people (see Acts 7:19; 2 Cor 11:26; Gal 1:14; Phil 3:5; 1 Pet 2:9), or it can mean class, sort, kind (see 1 Cor 12:10, 28). For a full definition, see "γένος," in LSJ, 344.

104 1 Pet 2:9. Cf. Acts 7:19; 2 Cor 11:26; Gal 1:14; Phil 3:5.

105 Herm. *Sim.* 9.15.1–3.

106 Carolyn Osiek, "An Early Tale That Almost Made it into the New Testament," *BRev* 10 (1994): 48–54, esp. 54.

107 J.B. Lightfoot and J.R. Harmer, *The Apostolic Fathers: Greek Texts and English Translations of Their Writings* (Grand Rapids: Baker, 1992), 12.

108 John J. Collins, *The Apocalyptic Imagination: An Introduction to the Jewish Matrix of Christianity* (New York: Crossroad, 1984), 215.

109 Rudolph Arbesmann, *Tertullian: Disciplinary, Moral and Ascetical Works* (Washington, D.C.: Catholic University of America, 1977), 43. Quasten suggests that 197 CE is the most probable date of this text. See Johannes Quasten, *Patrology* (4 vols.; Westminster, Md.: Christian Classics, 1951–86), 2:293.

110 There were four kinds of spectacles in Roman antiquity: (1) circus, (2) amphitheater, (3) stadium, and (4) theater.

111 Tertullian, *De spectaculis* 3.2 "Now, to be sure, nowhere do we find it laid down with the same precision as 'Thou shalt not kill,' 'Thou shalt not worship an idol,' 'Thou shalt not commit adultery,' 'Thou shalt not commit fraud' – nowhere do we find it thus clearly declared: 'Thou shalt not go to the circus,' 'Thou shalt not go to the theater,' 'Thou shalt not watch a contest or show of gladiators.'" For a

useful discussion on Tertullian's response to the silence of scriptures, see T.P. O'Malley, *Tertullian and the Bible: Language – Imagery – Exegesis* (Utrecht: Dekker & Van de Vegt, N.V. Nijmegen, 1967), 129–30.

112 See Arbesmann, *Tertullian*, 53, n. 2. Arbesmann suggests that Tertullian is under the influence of the sophistic methods of argumentation, which hold that everything is capable of proof. Tertullian distorts the meaning of Ps 1:1 to fit his purpose of discrediting the spectacles. Cf. Clement, *Paedagogus* 3.11.76.3.

113 Tertullian, *De spectaculis* 3.3 (trans. T.R. Glover; LCL; Cambridge, Mass.: Harvard University Press, 1977). "But we do find that to this special case there can be applied that first verse of David, where he says: 'Happy is the man who has not gone to the gathering of the ungodly, nor stood in the ways of sinners, nor sat in the chair of pestilence.'"

114 Tertullian, *De spectaculis* 1.4.

115 Tertullian, *De spectaculis* 4–13.

116 Chapters 1 and 2 of this text elaborate upon the excuses Gentiles (or pagans) used to justify their support of the spectacles. Both Glover and Arbesmann translate this phrase as "heathen opinion." I have chosen to translate *ethnicorum* as "Gentiles" (or "pagans").

117 Cf. *De spectaculis* 20.1. For a discussion on Tertullian's understanding of "Scriptures," see O'Malley, *Tertullian and the Bible*, 119–25.

118 Tertullian, *De spectaculis* 3.1–7.

119 Tertullian, *De spectaculis* 3.3–7.

120 Tertullian, *De spectaculis* 3.8.

121 Tertullian, *De spectaculis* 3.8. (English translation in Arbesmann, *Tertullian*, 55–56.)

122 See esp. Ezek 30:4 "A sword shall come upon Egypt, and anguish shall be in Ethiopia, when the slain fall in Egypt, and its wealth is carried away, and its foundations are torn down."

123 Tertullian's association of Egypt and Ethiopia with sin is not unique. Within the LXX, many of the prophets, especially Isaiah, made this association.

124 O'Malley, *Tertullian and the Bible*. O'Malley claims that Tertullian's rhetorical training is evident throughout his writings. See Tertullian and the Bible, 137–41.

125 Courtès, "'Ethiopians' in Patristic Literature," 25–26. Courtès claims that the use of Egypt and Ethiopia in this context is an example of the author's "rhetorical style."

126 Tertullian, *Ad nationes* 1.8; 1.20. See Harnack, "Christians as a Third Race," 1:336–52, esp. 343–47. Harnack argues that *tertium genus* refers to Christian worship and religion. David M. Olster, in his study on classical ethnography and early Christianity, challenges this basic premise. Olster suggests that *tertium genus* has extensive cultural and social implications and argues that classical ethnography might provide a hermeneutical key for understanding Tertullian's use of this phrase. See Olster, "Classical Ethnography," 11–12.

127 Tertullian, *Ad nationes* 1.8. Text and translation from Harnack, "Christians as a Third Race," 344–45.

128 Cf. *Passio Sanctarum Perpetuae et Felicitatis* 10.8–14. In this text, Perpetua has a fight with *ho Aigyptios* (the Egyptian) before her martyrdom. For a useful discussion on ethnic and color differences in North Africa, see L.C. Brown, "Color in Northern Africa," in *Color and Race* (ed. John Hope Franklin; Boston: Houghton Mifflin, 1968), 186–204.

129 Origen, *De principiis* 4.1.11. Origen, *De principiis*, in *Origène: Traité; des Principes* (SC; ed. H. Crouzel and M. Simonetti; Paris: Cerf, 1978–84). For an English translation, see *Origen: On First Principles* (ed. and trans. G.W. Butterworth; New York: Harper & Row, 1966).

130 Origen, *De principiis* 4. To explain this level, Origen cites 1 Cor 9:9 where Paul interprets a verse from Deuteronomy about muzzling the mouth of the ox: "Is it for oxen that God is concerned? Does he not speak entirely for our sake?"

131 Origen, *De principiis* 4.1.15.

132 Origen, *De principiis* 4.1.27.

133 Song 1:5–6 (LXX). English translation mine. Frank Snowden has reviewed this text in detail. He identified the black–white color symbolism in Origen's interpretation of the black bride. See Snowden, *Blacks in Antiquity*, 201–204; *Before Color Prejudice*, 101–103. For commentary of the Song of Songs, see Renita J. Weems, 'Song of Songs,' in *The New Interpreter's Bible* (vol. 5; Nashville: Abingdon, 1997), 363–434 and Jacqueline de Weever, *Sheba's Daughters: Whitening and Demonizing the Saracen Woman in Medieval French Literature* (New York and London: Garland 1998).

134 For the Latin texts, see *Origenes Werke* (GCS 8; ed. W.A. Baehrens; Leipzig: J.C. Hinrichs, 1925), xiv–xx and 26–60 for the homilies; xx–xxviii and 61–241 for the commentary. For another edition of the homilies and commentary, see *Origène: Homélies sur le Cantique des Cantiques* (SC 37; ed. O. Rousseau; Paris: Cerf, 1954); and *Commentarium in Canticum Canticorum* (2 vols.; Commentaire sur le Cantique des Cantiques; texte de la version latin de Rufinus; introduction, traduction et notes par Luc Brésard et Henri Crouzel avec la collaboration de Marcel Borret; SC 375 et 376; Paris: Cerf, 1991–92). For an English translation of the commentary and the homilies, see *Origen: The Song of Songs, Commentary and Homilies* (Ancient Christian Writers 26; trans. R.P. Lawson; New York: Newman, 1956). I follow this translation with slight modifications. Only a few Greek fragments of the *Commentary* survive and there are no remaining Greek fragments of the *Homilies*. See Lawson, *Origen*, 3–4.

135 Rom 11:28.

136 Origen, *Commentarium* 2.1.3. English translation in Lawson, *Origen*, 92.

137 Lawson, *Origen*, 92.

138 Origen, *Commentarium* 2.1.4. Lawson, *Origen*, 92.

139 Origen, *Commentarium* 2.1.6. Lawson, *Origen*, 93.

140 Lawson, *Origen*, 93–96. Origen refers to Num 12:1–15 (The Ethiopian wife of Moses); 1 Kgs 10:1–13 (Queen of Sheba); Josephus, *Ant.* 8.165–75; Ps 67(68): 31–33; Soph. 3:8–11; Jer 38(45):10 and 39(46):15, 18. For a summary of Origen's use of these sources in Song of Songs, see Snowden, *Blacks in Antiquity*, 201–204; Courtès, "'Ethiopians' in Patristic Literature," 14–16.

141 Courtès, "'Ethiopians' in Patristic Literature," 28–29.

142 Rom 1:18–21.

143 Courtès, "'Ethiopians' in Patristic Literature," 15.

144 Origen, *Homiliae* 1.6 (GCS 8.37). English translation in Lawson, *Origen*, 277. Baehrens suggests that the bracketed section is a gloss.

145 Lawson, *Origen*, 17–19. These homilies were translated by Jerome while he was in Rome around the year 383 CE.

146 Cf. 2 Cor 2:14ff.

147 Ps 37:6.

148 Origen, *Homiliae* 1.2 (GCS 8.30); Lawson, *Origen*, 269.

149 Snowden, *Blacks in Antiquity*, 205. Cf. Augustine, *Enarrationes in Psalmos* 71.12 (CC 39.980).

150 *The Poems of St. Paulinus of Nola* (Ancient Christian Writers 40; trans. P.G. Walsh; New York: Newman, 1975), 302–303; Latin text in CSEL 30 (ed. G. de Hartel; Vienna: Academiae Litterarum Caesareae Vindobonensis, 1894), 301–302.

4 "STIRRING UP THE PASSIONS": ETHNO-POLITICAL RHETORICS DEFINING SEXUAL THREATS

1 There are many studies that discuss how Ethiopians were depicted as a source of sexual temptations, especially in the monastic literature from the third to fifth centuries CE. See, for example, Hood, "Blackness as Evil and Sex in Early Christian Thought," in *Begrimed and Black*, 73–90; Mayerson, "Anti-Black Sentiment," 304–11; Frost, "Attitudes toward Blacks," 1–11; and Courtès, "'Ethiopians' in Patristic Literature," 9–32. These studies, however, do not explore the discursive strategies the Christian writers used in developing their stories. For an insightful study that classifies rhetorics of sexuality in ancient rabbinical sources, see Michael L. Satlow, *Tasting the Dish: Rabbinic Rhetorics of Sexuality* (BJS 303; Atlanta: Scholars Press, 1995). Satlow examines the rhetoric that the rabbis of late antiquity used to promote their sexual mores and to persuade their respective communities to practice only "sanctioned" sexual behavior. For a well-documented description of *porneia* in the ancient world, see Aline Rousselle, *Porneia: On Desire and the Body in Antiquity* (ed. Felicia Pheasant; Cambridge and Oxford: Blackwell, 1988).

2 For an excellent discussion of asceticism (including definitions, approaches, and geographical regions), see Elizabeth A. Clark, *Reading Renunciation: Asceticism and Scripture in Early Christianity* (Princeton: Princeton University Press, 1999), 14–42. See also Vincent L. Wimbush, ed., *Ascetic Behavior in Greco-Roman Antiquity* (Minneapolis: Fortress, 1990).

3 For a discussion on the use of sexual slander in political invective, see Long, *Claudian's In Eutropium*. See also, Jennifer Wright Knust, "God Has Abandoned Them to Their Lust: The Politics of Sexual Vice in Early Christian Discourse" (Ph.D. diss., Columbia University, 2000).

4 Frost, "Attitudes toward Blacks," 8. Frost argues that the use of the Ethiopian woman to epitomize undesirability is particularly noticeable in the literature left by the monks of the Egyptian desert. Frost leads the reader to several examples within monastic literature in which Ethiopian women are used for "harboring disgust for the pleasures of the flesh".

5 Anonymous, *Apophthegmata patrum*, in *Les sentences des pères du désert: nouveau recueil* (ed. L. Regnault; 2nd ed.; Sarthe: Solesmes, 1985), 184.

6 *Apophthegmata patrum* 5.5. For background on the significance of odors in the ancient world, see Marcel Detienne, *The Gardens of Adonis: Spices in Greek Mythology* (trans. Janet Lloyd; Hassocks, Sussex: Harvester, 1977); Constance Classen, David Howes, and Anthony Synnott, *Aroma: The Cultural History of Smell* (New York: Routledge, 1994); and W. Deonna, "ΕΥΩΔΙΑ: Croyances antiques et modernes: l'odeur suave des dieux et des élus," *Genava* 17 (1939): 167–263. For early Christian understandings of smell, see Susan Ashbrook Harvey, "Olfactory Knowing: Signs of Smell in the *Vitae* of Simeon Stylites," in *After Bardaisan: Studies on Continuity and Change in Syriac Christianity in Honour of Professor Han J.W. Drijvers* (ed. G.J. Reinink and A.C. Klugkist; Leuven: Peeters, 1999), 23–34; and "St. Ephrem on the Scent of Salvation," *JTS* 49 (1998): 109–28.

7 Palladius, *Historia Lausiaca* 23.5.

8 Adele Logan Alexander, "'She's No Lady, She's a Nigger': Abuses, Stereotypes, and Realities from the Middle Passage to Capitol (and Anita) Hill," in *Race, Gender, and Power in America: The Legacy of the Hill-Thomas Hearings* (ed. Anita Faye Hill and Emma Coleman Jordan; New York: Oxford University Press, 1995), 3–25.

9 Frank Snowden correctly indicates that for Egyptians, the people of Nubia and Syria had become "the Others," who represented an *ethnic* type differing from themselves. See Snowden, "Bernal's 'Blacks'", 123. For a discussion about ethnic relations between Egyptians and Ethiopians, see V. Christides, "Ethnic Movements in Southern Egypt and Northern Sudan," *Listy Filologicke* 103 (1980): 129–43; L.P. Kirwan, "Rome Beyond the Southern Egyptian Frontier," *Geographical Journal* 123 (1957): 13–19; and Anthony Leahy, "Ethnic Diversity in Ancient Egypt," in *Civilizations of the Ancient Near East* (ed. Jack M. Sasson; New York: Scribner, 1995), 1:225–34.

10 Adams, "The Invention of Nubia," 17–22, esp. 17.

11 See, for example, Athanasius, *Vita Antonii*, 6.

12 Philostratus, *Vita Apoll.* 6.2.

13 Thompson, *Romans and Blacks*, 62–85, 105.

14 The use of the generic term "Egyptians" is admittedly problematic. The term could be used to describe indigenous Egyptians (Copts) and immigrant Greeks who settled in various parts of late antique Egypt (especially Alexandria). Examination of Coptic sources is beyond the scope of this chapter. For a concise explanation of the problem, see Robert Steven Bianchi, "Postdynastic Egypt," in *The Oxford Encyclopedia of Archaeology in the Near East* (ed. Eric M. Meyers; New York: Oxford University Press, 1997), 2:201–205.

15 Bowman, *Egypt After the Pharaohs*.

16 For a useful study on Alexandria in late antiquity, see Christopher Haas, *Alexandria in Late Antiquity: Topography and Social Conflict* (Baltimore: Johns Hopkins University Press, 1997). See also Roger S. Bagnall, *Egypt in Late Antiquity* (Princeton: Princeton University Press, 1993), 148–80. Bagnall argues that it is impossible to discuss the desert of Egypt without dealing with the city of Alexandria.

17 Peter Brown, "The Rise and Function of the Holy Man in Late Antiquity," in *Society and Holy in Late Antiquity* (Berkeley: University of California Press, 1982), 103–52; originally published in *JRS* 61 (1971): 80–101.

18 N.B. Egypt was not the only center of ascetic activity. Ascetic movements were located in several geographical regions within the Roman Empire by the fourth century CE (e.g., Asia Minor, Syria, Palestine, North Africa, Italy, southern France, and Spain). See Susanna Elm, *"Virgins of God": The Making of Asceticism in Late Antiquity* (New York: Oxford University Press, 1994), 18; and Clark, *Reading Renunciation*, 27–33.

19 Brown, "Rise and Function of the Holy Man," 109.

20 See John Cassian, *Conferences* 11.1, "On Perfection," *John Cassian: Conferences* (trans. Colm Luibheid; New York: Paulist Press, 1985), 141.

21 See Samuel Rubenson, "Christian Asceticism and the Emergence of the Monastic Tradition," in *Asceticism* (ed. Vincent L. Wimbush and Richard Valantasis; New York: Oxford University Press, 1995), 49–57; Susanna Elm, *"Virgins of God"*; and James E. Goehring, "The World Engaged: The Social and Economic World of Early Egyptian Monasticism," in *Gnosticism and the Early Christian World: Essays in Honor of James M. Robinson* (ed. J. Goehring et al.; Sonoma, Calif.: Polebridge, 1990), 134–44.

22 See Douglas Burton-Christie, *The Word in the Desert: Scripture and the Quest for Holiness in Early Christian Monasticism* (New York: Oxford University Press, 1993), 39–43, esp. 41. Burton-Christie claims that "*anachōrēsis*, whether as an act of desperation by people who could not pay their debts, or as flight from the overwhelming burden of taxation, or as a refuge from other heavy responsibilities, was a common feature in the life of Roman Egypt."

23 Athanasius, *Vita Antonii* 14: "The desert was made a city by monks, who left their

own people and registered themselves for citizenship in the heavens." Cf. Derwas Chitty, *The Desert A City: An Introduction to the Study of Egyptian and Palestinian Monasticism Under the Christian Empire* (Oxford: Basil Blackwell, 1966).

24 See Arthur Vööbus, *A History of Asceticism in the Syrian Orient* (CSCO 184; Subsidia 14; Louvain: CSCO, 1958); Sabastian P. Brock and Susan Ashbrook Harvey, eds. and trans., *Holy Women of the Syrian Orient* (Berkeley: University of California Press, 1987); John Binns, *Ascetics and Ambassadors of Christ: The Monasteries of Palestine 314–631* (New York: Oxford University Press, 1994); G. Folliet, "Aux origines de l'ascétisme et du cénobitisme africain," SA 46 (1961): 25–44; and Elm, *"Virgins of God."*

25 See, for example, Wimbush, *Ascetic Behavior in Greco-Roman Antiquity*, 6–8; Benedicta Ward, *The Sayings of the Desert Fathers: The Alphabetical Collection* (Kalamazoo, Mich.: Cistercian, 1984 [1975]), xvii–xxvii; Benedicta Ward, *The Lives of the Desert Fathers: The Historia Monachorum in Aegypto* (intro. Benedicta Ward; trans. Norman Russell; Kalamazoo, Mich.: Cistercian, 1981), 20–28; and James E. Goehring, "Through a Glass Darkly: Diverse Images of the APOTAKTIKOI(AI) of Early Egyptian Monasticism," *Semeia* 58 (1992): 25–45. For another survey of the history of monasticism, admittedly not intended for a scholarly audience, see *An Unbroken Circle: Linking Ancient Christianity to the African-American Experience* (ed. Paisius Altschul; St. Louis, Mo.: Brotherhood of St. Moses the Black, 1997), esp. 3–43.

26 Matt 19:21: "If you wish to be perfect, go, sell your possessions, and give the money to the poor, and you will have treasure in heaven; then come, follow me." Cf. Athanasius, *Vita Antonii* 2.

27 *Pachomian Koinonia: The Life of Saint Pachomius and his Disciples* (3 vols.; trans. Armand Veilleux; Kalamazoo, Mich.: Cistercian, 1980).

28 *Pachomian Koinonia*, 1.xxi.

29 Ward, *Sayings of the Desert Fathers*, xviii.

30 Ward, *Sayings of the Desert Fathers*. Many of the sayings of the desert fathers influenced Cassian's sermons. See Cassian, *The Conferences* (trans. Boniface Ramsey, Ancient Christian Writers 57; New York: Paulist Press, 1997). See also Columba Stewart, *Cassian the Monk* (New York: Oxford University Press, 1998).

31 Ward, *Sayings of the Desert Fathers*, xiv; DeLacy O'Leary, *The Saints of Egypt* (London: SPCK; New York: Macmillan, 1937), 29–30.

32 Elizabeth Clark offers a summary of some of the different models for ascetic living, giving special attention to women renunciants. See Clark, *Reading Renunciation*, 33–38. See also Bagnall's discussion about monasticism in *Egypt in Late Antiquity*, 293–303; Goehring, "World Engaged"; and Douglas Burton-Christie, *Word in the Desert*, 34–48.

33 Bagnall, *Egypt in Late Antiquity*, 295.

34 David Brakke, *Athanasius and the Politics of Asceticism* (New York: Oxford University Press, 1995; repr. Baltimore: Johns Hopkins University Press, 1998), 15.

35 Bagnall identifies a fourth type of monasticism: "a celibate and distinct life by separate communities of men and women carried on in the midst of regular society." See Bagnall, *Egypt in Late Antiquity*, 297.

36 Robert Riall, "Athanasius Bishop of Alexandria: The Politics of Spirituality" (Ph.D. diss., University of Cincinnati, 1987).

37 Goehring, "World Engaged," 134–44. Goehring suggests that the *Apophthegmata patrum* contains numerous indications of commercial dealings.

38 Goehring, "World Engaged," 138.

39 Many of the monastic documents refer to taxes, wills, leases, legal disputes, etc. See Goehring, "World Engaged," 142. See also Henry A. Green, "The Socio-

Economic Background of Christianity in Egypt," in *Roots of Egyptian Christianity* (ed. Birger A. Pearson and James E. Goehring; Philadelphia: Fortress, 1986), 100–113; and Dominic W. Rathbone, "The Ancient Economy and Graeco-Roman Egypt," in *Egitto e Storia Antica Dall'Ellenismo All'età Araba: Bilancio di un Confronto* (ed. Lucia Criscuolo and Giovanni Geraci; Bologna: Clueb, 1989), 159–76.

40 Peter Brown, "From the Heavens to the Desert: Anthony and Pachomius," in *The Making of Late Antiquity* (Cambridge, Mass.: Harvard University Press, 1978), 82.

41 Kallistos Ware, "The Way of the Ascetics: Negative or Affirmative?" in *Asceticism* (ed. Vincent L. Wimbush and Richard Valantasis; New York: Oxford University Press, 1995), 3–15.

42 Ware, "Way of the Ascetics," 4–8. On the presence of monks in cities, villages, and countryside, see Goehring, "World Engaged," 138.

43 Wimbush, *Ascetic Behavior in Greco-Roman Antiquity*, 2. Wimbush argues that "ascetic behavior represents a range of responses to social, political, and physical worlds often perceived as oppressive or unfriendly, or as stumbling blocks to the pursuit of heroic personal or communal goals, life styles, and commitments."

44 Naphtali Lewis, *Life in Egypt Under Roman Rule* (Oxford: Clarendon, 1983), 107–33; Lellia Cracco Ruggini, "Leggenda e realtà degli Etiopi nella cultura-tardoimperiale." *Atti del IV congresso internazionale di studi etiopici – 10–15 Aprile 1972* (vol. 1; Rome: Accademia Nazionale dei Lincei, 1974), 141–93; and "Il Negro buono e il negro malvagio," 120–21.

45 For an important assessment of the political history between Egypt and Nubia (Ethiopia), see László Török, *The Kingdom of Kush: Handbook of the Napatan-Meriotic Civilization* (New York: E.J. Brill, 1997), 448–87; see also by Török, *Late Antique Nubia: History and Archaeology of the Southern Neighbor of Egypt in the 4th–6th c. A.D.* (Antaeus 16; Budapest: Archaeological Institute of the Hungarian Academy of Sciences, 1988), 49–63.

46 For a comprehensive historical study on the Blemmyes, see R. Updegraff and L. Török, "The Blemmyes I: The Rise of the Blemmyes and the Roman With-drawal from Nubia under Diocletian," *ANRW* 10.1, 44–106.

47 Strabo, *Geography*, 17.1.53. See English translation in Strabo, *Geography* (8 vols.; trans. Horace Leonard Jones; LCL; Cambridge, Mass.: Harvard University Press, 1969).

48 *Geographi Graeci Minores* (ed. Carolus Müller; Paris, 1855 and 1861), 2.114, lines 217 ff. English translation in Updegraff and Török, "The Blemmyes I," 65.

49 *Geographi Graeci Minores* 2.180, lines 329–33.

50 Snowden, *Blacks in Antiquity*, 137. Cf. *Chronicon Paschale* in *Corpus Scriptorum Historiae Byzantinae*, I (Bonn: E. Weber, 1832), 504–505.

51 Procopius, *De bello Persico* 1.19.29–33. According to the sixth-century historian Procopius, Diocletian (1) abandoned Lower Nubia and withdrew the Roman frontier to the First Cataract; (2) invited the Nobades to occupy the Roman settle-ments on both sides of the Nile beyond the city of Elephantine; (3) gave an annual grant of money to both the Nobades and the Blemmyes with the stipulation that they were no longer to plunder Roman territory; and (4) instituted an inter-cultural and interreligious venture whereby he set up certain temples and altars and settled priests from among the Romans, Blemmyes, and Nobades. Cf. Snowden, *Blacks in Antiquity*, 137.

52 Bowman, *Egypt after the Pharaohs*, 51, esp. n. 59.

53 Bagnall, *Egypt in Late Antiquity*, 146–47. Bagnall acknowledges that the relationship of these tribes to Egyptian civilization and religion was complex. The Blemmyes were at times involved in diplomatic contact with the court at Constantinople. At other times, however, they acted as "the unpredictable enemy

of settled life – even occasionally of the ascetic desert-dwellers." Bagnall is skeptical of the sources from antiquity that describe the military activities of the Blemmyes. He refers the reader to a study that analyzes the primary sources about the Blemmyes. See Anna Maria Demicheli, *Rapporti di pace e di guerra dell'Egitto romano con le popolazioni dei deserti africani* (Univ. di Genova, Fondazione Nobile Agostino Poggi 12; Milan: A. Giuffre, 1976). Another classicist, Frank Snowden, presents a more monolithic picture of Egypt's relationship with the Blemmyes. His intent is to demonstrate that the Blemmyes presented a persistent military threat to Roman Egypt. Snowden relies heavily on the primary sources in his reconstruction of the military presence of Blacks in antiquity during the Roman period. See Snowden, *Blacks in Antiquity*, 130–43.

54 For a general description of the Blemmyes, see Adams, *Nubia*, 56–60; and "Beja Tribes," in *The Coptic Encyclopedia* (8 vols.; ed. Aziz S. Atiya; New York: Macmillan, 1991), 1:373–74.

55 Pliny, *Naturalis historia* 6.35.182. See English translation in Pliny, *Natural History* (10 vols.; trans. H. Rackham; LCL; Cambridge, Mass.: Harvard University Press, 1979), 2:475.

56 Evagrius, *Historia ecclesiastica* 1.7.259–60; Cf. Snowden, *Blacks in Antiquity*, 138.

57 Snowden, *Blacks in Antiquity*, 139.

58 Given the paucity of primary evidence during the fourth and fifth centuries related to the Blemmyes, *pace* Snowden, it is difficult to determine whether the presence of the Blemmyes was persistent or episodic.

59 See *Scholia in Theocritum Vetera* 7.114a (ed. Carl Wendel; Leipzig: Teubneri, 1967 [1914]). This text describes Blemmyes as a black-skinned Ethiopian nation (*ethnos Aithiopikona melanochroun*).

60 Palladius, *Historia Lausiaca* 32. For Greek text see Butler, *Lausiac History*, 2:95.

61 Palladius, *Dialogus* 20. See *The Dialogue of Palladius* (trans. Herbert Moore; New York: Macmillan, 1921), 174–75.

62 Rufinus, *Historia monachorum in Aegypto* 1.2 *Historia monachorum in Aegypto: édition critique du texte grec et traduction annotée* (ed. André-Jean Festugière; Brussels: Société des Bollandistes, 1971), 9–10.

63 For an excellent assessment of the different regions around the Nile, especially Syene, see Josef Locher, *Topographie und Geschichte der Region am Ersten Nilkatarakt in Griechisch-Romischer Zeit* (APF 5; Stuttgart: B.G. Teubner, 1999), 58–89.

64 Peter Brown, *The Body and Society: Men, Women, and Sexual Renunciation in Early Christianity* (New York: Columbia University Press, 1988), 242.

65 Mayerson, "Anti-Black Sentiment," 304–11.

66 Geoffrey Galt Harpham, "The Signs of Temptation," in *The Ascetic Imperative in Culture and Criticism* (Chicago: University of Chicago Press, 1987), 45–66.

67 Athanasius composed this hagiography during his third exile (355–62 CE). *Athanasius: The Life of Anthony and the Letter to Marcellinus* (trans. Robert Gregg; New York: Paulist Press, 1980), xi.

68 Averil Cameron, *The Mediterranean World in Late Antiquity AD 395–600* (London: Routledge, 1993), 72.

69 Athanasius, *Vita Antonii*, Prologue 13: "I feel that you also, once you have heard the story, will not merely admire the man but will wish to emulate his resolution as well. For monks, the life of Antony is an ideal pattern of the ascetical life." On the difference between biography and hagiography in ascetic literature, see Patricia Cox, *Biography in Late Antiquity: A Quest for the Holy Man* (Berkeley: University of California Press, 1983).

70 Johann List suggests that this work conforms to the prescription of a Greco-Roman *encomium*, which relates the nationality, education, training, and deeds of a celebrated personage who has died. See Johann List, *Das Antoniusleben des hl.*

Athanasius des Grossen: eine literarhistorische Studie zu den Anfängen der byzantinischen Hagiographie (Athens: P.D. Sakellarios, 1931).

71 Athanasius, *Vita Antonii*, 69.

72 Athanasius does not refer to Ethiopians in the *Vita Antonii*. In chapter 6 he uses *melas* to describe the ethnic identity of the boy.

73 Athanasius, *Vita Antonii*, 1.

74 The use of *genos* combined with a nation of people was a common way to express ethnic identity in antiquity. For a useful discussion on the possible ethnic and geographic meanings of *Ioudaios to genos* in the writings of Josephus, see Shaye J.D. Cohen, "Ἰουδαῖος το γένος and Related Expressions in *Josephus*," in *Josephus and the History of the Greco-Roman Period: Essays in Memory of Morton Smith* (ed. F. Parente and J. Sievers; Leiden: E.J. Brill, 1994), 23–38. See also, Obery M. Hendricks, "A Discourse of Domination: A Socio-Rhetorical Study of the Use of *Ioudaios* in the Fourth Gospel" (Ph.D. diss., Princeton University, 1995).

75 N.B. *drakōn* may be translated as a dragon or serpent. See G.W.H. Lampe, *A Patristic Greek Lexicon* (Oxford: Clarendon, 1961), 386.

76 Ps 111:10; Mark 9:17.

77 Robert Meyer's translation (cited below in note 81) is as follows: "he changed his person, so to speak. As he is in his heart, precisely so did he appear to him – as a black boy."

78 Meyer's translation says, "I am a lover of fornication."

79 Hos 4:12.

80 Ps 117:7.

81 Athanasius, *Vita Antonii* 6 (PG 26.835–976). Translation mine. For other English translations, see Gregg, *Athanasius*; and *St. Athanasius: The Life of Saint Antony* (trans. Robert T. Meyer; New York: Newman, 1978). For an English translation of the Syriac version, see *The Life of Antony* in *The Paradise of the Holy Fathers* (2 vols.; trans. E.A. Wallis Budge; London: Chatto & Windus, 1907), 1:3–76. The Syriac version depicts the "enemy" as an "Indian boy" who is "black in thy nature." See Budge, *Life of Antony*, 11.

82 P. Basilius Steidle, "Der 'schwarze kleine Knabe' in der alten Mönchserzählung," *Benediktinische Monatschrift* 34 (1958): 339–50.

83 Courtès, "'Ethiopians' in Patristic Literature," 19.

84 Brakke, *Athanasius*, 229.

85 Brakke, *Athanasius*, 229.

86 For discussions on pederasty in the ancient world, see Martti Nissinen, *Homoeroticism in the Biblical World: A Historical Perspective* (Minneapolis: Fortress, 1998); Robin Scroggs, *The New Testament and Homosexuality: Contextual Background for Contemporary Debate* (Philadelphia: Fortress, 1983); John Boswell, *Christianity, Social Tolerance, and Homosexuality: Gay People in Western Europe from the Beginning of the Christian Era to the Fourteenth Century* (Chicago: University of Chicago Press, 1980); and Michel Foucault, *The History of Sexuality: An Introduction* (3 vols; trans. Robert Hurley; New York: Vintage, 1978–86), 3.189–232.

87 Brakke, *Athanasius*, 230.

88 For a more recent interpretation of this text by Brakke, which identifies the erotic power of the black boy, see Brakke, "Ethiopian Demons."

89 Athanasius, *Vita Antonii* 7.1.

90 See Richard Valantasis, "Demons and the Perfecting of the Monk's Body: Monastic Anthropology, Daemonology, and Asceticism," *Semeia* 58 (1992): 47–79. See also Henry A. Kelly, "The Devil in the Desert," *CBQ* 26, no. 2 (1964): 190–220.

91 Pseudo-Athanasius, *Life and Activity of Syncletica* 28 (PG 28, cols. 1487–1558). English translation by Elizabeth A. Castelli, "Pseudo-Athanasius: The Life and

Activity of the Holy and Blessed Teacher Syncletica," in *Ascetic Behavior in Greco-Roman Antiquity*, 265–311, esp. 279.

92 See, for example, the many sayings under the rubric of fornication in the anonymous series of *Sayings of the Desert Fathers* in Benedicta Ward, trans. *The Wisdom of the Desert Fathers: Apophthegmata Patrum – The Anonymous Series* (Fairacres, Oxford: SLG, 1975), 7–21.

93 Athanasius did not simply use *ho melas* in this text. He added to this ethnic marker *pais* to further emphasize power relationships within Greco-Roman culture.

94 This same formula is found in non-Christian Greco-Roman sources, as well as other Christian texts.

95 Athanasius, *Vita Antonii* 7 (PG 26.852).

96 Burton-Christie describes *rhēma* as follows: "The word *rhēma* corresponds to the Hebrew *dabar* and has a similar connotation of a deed or an 'event' which is announced by a word. It expresses both the close relation between life and action which characterized these words as well as the weight and authority they possessed. Furthermore, it was commonly understood in the desert that one did not speak these words apart from an inspiration from God, nor did one convey such a word to a listener unless that person showed a willingness to put the word into action." Burton-Christie, *Word in the Desert*, 77–78.

97 Burton-Christie, *Word in the Desert*, 77. Burton-Christie admits that other geographical locations are represented in the *Sayings*; but following the scholarship of Chitty, *Desert a City*, he concludes that Scetis is the geographical center of the *Sayings*.

98 This story has not been published in the original languages. See French version in *Les sentences des pères du désert: série des anonymes* (ed. L. Regnault; Sarthe: Solesmes, 1985), 141. Regnault's translation is based on *Apophthegmata patrum* published by Nau in *Revue de l'orient chrétien* 18, 1913. For an English translation of the Syriac version, see Palladius, "On Fornication," 579, in *The Wit and Wisdom of the Christian Fathers of Egypt* (trans. E.A. Wallis Budge; London: Oxford University Press, 1934), 170–71. The same English translation is also in Palladius, *The Sayings of the Holy Fathers*, "Of Fornication," 579, in *The Paradise or Garden of the Holy Fathers* (2 vols.; trans. E.A. Wallis Budge; London: Chatto & Windus, 1907), 2:130. Budge has translated the Syriac version of the *Sayings of the Fathers* by the sixth/seventh-century monk Ânân-Îshô. For a detailed discussion of the Syriac versions of Palladius's works, see Butler, *Lausiac History*, 77–96. My English translation is based upon the French and English versions mentioned above.

99 This *Saying* is cited in Mayerson, "Anti-Black Sentiment," 308–309; Frost, "Attitudes toward Blacks," 8.

100 PL 73, cols. 874–75. English translation in Helen Waddell, *The Desert Fathers* (New York: H. Holt, 1936), 103–105 (modified slightly); this text is also cited in Mayerson, "Anti-Black Sentiment," 309. For Greek text, see *Les apophtegmes des pères: collection systématique* (SC 387; ed. Jean-Claude Guy; Paris: Cerf, 1993).

101 PL 73, cols. 874–75. English translation in Waddell, *Desert Fathers*, 103–105 (modified slightly).

102 Snowden, *Blacks in Antiquity*, 121–43.

103 Cf. Palladius, *Historia Lausiaca* 32; Palladius, *Dialogus* 20.

104 See A.H. Zayed, "Egypt's Relations with the Rest of Africa," in *Ancient Civilizations of Africa* (ed. G. Mokhtar; Berkeley: University of California Press, 1981), 2:136–52. He argues that Egyptians in antiquity were conscious of their difference from darker Africans based on skin color. See also Martin Bernal, *Black Athena: The Afroasiatic Roots of Classical Civilization* (2 vols.; New Brunswick, N.J.: Rutgers University Press, 1987), 1:15.

105 See "Excursus" above on the Blemmyes.

106 Gillian Clark, "Women and Asceticism in Late Antiquity: The Refusal of Status and Gender," in *Asceticism* (ed. Vincent L. Wimbush and Richard Valantasis; New York: Oxford University Press, 1995), 33–48.

107 Clark, "Women and Asceticism," 37. N.B. Clark also discusses how the presence of men was distracting for the women ascetics as well.

108 Norman Russell, *The Lives of the Desert Fathers* (Oxford: Mowbray, 1980), 36.

109 *Apophthegmata patrum*, Sisoes 3: PG 65.392D.

110 Clark, "Women and Asceticism," 38; Collationes Patrum (CSEL 13).

111 Clark, "Women and Asceticism," 37.

112 Brown, *Body and Society*, 243.

113 Brown, *Body and Society*, 242.

114 Brown, *Body and Society*, 243.

115 Brown, *Body and Society*, 244.

116 Brown, *Body and Society*, 247. According to Brown, "only cautionary tales of nightmarish sexual encounters were considered effective in blocking the way that led back, with such ease, from the desert into what were perfectly legitimate forms of Christian devotion in the settled land."

117 Both Courtès and Frost translate this couplet as follows: "do not let the body of a black girl soil yours, nor lie with her for her Hell-black face." The Latin term *Tartareus* simply means "of or belonging to the underworld." The translations of Frost and Courtès reflect their ideological assumptions related to ethnic and color difference.

118 Or "water of Baptism."

119 Translation mine. I want to thank classicist Reinaldo Pérez (University of Michigan-Dearborn) and medievalist Charles Terbile (University of Toledo) for the generous assistance they gave me in translating this text. Their suggestions about other Latin sources and possible translations of this text helped clarify my understanding of the black (literally, "blackening") girl.

120 N.B. The Virgin Mary is referred to as the *Immaculata* (i.e., one without sin).

121 Elizabeth A. Clark, "Ideology, History, and the Construction of 'Woman' in Late Ancient Christianity," *JECS* 2 (1994): 155–84.

122 Frost, "Attitudes toward Blacks," 7. Cf. Noliwe M. Rooks, *Hair Raising: Beauty, Culture, and African American Women* (New Brunswick, N.J.: Rutgers University Press, 1996). Rooks analyzes aesthetic values reflected in nineteenth- and twentieth-century advertisements and other discourses about the hair and beauty of African American women.

123 Frost, "Attitudes toward Blacks," 7. For a recent study that explores similar aesthetic views in medieval western thought, see Jacqueline de Weever, *Sheba's Daughters: Whitening and Demonizing the Saracen Woman in Medieval French Literature* (New York: Garland, 1998).

124 Anonymous, *Apophthegmata patrum* 1596, 10 in Regnault, *Pères du désert*, 241.

125 Greek text in R. Draguet, "Un Paralipomenon Pachômien Inconnu dans le Karakallou 251," *Mélanges Eugène Tisserant* 2 (1964): 55–61, esp. 59. English translation in *Pachomian Koinonia*, 2.117.

126 Rufinus, *Historia monachorum in Aegypto* 1 (PL 21.387).

127 Ward, *Wisdom of the Desert Fathers*, 18.

128 PL 73, col. 879. Translation mine. For another English translation, see Ward, *Wisdom of the Desert Fathers*, 10.

129 Classen, "The Aromas of Antiquity," chap. 1 of Classen et al., *Aroma*, 13–50.

130 Martial, *Epigrams* 6.93.

131 Classen et al., *Aroma*, 36–37. Classen et al. claim that the foul smell accorded to prostitutes was indicative both of the filthiness of the conditions in which they worked, and of their very low social status.

132 Martial, *Epigrams* 3.93.

133 Juvenal, *Satires* 6 (and 11).

134 Classen et al., *Aroma*, 38.

135 Harvey, "Olfactory Knowing."

136 John Climacus, *The Ladder of Divine Ascent*, Step 15 (PG 88, cols. 632–1208). English translation in John Climacus, *The Ladder of Divine Ascent* (trans. Lazarus Moore; Boston: Holy Transfiguration Monastery, 1978), 109.

137 Ward, *Wisdom of the Desert Fathers*, 8.

138 Ward, *Wisdom of the Desert Fathers*, 10.

139 Classen et al., *Aroma*, 169.

140 See Young, *Justice and the Politics of Difference*, 123.

141 Palladius, *Historia Lausiaca* 23.4–5 (PL 74.347).

142 Some scholars doubt the historicity of these two works. For a brief discussion on this point, see Butler, *Lausiac History*, 1–6.

143 Courtès, "'Ethiopians' in Patristic Literature," 22. He incorrectly labels this text 2 instead of 23, see Courtès, 211, n. 90. N.B. The original text does not describe the woman as "pretty."

144 Frost, "Attitudes toward Blacks," 8.

145 Ps 103:20. Translator's emphasis.

146 Butler, *Lausiac History*, 2.76. English translation in *Palladius: The Lausiac History* (trans. Robert T. Meyer; Ancient Christian Writers 34; New York: Newman, 1965), 82 (modified slightly).

147 Butler, *Lausiac History*, 2.76–77.

148 Palladius, *Historia Lausiaca*; Prooem.; and *Ad Laus.* in Butler, *Lausiac History* 2.3–7.

149 See Robert T. Meyer, "Palladius as Biographer and Autobiographer," StPatr 17, pt. 1. (ed. Elizabeth A. Livingstone; Oxford: Pergamon, 1982), 66–71.

150 Scott, "Gender," 169–70.

151 Anne Carson, "Putting Her in Her Place: Women, Dirt, and Desire," in *Before Sexuality: The Construction of Erotic Experience in the Ancient Greek World* (ed. David M. Halperin, John J. Winkler, and Froma I. Zeitlin; Princeton: Princeton University Press, 1990), 135–70.

152 Godelier, "Origins of Male Domination," 17.

153 Brown, *Body and Society*, 19.

154 Epiphanius, *The Panarion of Epiphanius of Salamis* (2 vols.; Nag Hammadi Studies 35 and 36; trans. Frank Williams; Leiden: E.J. Brill, 1987–94), 2:64.2.

5 "BEYOND THE RIVERS OF ETHIOPIA": ETHNO-POLITICAL RHETORICS DEFINING INSIDERS AND OUTSIDERS

1 Melania's name is derived from *melas*. See Hans-Veit Beyer, *Prosopographisches Lexikon der Palaiologenzeit* 7 (Vienna: Verlag der Österreichischen Akademie der Wissenschaften, 1985).

2 See Wimbush, "Ascetic Behavior and Color-ful Language," 81–92. Wimbush argues that the color symbolization associated with Ethiopian Moses is overworked by the monastic fathers; the ascetic life is advanced at the expense of Moses.

3 Ethiopians/Ethiopia and Blacks/blackness are used throughout Christian writings to demonize groups considered heretical. See Jeffrey Burton Russell, "Satan and

NOTES

Heresy," chap. 5 in *The Prince of Darkness: Radical Evil and the Power of Good in History* (Ithaca: Cornell University Press, 1988), 56–81; Pagels, "The Enemy Within: Demonizing the Heretics," chap. 6 in *Origin of Satan*, 149–78.

4 Jerome, *Commentary on Isaiah* 7.18.1–3. Cf. Zeph 3:10 "From beyond the rivers of Ethiopia my suppliants, even the daughter of my dispersed, shall bring mine offering." For an example of how this theme is used in modern studies about the Bible, see Mensa Otabil, *Beyond the Rivers of Ethiopia: A Biblical Revelation of God's Purpose for the Black Race* (Accra, Ghana: Altar International, 1992).

5 Ambrose, *Expositio Psalmi* 118.

6 Jerome, *Letter to Mark* 2 in *The Letters of St. Jerome* (Ancient Christian Writers 33; trans. C.C. Mierow; New York: Newman, 1963), 76–77.

7 Women were also used as symbols of heresy within ancient Christian writings. For examples, see two essays by Virginia Burrus, "The Heretical Woman as Symbol in Alexander, Athanasius, Epiphanius, and Jerome," *HTR* 84 (1991): 229–48; and "Word and Flesh," 27–51.

8 For a discussion about the violence among rival groups of Christians during the fifth century, see Cameron, "Conflicts between Christians: Church Councils," in *Mediterranean World*, 64–67.

9 Walter Bauer, *Rechtgläubigkeit und Ketzerei im ältesten Christentum* (BHT 10; Tübingen: J.C.B. Mohr/P. Siebeck, 1964 [1934]). English translation, *Orthodoxy and Heresy in Earliest Christianity* (ed. and trans. Robert A. Kraft, Gerhard Krodel, et al., Philadelphia: Fortress, 1971). The terms "orthodoxy" and "heresy" are intrinsically polemical. In this chapter the term "orthodoxy" is used for those theological positions that came to be incorporated into the developing Catholic Church; "heresy" is used for those theological positions that were excluded from the developing Catholic Church. See discussion on the challenges of terminology in Thomas Robinson, *The Bauer Thesis Examined: The Geography of Heresy in the Early Christian Church* (Lewiston: Edwin Mellen, 1988), 30–32.

10 Bauer, *Orthodoxy and Heresy*, 229.

11 Robinson, *Bauer Thesis Examined*, 28.

12 Tertullian, *Against Marcion* 4.7; 5.19. See text in *Against Marcion* (The Ante-Nicene Fathers; Grand Rapids: Eerdmans, 1978).

13 New Testament scholars such as Rudolf Bultmann agreed with Bauer's conclusions. He says, "Bauer has shown that the doctrine which in the end won out in the ancient church as the 'right' or 'orthodox' doctrine stands at the end of a development or, rather, is the result of a conflict among various shades of doctrine, and the heresy was not, as the ecclesiastical tradition holds, an apostasy, a degeneration, but was already present at the beginning – or, rather that by the triumph of a certain teaching as the 'right doctrine' divergent teachings were condemned as heresy." See Rudolf Bultmann, *Theology of the New Testament* (2 vols.; trans. K. Grobel; New York: Charles Scribner's Sons, 1955), 2:137. Cf. H. von Campenhausen, *Formation of the Christian Bible* (Philadelphia: Fortress, 1972).

14 Helmut Koester also identified the diversity of ancient Christianity. See Helmut Koester, "GNOMAI DIAPHOROI: The Origin and Nature of Diversification in the History of Early Christianity," *HTR* 58 (1965): 279–318.

15 Elizabeth A. Clark, *The Life of Melania the Younger: Introduction, Translation, and Commentary* (Studies in Women and Religion 14; New York: Edwin Mellen, 1984).

16 See Clark's summary of the debate in *Life of Melania*, 4–13. Clark sides with the Greek priority argument (10–13). Commentators generally agree that neither the Greek nor the Latin was the original, and that both derive from an "Ur-text" now lost (5). For the Greek text, see *Vie de Sainte Mélanie* (SC 90; ed. Denys Gorce; Paris: Cerf, 1962), 232–35. For the Latin text, see *Santa Melania Giuniore, senatrice*

168

romana: documenti contemporei e note (ed. Mariano del Tindaro Rampolla; Rome: Tipografia Vaticana, 1905), 30–31.

17 *Vita Melaniae Junioris* 54. Greek text in *Vie de Sainte Mélanie* 232, 234; English translation in Clark, *Life of Melania*, 66–67.

18 For a brief description of Nestorianism, see C. FitzSimons Allison, *The Cruelty of Heresy: An Affirmation of Christian Orthodoxy* (Harrisburg, Pa.: Morehouse, 1994), 119–37.

19 Clark, *Life of Melania*, 141.

20 Clark, *Life of Melania*, 141–45. Clark reviews primary evidence to support that Melania was linked to Origenism, Pelagianism, and Donatism.

21 Clark, *Life of Melania*, 141. Clark claims that many of the *Vitae* from the fourth and fifth centuries were manipulated by their authors to adhere to certain doctrinal teachings.

22 *Santa Melania Giuniore* 30–31. I want to express my deep appreciation to Professor Elizabeth A. Clark for sending me a copy of the Latin text.

23 Clark, *Life of Melania*, 24.

24 See Henry Chadwick, *Heresy and Orthodoxy in the Early Church* (Brookfield, Vt.: Gower, 1991); and David Christie-Murray, *A History of Heresy* (2nd ed.; Oxford: Oxford University Press, 1990).

25 Snowden, *Blacks in Antiquity*, 196.

26 Snowden claims, "the Ethiopian's blackness and other physical characteristics conspicuously called him to the attention of a predominantly white society." See Snowden, *Blacks in Antiquity*, 196.

27 Martin, "Chamberlain's Journey," 105–35.

28 For historical readings of the text, see Martin Dibelius, *Studies in the Acts of the Apostles* (ed. Heinrich Greeven; London: SCM Press, 1956); and Ernst Haenchen, *Acts of the Apostles: A Commentary* (Philadelphia: Westminster, 1971). For a literary reading of this text, see Smith, "'Do You Understand?'" 48–70; for a social-scientific analysis of the text, see Spencer, "Ethiopian Eunuch," 155–65; for a discussion on the political significance of the eunuch, see Keith Hopkins, "The Political Power of Eunuchs," in *Conquerors and Slaves* (Sociological Studies in Roman History 1; Cambridge: Cambridge University Press, 1978), 172–96; For an examination of racial motifs in the text, see Felder, "Racial Motifs in the Biblical Narratives," chap. 3 in *Troubling Biblical Waters*, 37–48 (esp. 46–48); for economic considerations of the Ethiopian eunuch story, see Dieter Georgi, "The Resurrection and the South," Lecture 12 of a course entitled "Cash and Creed in Early Christianity," at Union Theological Seminary, spring 1997, where Dieter Georgi was Visiting Professor. I want to thank Professor Georgi for sharing his lecture notes with me and for offering many helpful suggestions for conceptualizing my findings in this section.

29 See, for example, William Frank Lawrence, Jr., "The History of the Interpretation of Acts 8:26–40 by the Church Fathers Prior to the Fall of Rome" (Ph.D. diss., Union Theological Seminary, 1984); Martin, "Function of Acts 8:26–40"; Carson, "'Do You Understand?'"

30 Haenchen, *Acts of the Apostles*, 309–15.

31 Snowden, *Blacks in Antiquity*, 205.

32 Snowden, *Blacks in Antiquity*, 206.

33 Gier, "The Color of Sin/The Color of Skin," 42–52, esp. 43. Cf. Col 3:11.

34 Hood, *Begrimed and Black*, 63.

35 Felder, "Racial Motifs," 37–48; Martin, "Chamberlain's Journey," 105–35.

36 Felder, "Racial Motifs," 46–48. Felder defines "secularization" as a process of diluting a rich religious concept under the weighty influence of secular (i.e., social and political) pressures. This broad, anachronistic category of "secularization" is

not adequately defined by Felder. He admits that "secularization in the New Testament needs much fuller exploration in terms of its racial dimensions" (48). See also William R. Herzog, II, "The New Testament and the Question of Racial Injustice," *ABQ* 5 (1989): 12–32.

37 Felder, "Racial Motifs," 46.
38 Felder, "Racial Motifs," 48.
39 Felder, "Racial Motifs," 46.
40 Felder, "Racial Motifs," 47.
41 Felder, "Racial Motifs," 47. Felder apparently concludes that the Holy Spirit is not involved in the Ethiopian's baptism. Martin highlights the action of the Holy Spirit throughout Acts 8:26–40. See Martin, "Chamberlain's Journey," 106–107, esp. n. 2.
42 See, for example, Haenchen, *Acts of the Apostles*, 309–17; F.F. Bruce, *The Acts of the Apostles: The Greek Text with Introduction and Commentary* (Grand Rapids: Eerdmans, 1984), 198; and I. Howard Marshall, *The Acts of the Apostles* (Grand Rapids: Eerdmans, 1983), 160–66.
43 Martin, "Chamberlain's Journey," 110. Martin analyzes the impact of a "politics of omission" in biblical scholarship that results in an ongoing lack of familiarity with Ethiopians both in antiquity and in contemporary culture.
44 These three approaches include (1) uncertainty, (2) cursory discussion of Nubia, and (3) ethnographic identity. See Martin, "Chamberlain's Journey," 110–11. She is particularly concerned with approaches that ignore the eunuch's ethnic origins such as that suggested by Nils Dahl: "What made his [the Ethiopian eunuch's] conversion to be remembered and told as a legend was neither his African provenance nor his black skin. (It is quite possible that he was black, but that is never said . . .). In the Lucan composition his story has been placed between the evangelization among the Samaritans and the vocation of Paul, preparing for the mission to the Gentiles. Thus we get a picture of a progressive widening of the circle reached by the gospel; *but the question of nationality has no special importance* [emphasis mine]." See Nils A. Dahl, "Nations in the New Testament," in *New Testament Christianity for Africa and the World: Essays in Honor of Harry Sawyer* (ed. Mark E. Glaswell and Edward Fasholé-Luke; London: SPCK, 1974), 54–68, esp. 62–63; cited in Martin, "Chamberlain's Journey," 110.
45 Martin, "Chamberlain's Journey," 114.
46 Martin, "Chamberlain's Journey," 111–14.
47 Martin, "Chamberlain's Journey," 116. Martin agrees with the conclusions of Snowden (198) and uses Augustine and Athanasius to support her argument. Cf. Courtès, "'Ethiopians' in Patristic Literature," 22, nn. 82–84.
48 Martin, "Chamberlain's Journey," 117.
49 Martin, "Chamberlain's Journey," 118.
50 Martin, "Chamberlain's Journey," 118–20. Cf. Homer, *Iliad* 23.205–207; Herodotus 3.114–15; Strabo, *Geography* 1.2.27.
51 For a study that explores the cultural and ideological significance of the eunuch, see Carson, "'Do You Understand?'"
52 Acts 2:5.
53 Acts 2:10. For an excellent historical study about Jews in Egypt, see Modrzejewski, *Jews of Egypt*.
54 Acts 2:9–11.
55 Acts 2:37b.
56 Acts 2:38–39.
57 This reference to the "far away" could also indicate Luke's awareness of biblical language from Isaiah. For example, Isa 57:19 mentions the far and the near, or

those in Judah and those still in exile: "Peace, peace, to the far and the near, says the LORD; and I will heal them."

58 Cf. Herodotus, 7.69.2, 4; Homer, *Odyssey* 24.351.

59 See Bruce W. Winter and Andrew D. Clarke (eds.), *The Book of Acts in its Ancient Literary Setting* (Grand Rapids: Eerdmans, 1993).

60 Acts 1:8c.

61 The queens of Ethiopia bore the title *Kandakē* or "Candace." Cf. Pliny, *Naturalis historia* 6.35.186.

62 Cassius Dio, 54.5.4; Strabo, *Geography* 17.1.54; Pliny, *Naturalis historia* 6.35. 181–82.

63 Seneca, *Naturales Quaestiones* 6.8.3; Tacitus, *Annales* 15; Cassius Dio 68.8.1.

64 Edward Ullendorff, "Candace (Acts VIII.27) and the Queen of Sheba," *NTS* 2 (1955–56): 53–56, esp. 53. See also by Ullendorff, *The Ethiopians: An Introduction to the Country and People* (Oxford: Oxford University Press, 1973).

65 Beverly Gaventa argues that the Ethiopian eunuch is a *symbolic* convert. By this she means, "he does not establish a pattern that later conversions must follow. Instead as one who comes from the limits of Luke's geographical world (an Ethiopian) and beyond Luke's religious community (a eunuch), he symbolizes all those whose inclusion has been announced in Acts 1:8." See Beverly R. Gaventa, *From Darkness to Light: Aspects of Conversion in the New Testament* (Philadelphia: Fortress, 1986), 106. I also view the Ethiopian eunuch as a symbolic convert for the reasons noted by Gaventa, as well as the political factors that were prevalent in Luke's world.

66 The term *eunouchos* occurs in vv. 34, 36, 38, and 39.

67 For a brief summary of eunuchs in the ancient Mediterranean world, see Spencer, "Ethiopian Eunuch," 156–57. Spencer provides several primary sources to support his argument that there were antagonistic attitudes against eunuchs in the ancient world. For a more detailed treatment of the subject, see Long, *Claudian's In Eutropium*; Carson, "'Do You Understand?'"; and Mathew Kuefler, *The Manly Eunuch: Masculinity, Gender Ambiguity, and Christian Ideology in Late Antiquity* (Chicago: University of Chicago Press, 2001).

68 Lucian, *The Eunuch* (vol. 5; trans. A.M. Harmon; LCL; Cambridge, Mass.: Harvard University Press, 1972).

69 Lucian, *Eunuch* 6–11.

70 Deut 23:1.

71 Lev 21:20; cf. 22:24.

72 Josephus, *Ant.* 4.290–91.

73 Philo, *Special Laws* 1.324–25.

74 A contrary view is represented in Isa 56:1–7. "Do not let the foreigner joined to the LORD say, 'The Lord will surely separate me from his people'; and do not let the eunuch say, 'I am just a dry tree.' For thus says the LORD: To the eunuchs who keep my sabbaths, who choose the things that please me and hold fast my covenant, I will give, in my house and within my walls, a monument and a name better than sons and daughters; I will give them an everlasting name that shall not be cut off" (vv. 3–5). It is possible that Luke's account of the Ethiopian eunuch in Acts 8:26–40 is an intentional allusion to the Isaiah text, thus a "fulfillment of prophecy" story.

75 The Ethiopian eunuch is used by Luke as an ethnic trope for the purpose of idealizing the Christian message. One of the chief aspects of this message is the universal appeal it has for all ethnic groups (cf. Gal 3:28; Col 3:11).

76 Acts 8:26–27a.

77 Gen 18:1; 43:16; Deut 28:29; 1 Kgs 18:26–27; Jer 6:4. Cf. Acts 22:6 and 26:13.

78 Acts 8:27b–28.

79 Cf. Acts 10:1. Bauer, BAGD, 66.
80 Cf. Acts 1:11 (*andres Galilaioi*); 1:16 (*andres adelphoi*); 2:5 (*Ioudaioi, andres eulabeis*); 17:22 (*andres Athēnaioi*).
81 Cf. Acts 6:3, 5.
82 Isa 53:7–8. Emphasis provided in the original text.
83 See Burton-Christie, *Word in the Desert*, 146–50, 236–60.
84 For an important resource dealing with the topic, see *Asceticism and the New Testament* (ed. Leif Vaage and Vincent L. Wimbush; New York: Routledge, 1999). None of the essays in this volume examine the Ethiopian eunuch story.
85 Acts 10:34–35.
86 Spencer, "Ethiopian Eunuch," 157.
87 Ethiopian Moses is not to be confused with Abba Moses, whom Cassian claimed to have met during his travels in the desert (Cassian, *Inst.* 10.25).
88 Sozomen, *Historia ecclesiastica* 6.29. Little is known of the origins of Ethiopian Moses. Kathleen O'Brien Wicker suggests that he may have come from one of the Nilotic cattle-raising and raiding tribes, who were characteristically tall and dark. See Wicker, "Ethiopian Moses," 331. See also E.E. Evans-Pritchard, *The Nuer: A Description of the Modes of Livelihood and Political Institutions of the Nilotic People* (Oxford: Clarendon, 1940).
89 Sozomen, *Historia ecclesiastica* 6.29.
90 *Apophthegmata patrum* 8 (PG 65.285).
91 Palladius, *Historia Lausiaca* 19, Greek text in Butler, *Lausiac History* 2.58–62; Sozomen, *Historia ecclesiastica* 6.29, Greek text in *Sozomenus Kirchengeschichte* (GCS 50; ed. Joseph Bidez and Günther Christian Hansen; Berlin: Akademie, 1960), 280–82; *Apophthegmata patrum* (PG 65.281–89); "Vita S. Moyse Aethiopie," in *Acta Sanct.* (Augusti Tomus Sextus; ed. Joannes Bollandus et al.; Paris: Victor Palme, 1868): 199–212. For English translations of these texts, see Wicker, "Ethiopian Moses," 329–48.
92 Wicker, "Ethiopian Moses," 334.
93 Wimbush, "Ascetic Behavior and Color-ful Language," 88. See also Wicker, "Ethiopian Moses," 334.
94 Mayerson, "Anti-Black Sentiment," 305.
95 Mayerson, "Anti-Black Sentiment," 306–307. Lloyd Thompson renders this view "unacceptable." See Thompson, *Romans and Blacks*, 139, esp. n. 200.
96 Cracco Ruggini, "Il negro buono e il negro malvagio," 115–17; Cracco Ruggini agrees with the findings of Snowden, *Blacks in Antiquity*, 209–11.
97 Gier, "The Color of Sin/The Color of Skin," 42.
98 Gier, "The Color of Sin/The Color of Skin," 45.
99 Gier, "The Color of Sin/The Color of Skin," 42.
100 Gier, "The Color of Sin/The Color of Skin," 42.
101 Gier, "The Color of Sin/The Color of Skin," 42.
102 See, for example, his discussion of the *Epistle of Barnabas*: "As early as the Epistle of Barnabas, the Christian devil appears as a black Ethiopian, and later Christian art portrays those who crucify Christ as black – for example, one painting shows the impenitent thief as black and the penitent one as white. But, with few exceptions, *demons and evil people in Christian art do not have Negroid features. Instead, they are white people or monsters painted the color of evil* [emphasis mine]." Gier, "The Color of Sin/The Color of Skin," 45.
103 Gier, "The Color of Sin/The Color of Skin," 45.
104 Thompson, *Romans and Blacks*, 42.
105 Thompson, *Romans and Blacks*, 41–43, 139.
106 Hood, *Begrimed and Black*, 87–89. Hood claims that "the abuse of Moses because of his color could indicate (1) [that a] caste system [may have existed] within the

Egyptian Christian community, (2) the Egyptian monks may have internalized the Christian belief that blackness and black skin represented a stain and symbol of evil and carnality, (3) the Egyptian monks may have been exhibiting cultural ethnocentric behavior, (4) prior to Moses' conversion, the tradition linked his blackness to negative behavior and to carnal lust."

107 Wimbush, "Ascetic Behavior and Color-ful Language," 86. See Snowden, *Blacks in Antiquity*, 201, 209–11, esp. 211. Snowden cites an anonymous Byzantine text to summarize early Christian attitudes toward the Ethiopian. See Vita S. Moysis, *Aethiopis in Menologium fasc.* 2 (V. Latyshev), 330–34. See also Snowden, *Before Color Prejudice*, 106.

108 Wimbush, "Ascetic Behavior and Color-ful Language," 89.

109 Wimbush, "Ascetic Behavior and Color-ful Language," 83. See also by Wimbush, "'. . . Not of This World . . .': Early Christianities as Rhetorical and Social Formation," in *Reimagining Christian Origins: A Colloquium Honoring Burton L. Mack* (ed. Elizabeth A. Castelli and Hal Taussig; Valley Forge, Pa.: Trinity Press International, 1996), 23–36.

110 The Syriac version says, "because certain people wished to see Abba Moses, they treated him with contempt." The Greek text does not mention "certain people." See Mayerson, "Anti-Black Sentiment," 305.

111 PG 65.284. English translation in Wicker, "Ethiopian Moses," 339 (modified slightly).

112 According to Mayerson, Moses had demonstrated spiritual excellence in maintaining silence and in not showing his inner anger. Mayerson, "Anti-Black Sentiment," 306–307.

113 Burton-Christie, *Word in the Desert*, 147–48.

114 PG 65.284. English translation in Wicker, "Ethiopian Moses," 340.

115 Thompson, *Romans and Blacks*, 139. Cf. Philip Mason, *Patterns of Dominance* (London: Oxford University Press, 1970), 1, 11–12.

116 Thompson, *Romans and Blacks*, 139. Thompson strongly disagrees with the conclusions of Mayerson, "Anti-Black Sentiment," 307; Courtès, "'Ethiopians' in Patristic Literature," 20; and Jean Devisse, "Christians and Blacks," in *The Image of the Black in Western Art*, vol. 2.1. From the Early Christian Era to the "Age of Discovery" (gen. ed. Jean Devisse; New York: W. Morrow, 1979), 37–80, esp. 50–51.

117 PG 65.285. English translation in Wicker, "Ethiopian Moses," 341.

118 PG 65.285. Wicker, "Ethiopian Moses," 341.

119 Palladius, *Historia Lausiaca* 32. For Greek text see Butler, *Lausiac History*, 2:95.

120 Rufinus, *Historia monachorum in Aegypto* 7 (PL 21.415).

121 For a detailed treatment of the language of conversion in the New Testament, see Gaventa, *From Darkness to Light*.

122 Dibelius, *Studies in the Acts of the Apostles*, 315–16; Wicker, "Ethiopian Moses," 333.

123 Frost, "Attitudes toward Blacks," 1–11, esp. 2.

124 Frost, "Attitudes toward Blacks," 2.

CONCLUSION

1 *Apophthegmata patrum* 3.

2 *Apophthegmata patrum* 3.

3 Bourdieu, *Language and Symbolic Power*.

4 The historical development is not as neat and clean as might be expected. Because of the focus on classifying the rhetorics, I have developed the historical

background around the themes generated by the taxonomy. Given the complex nature of the rhetorics, a mere diachronic analysis starting in the first century CE and proceeding through late antiquity could not be achieved. The rhetorics overlap different time periods.

5 An entire book could easily have been devoted to a particular author, genre, geographical location or time period contained in this study.

6 Patrick J. Geary, "Barbarians and Ethnicity," in *Late Antiquity: A Guide to the Postclassical World* (ed. G.W. Bowersock, Peter Brown, and Oleg Grabar; Cambridge, Mass.: Harvard University Press, 1999), 107–29.

7 Kelly Brown Douglas, *Sexuality and the Black Church: A Womanist Perspective* (Maryknoll, N.Y.: Orbis, 1999); Phillis Sheppard, "Fleshing the Theory: A Critical Analysis of Theories of the Body in Light of African American Women's Experiences" (Ph.D. diss., Chicago Theological Seminary, 1997).

8 Michael Mann, *The Sources of Social Power: A History of Power from the Beginning to A.D. 1760* (vol. 1; Cambridge: Cambridge University Press, 1986).

9 In 1903 W.E.B. DuBois prophetically summarized the major challenge of the twentieth century: "the problem of the twentieth century is the problem of the color line." See W.E.B. DuBois, *Souls of Black Folk* (New York: Signet Classics, 1969 [1903]), xi. In 1992, Henry Louis Gates likewise summarized the major challenge of the twenty-first century: "the problem of the twenty-first century will be the problem of *ethnic differences* [emphasis mine], as these conspire with complex differences in color, gender, and class." See Henry Louis Gates, Jr., *Loose Canons: Notes on the Culture Wars* (New York: Oxford University Press, 1992), xii.

10 Randell Balmer, "Casting Aside the Ballast of History and Tradition: White Protestants and the Bible in the Antebellum Period," in *African Americans and the Bible* (ed. Vincent L. Wimbush; New York: Continuum, 2000), 193–200.

11 See, for example, Nancy Gibbs, "Death and Deceit," *Time Magazine* (November 14, 1994): 43–51.

12 Other cases include Charles Stuart of Boston, who in 1989 accused a Black man of killing his wife, who was eight months pregnant; Robert Harris of Baltimore, who told police a Black man killed his fiancée; and Tanya Dacri of Northeast Philadelphia, who said three Black kidnappers snatched her baby. See Phillip Brian Harper, *Are We Not Men: Masculine Anxiety and the Problem of African-American Identity* (New York: Oxford University Press, 1996); and John Harvey, *Men in Black* (Chicago: University of Chicago Press, 1995).

13 Long, *Significations*; and Gates, Jr., *Signifying Monkey*.

14 Long, *Significations*, 7–8. Long's discussion indicates that "signifying" is not only advanced by those in power over subordinate groups, but can be carried forth among members within subordinate groups as a strategy for distancing others within the group and establishing proper standards and values. This is especially applicable to early Christians who represented a minority group within the Roman Empire. Those in power were the ones in a position to define the symbolic language world that determined the proper standards and behaviors of early Christians.

15 Long, *Significations*, 7.

16 Martin, "Womanist Interpretations," 41–61, esp. 53.

17 Martin, "Womanist Interpretations," 53.

18 Alexander, "'She's No Lady,'" 3–25.

19 Vincent L. Wimbush, "The Ecclesiastical Context of the New Testament," in *NIB*, 8:43–55.

20 Wimbush, "Ecclesiastical Context," 55.

BIBLIOGRAPHY

PRIMARY SOURCES

Most translations in this book are based on the works listed below, with some modifications; others, as indicated in the endnotes, are my own.

Acta Apostolorum Apocrypha. Ed. Ricardus A. Lipsius and Maximilianus Bonnet. 2 vols. Hildesheim: G. Olms, 1959.

Aeschylus. *Prometheus Bound*. Ed. Mark Griffith. Cambridge Greek and Latin Classics. Cambridge: Cambridge University Press, 1983.

Ambrose. *De paradiso* 16. Trans. J.J. Savage. The Fathers of the Church 42. New York: Catholic University of America Press, 1961.

——. *Expositio Psalmi* 118. PL 15.1257–1603. Ed. M. Petschenig. CSEL 62. Vienna: F. Tempsky, 1913.

Amherst Papyri. Ed. B.P. Grenfell and A.S. Hunt. London: Oxford University Press, 1901.

Ammianus Marcellinus. Trans. John C. Rolfe. 3 vols. LCL. Cambridge, Mass.: Harvard University Press, 1972.

Antologia Erotica Pompeiana. Ed. Matteo Della Corte. Cava dei Tirreni: E. Di Mauro, 1958.

Antony. *The Letters of Saint Antony the Great*. Trans. D.J. Chitty. Oxford: SLG, 1977.

Apophthegmata patrum. PG 65.72–440. English translations in *The Sayings of the Desert Fathers*. Trans. Benedicta Ward. Cistercian Studies 59. Kalamazoo, Mich.: Cistercian Publications, 1975; *The Desert Fathers*. Trans. Helen Waddell. New York: H. Holt, 1936.

——. *Les sentences des pères du désert: nouveau recueil*. Ed. and trans. L. Regnault. 2nd ed. Sarthe: Solesmes, 1985.

Apostolic Fathers. Trans. Kirsopp Lake. 2 vols. LCL. Cambridge, Mass.: Harvard University Press, 1976–85.

Appian of Alexandria. *Civil Wars*. Trans. Horace White. 2 vols. LCL. Cambridge, Mass.: Harvard University Press, 1972.

Aristotle. *De generatione animalium*. Trans. A.L. Peck. LCL. Cambridge, Mass.: Harvard University Press, 1979.

——. *Minor Works*. Trans. W.S. Hett. LCL. Cambridge, Mass.: Harvard University Press, 1963.

Aristotle. *Politica.* Trans. H. Rackham. LCL. Cambridge, Mass.: Harvard University Press, 1977.

——. *The "Art" of Rhetoric.* Trans. John Henry Freese. LCL. London: William Heinemann, 1926.

Athanasius. *Vita Antonii.* PG 26.835–976. *Vie D'Antoine.* SC 400. Earliest Latin translation: Ed. G.J.M. Bartelink, *Vita di Antonio.* Vite dei Santi I. Fondazione Lorenzo Valla: Mondadori, 1974. English translation in *Athanasius: The Life of Anthony and the Letter to Marcellinus.* Trans. Robert Gregg. New York: Paulist Press, 1980.

Augustine. *De civitate dei.* Libri 22. Ed. Emanuel Hoffmann. CSEL. New York, 1900.

——. *Enarrationes in Psalmos.* CC 39. English translation in *Augustine of Hippo: Selected Writings.* Trans. Mary T. Clark. New York: Paulist Press, 1984.

Augustus, *Res gestae divi Augusti.* English translation in *Res gestae divi Augusti: The Achievements of the Divine Augustus.* Introduction and Commentary by P.A. Brunt and J.M. Moore. Oxford: Oxford University Press, 1967.

Ausonius. *Parentalia.* Trans. Hugh G. Evelyn White. LCL. Cambridge, Mass.: Harvard University Press, 1977.

Cassian. *Conferences.* Trans. Colm Luibheid. New York: Paulist Press, 1985.

——. *On Impurity.* In *Les sentences des pères du désert.* Ed. L. Regnault. Sarthe: Solesmes, 1966.

——. *The Conferences.* Trans. Boniface Ramsey. Ancient Christian Writers 57. New York: Paulist Press, 1997.

Cassius Dio. Trans. Earnest Cary. 9 vols. LCL. Cambridge, Mass.: Harvard University Press, 1980–90.

CETEDOC Library of Christian Latin Texts. CLCLT-3. Universitas Catholica Lovaniensis. Turnhout: Brepols, 1996.

Cicero. *De senectute.* Trans. William Armistead Falconer. 28 vols. LCL. Cambridge, Mass.: Harvard University Press, 1979.

Clement. *Protrepticus, Paedagogus.* GCS 12. Ed. Otto Stählin. Berlin: Akademie, 1972.

——. *Stromateis: Books 1–3.* Trans. John Ferguson. The Fathers of the Church 85. Washington, D.C.: Catholic University of America Press, 1991.

Climacus, John. *The Ladder of Divine Ascent.* PG 88, cols. 632–1208. Trans. L. Moore. Boston: Holy Transfiguration Monastery, 1978.

Diodorus Siculus. *History.* Trans. C. H. Oldfather. 12 vols. LCL. Cambridge, Mass.: Harvard University Press, 1968.

Diogenes Laertius. *Lives of Eminent Philosophers.* Trans. R.D. Hicks. 2 vols. LCL. Cambridge, Mass.: Harvard University Press, 1979–80.

Ennodius. *Epistulae.* In *Monumenta Germaniae Historica: Auctores Antiquissimi* 7. Ed. F. Vogel. Berlin: Monumenta Germaniae Historica, 1885.

Ephraem Syrus, *The Pearl, or Seven Rhythms on the Faith.* Library of the Fathers 41. Ed. and trans. J.B. Morris. Oxford: J.H. Parker, 1847.

Epiphanius. *The Panarion of Epiphanius of Salamis.* Trans. Frank Williams. 2 vols. Nag Hammadi Studies 35 and 36. Leiden: E.J. Brill, 1987–94.

Epistle of Barnabas. In *The Apostolic Fathers.* Vol. 1. Trans. Kirsopp Lake. LCL. Cambridge, Mass.: Harvard University Press, 1985.

Ethiopian Moses. Apophthegmata Patrum. PG 65, cols. 281–89. "Vita S. Moysis Aethiopis," in *Menologium fasc.* 2 (V. Latyshev) 330–34. "Vita S. Moyse Aethiope," in *Acta Sanct.* Augusti Tomus Sextus. Ed. Joannes Bollandus et al. Paris: V. Palme, 1868. English translations by Kathleen O. Wicker. "Ethiopian Moses (Collected

Sources)." Pages 329–48 in *Ascetic Behavior in Greco-Roman Antiquity: A Source Book*. Ed. Vincent L. Wimbush. Minneapolis: Fortress, 1990.

Eusebius. *Ecclesiastical History*. Trans. Kirsopp Lake. 2 vols. LCL. London: W. Heinemann; New York: G.P. Putnam's Sons, 1926–32.

Evagrius, *Historia ecclesiastica* 1.7.259–60.

Galen. *On The Natural Faculties*. Trans. Arthur John Brock. LCL. Cambridge, Mass.: Harvard University Press, 1979.

Geographi Graeci Minores. Ed. Karl Müller. 2 vols. Paris: Firmin Didot, 1855–61. Repr. Hildesheim: Georg Olms, 1990.

Gregory of Elvira. *In Canticum Canticorum*. CC 69.176–79.

Gregory the Great. *Moralia in Iob*. PL 75.509–1162 and CCSL 26.

Heliodorus. *Aethiopica*. Ed. A. Colonna. Rome: Regiae Officinae Polygraphicae, 1938.

Herodotus. Trans. A.D. Godley. 4 vols. LCL. Cambridge, Mass.: Harvard University Press, 1981–82. English translation in *Herodotus: The Histories*. Trans. Robin Waterfield. Oxford: Oxford University Press, 1998.

Homer. *The Iliad*. Trans. A.T. Murray. Rev. William F. Wyatt. 2 vols. LCL. Cambridge, Mass.: Harvard University Press, 1999.

———. *The Odyssey*. Trans. A.T. Murray. 2 vols. LCL. Cambridge, Mass.: Harvard University Press, 1976–80.

Jerome. *Commentaires de Jerome sur le Prophète Isaïe*. Intro. Roger Gryson. Livres I–IV. Freiburg: Herder, 1993.

———. *Commentary on Isaiah* 7.18.1–3. CC 73.274–75.

———. *De Psalmo* 86:137–57 (CC 78:114). English translation in Jerome, *Homily 18 on Psalm 86* in *St. Jerome: Homilies on the Psalms*. Ancient Christian Writers 48. Trans. Marie L. Ewald. Westminster, Md.: Newman, 1964.

———. *Letters* 60.17 (CSEL 54.572). English translation in J.H.D. Scourfield, *Consoling Heliodorus: A Commentary on Jerome, Letter 60*. New York: Oxford University Press, 1993; *The Letters of St. Jerome*. Ancient Christian Writers 33. Trans. C.C. Mierow. New York: Newman, 1963; and *Select Letters*. Trans. F.A. Wright. LCL. Cambridge, Mass.: Harvard University Press, 1954.

———. *Homilies on the Psalms*. S. Hieronymi Presbyteri Opera. Pars II Opera homiletica. Ed. E. Dekkers. CC 78. Turnhout, 1958.

———. *In Soph.* 3.10–13 (CC 76 A. 703–04).

Josephus. *Jewish Antiquities*. Trans. H. St. J. Thackeray, Ralph Marcus, Allen Wikgren, and H. Feldman. 7 vols. LCL. Cambridge, Mass.: Harvard University Press, 1978–81.

———. *Jewish War*. Trans. H. St. J. Thackeray. LCL. Cambridge, Mass.: Harvard University Press, 1996.

———. *The Life, Against Apion*. Trans. H. St. J. Thackeray. LCL. Cambridge, Mass.: Harvard University Press, 1976.

Juvenal. *Juvenal and Persius*. Trans. G.G. Ramsay. LCL. Cambridge, Mass.: Harvard University Press, 1979.

Lightfoot, J.B., and J.R. Harmer, eds. *The Apostolic Fathers: Greek Texts and English Translations of Their Writings*. Grand Rapids: Baker, 1998 (1992).

Lucian. *Philopatris*. Trans. M.D. MacLeod. Vol. 8. LCL. Cambridge, Mass.: Harvard University Press, 1979.

Lucian. *Rhetorum praeceptor*. Trans. A.M. Harmon. Vol. 4. LCL. Cambridge, Mass.: Harvard University Press, 1969.

------. *The Eunuch*. Trans. A.M. Harmon. Vol. 5. LCL. Cambridge, Mass.: Harvard University Press, 1972.

------. *The Ship or the Wishes (Navigium)*. Trans. K. Kilburn. Vol. 6. LCL. Cambridge, Mass.: Harvard University Press, 1968.

Manetho. *History of Egypt*. Trans. W.G. Waddell. LCL. Cambridge, Mass.: Harvard University Press, 1980.

Martial. *Epigrams*. Trans. D.R. Shackleton Bailey. LCL. Cambridge, Mass.: Harvard University Press, 1993.

Menander: The Principle Fragments. Trans. Francis G. Allison. LCL. Cambridge, Mass.: Harvard University Press, 1951 (1930).

Nestle-Aland. *Novum Testamentum Graece*. 26th ed. Stuttgart: Deutsche Bibel-gesellschaft, 1979. English trans.: NRSV New York: Oxford University Press, 1989.

New Testament Apocrypha. Trans. E. Hennecke and W. Schneemelcher. 2 vols. Rev. ed. Louisville: Westminster/John Knox, 1991–92.

Origen. *Commentarium in Canticum Canticorum*. Latin. Rufinus. Commentaire sur le Cantique des Cantiques. 2 vols. Texte de la version latin de Rufinus; introduction, traduction et notes par Luc Brésard et Henri Crouzel avec la collaboration de Marcel Borret. SC 375–76. Paris: Cerf, 1991–92.

------. *De principiis*. In *Origène: Traité des Principes*. SC. Ed. H. Crouzel and M. Simonetti. Paris: Cerf, 1978–84. English translation: *Origen: On First Principles*. Ed. and trans. G.W. Butterworth. New York: Harper & Row, 1966.

------. *Origène: Homélies sur le Cantique des Cantiques*. Ed. O. Rousseau. SC 37. Paris: Cerf, 1954.

------. *Origenes Werke*. Ed. W.A. Baehrens. GCS 8. Leipzig: J.C. Hinrichs, 1899–1955.

------. *The Song of Songs, Commentary and Homilies*. Trans. R.P. Lawson. Ancient Christian Writers 26. New York: Newman, 1956.

Pachomius. *Pachomian Koinonia: The Life of Saint Pachomius and his Disciples*. Trans. Armand Veilleux. 3 vols. Kalamazoo, Mich.: Cistercian, 1980–82. Greek text in R. Draguet, "Un Paralipomenon Pachômien Inconnu dans le Karakallou 251," *Mélanges Eugène Tisserant* 2 (1964): 55–61.

Palladius. *Apophthegmata Patrum*. French trans. in *Les Sentences des pères du désert: Série des anonymes*. Ed. D.L. Regnault. Sarthe: Solesmes, 1985. English trans. in *The Paradise or Garden of the Holy Fathers*. Trans. E.A. Wallis Budge. 2 vols. London: Chatto & Windus, 1907.

------. *Dialogue sur la Vie de Jean Chrysostome*. SC 341–42. Trans. Anne-Marie Malingrey. 2 vols. Paris: Cerf, 1988. English translation in *Palladius: Dialogue on the Life of St. John Chrysostom*. Trans. and ed. R.T. Meyer. Ancient Christian Writers 45. New York: Newman, 1985.

------. *Historia Lausiaca. The Lausiac History of Palladius: A Critical Discussion Together with Notes on Early Egyptian Monachism*. Ed. Cuthbert Butler. 2 vols. Hildesheim: G. Olms, 1967. English translation in *Palladius, Lausiac History*. Trans. R.T. Meyer. Ancient Christian Writers 34. New York: Newman, 1965.

Paulinus of Nola. *The Poems of St. Paulinus of Nola*. Ancient Christian Writers 40. Trans. P.G. Walsh. New York: Newman, 1975. Latin text in CSEL 30. Ed. G. de Hartel. Vienna: Academiae Litterarum Caesareae Vindobonensis, 1894.

Perpetua and Felicity. *Passio Sanctarum Perpetuae et Felicitatis*. Ed. Cornelius Ioannes Maria and Ioseph van Beek. Nijmegen: Dekker & Van De Vegt, 1936.

Philo. *Philo*. Trans. Francis H. Colson and George H. Whitaker. 12 vols. LCL. Cambridge, Mass.: Harvard University Press, 1929.

Philostratus. *Imagines*. Trans. Arthur Fairbanks. LCL. Cambridge, Mass.: Harvard University Press, 1960.

———. *The Life of Apollonius of Tyana*. Trans. F.C. Conybeare. 2 vols. LCL. Cambridge, Mass.: Harvard University Press, 1969.

Pindar. *Works*. Trans. William H. Race. 2 vols. LCL. Cambridge, Mass.: Harvard University Press, 1997.

Plautus. Trans. Paul Nixon. 5 vols. LCL. Cambridge, Mass.: Harvard University Press, 1965.

Pliny the Elder. *Naturalis historia*. Trans. H. Rackham. 10 vols. LCL. Cambridge, Mass.: Harvard University Press, 1979.

Pliny the Younger. *Letters and Panegyricus*. Trans. Betty Radice. 2 vols. LCL. Cambridge, Mass.: Harvard University Press, 1972–75.

Plutarch. *De Iside et Osiride*. Trans. F.C. Babbitt. LCL. Cambridge, Mass.: Harvard University Press, 1969.

———. *De Liberis Educandis*. In *Plutarch's Moralia* 1. Trans. Frank Cole Babbitt. LCL. Cambridge, Mass.: Harvard University Press, 1986.

Poeta Latini Minores. Ed. Aemilius Baehrens. Appendix Vergiliana rev. by F. Vollmer and W. Morel. Bibliotheca Scriptorum Graecorum et Romanorum Teubneriana. New York: Garland, 1979.

Procopius. *Works*. Trans. H.B. Dewing. 7 vols. LCL. Cambridge, Mass.: Harvard University Press, 1968–79.

Pseudo-Athanasius, *Life and Activity of Syncletica* 28. PG 28, cols. 1487–1558. English translation: Elizabeth A. Castelli. "Pseudo-Athanasius: The Life and Activity of the Holy and Blessed Teacher Syncletica." Pages 265–311 in *Ascetic Behavior in Greco-Roman Antiquity*. Ed. Vincent L. Wimbush. Minneapolis: Fortress, 1990.

Pseudo-Callisthenes. *Historia Alexandri Magni* 3.18.6. Ed. W. Kroll. Berlin, 1926.

Rufinus. *Historia monachorum in Aegypto*. PL 21.387–462.

Scholia in Theocritum Vetera. Ed. Carl Wendel. Stuttgart: Teubneri, 1967 (1914).

Seneca. *Naturales quaestiones*. Trans. Thomas H. Corcoran. 2 vols. LCL. Cambridge, Mass.: Harvard University Press, 1972.

Sextus Empiricus. *Adversus mathematicos*. Trans. R.G. Bury. LCL. Cambridge, Mass.: Harvard University Press, 1968.

Shepherd of Hermas. Der Hirt des Hermas. Trans. Molly Whittaker. GCS 48. Die Apostolischen Väter 1. 2nd ed. Berlin: Akademie, 1967. English translations: *Shepherd of Hermas: A Commentary*. Trans. Carolyn Osiek. Hermeneia Series. Minneapolis: Fortress, 1999; G. Snyder, *The Shepherd of Hermas*. Apostolic Fathers 6. Ed. Robert Grant. Camden, N.J.: T. Nelson, 1968; and *Shepherd of Hermas*. Trans. Kirsopp Lake. *The Apostolic Fathers*, vol. 2. LCL. Cambridge, Mass.: Harvard University Press, 1976.

Socrates. *Historia ecclesiastica*. Oxford: Clarendon, 1878. English translation in *Library of Nicene and Post-Nicene Fathers*, ser. 2, vol. 2. Ed. A.C. Zenos. Grand Rapids: Eerdmans, 1979.

Sozomen. *Historia ecclesiastica*. Paris: Cerf, 1983.

Strabo. *Geography*. Trans. Horace Leonard Jones. 8 vols. LCL. Cambridge, Mass.: Harvard University Press, 1967–83.

Suetonius. *Life of Caligula*. Trans. J.C. Rolfe. Vol. 1. 2nd ed. LCL. Cambridge, Mass.: Harvard University Press, 1997.

Tacitus. *Germania*. Vol 1. LCL. Cambridge, Mass.: Harvard University Press, 1970. English translation and commentary in *Germania*. Trans. James Rives. New York: Oxford University Press, 1999.

———. *Works*. 5 vols. LCL. Cambridge, Mass.: Harvard University Press, 1970–81.

Tertullian. *Ad nationes*. The Ante-Nicene Fathers. Grand Rapids: Eerdmans, 1973.

———. *Against Marcion*. The Ante-Nicene Fathers. Grand Rapids: Eerdmans, 1978.

———. *De spectaculis*. Ed. E. Dekkers. Tertulliani Opera. CC. Turnhout: Brepols, 1954. French translation in *Les spectacles*. SC 332. Trans. Marie Turcan. Paris: Cerf, 1986. English translation in *De spectaculis*. LCL. Trans. T.R. Glover. Cambridge, Mass.: Harvard University Press, 1977.

Thesaurus Linguae Graecae. CD-ROM Data Bank Version D. University of California at Irvine.

Thesaurus Linguae Latinae. Editus Auctoritate et Consilio Academiarum Quinque Germanicarum Berolinensis, Gottingensis, Lipsiensis, Monacensis, Vindobonensis. Vol. 1. Lipsiae: In Aedibus B.G. Teubneri, 1900– .

Vie de Sainte Mélanie. SC 90. Ed. Denys Gorce. Paris: Cerf, 1962. English trans.: Elizabeth A. Clark. *Life of Melania the Younger*. New York: Edwin Mellen, 1984.

Vita Melaniae Junioris. Santa Melania Giuniore, senatrice romana: documenti contemporei e note. Ed. Mariano del Tindaro Rampolla. Rome: Tipografia Vaticana, 1905.

Vita S. Mariae Aegyptiae. PG 87 (3), cols. 3693–726.

SECONDARY SOURCES

Adamo, David T. *Africa and the Africans in the Old Testament*. San Francisco: International Scholars, 1998.

Adams, William Y. "Beja Tribes." Pages 373–74 of vol. 1 in *The Coptic Encyclopedia*. 8 vols. Ed. Aziz S. Atiya. New York: Macmillan, 1991.

———. *Nubia: Corridor to Africa*. Princeton: Princeton University Press, 1977.

———. "The Invention of Nubia." Pages 17–22 in *Hommages à Jean Leclant* 2: Nubie, Soudan, Ethiopie (BdE 106/2). Ed. C. Berger et al. Cairo: IFAO, 1994.

Alexander, Adele Logan. "'She's No Lady, She's a Nigger': Abuses, Stereotypes, and Realities from the Middle Passage to Capitol (and Anita) Hill." Pages 3–25 in *Race, Gender, and Power in America: The Legacy of the Hill-Thomas Hearings*. Ed. Anita Faye Hill and Emma Coleman Jordan. New York: Oxford University Press, 1995.

Allison, C. FitzSimons. *The Cruelty of Heresy: An Affirmation of Christian Orthodoxy*. Harrisburg, Pa.: Morehouse, 1994.

Altschul, Paisius, ed. *An Unbroken Circle: Linking Ancient African Christianity to the African-American Experience*. St. Louis, Mo.: Brotherhood of St. Moses the Black, 1997.

Amador, J. David Hester. *Academic Constraints in Rhetorical Criticism of the New Testament: An Introduction to a Rhetoric of Power*. JSNTSup 174. Sheffield: Sheffield Academic Press, 1999.

Anderson, Victor. *Beyond Ontological Blackness: An Essay on African American Religious and Cultural Criticism.* New York: Continuum, 1995.

André, Jacques. *Étude sur les termes de couleur dans la langue latine.* Paris: C. Klincksieck, 1949.

Arbesmann, Rudolph, trans. *Tertullian: Disciplinary, Moral and Ascetical Works.* Washington, D.C.: Catholic University of America, 1977.

Arora, U.P. "India vis-à-vis Egypt-Ethiopia in Classical Accounts." *Graeco-Arabica* (1982): 131–40.

Asante, Molefi K. *Afrocentricity.* Trenton, N.J.: Africa World, 1988.

———. *Kemet, Afrocentricity, and Knowledge.* Trenton, N.J.: Africa World, 1990.

———. *The Afrocentric Idea.* Philadelphia: Temple University Press, 1987.

———. *The Painful Demise of Eurocentrism: An Afrocentric Response to Critics.* Trenton, N.J.: Africa World, 1999.

Asante, Molefi K., and Abu S. Abarry, eds. *African Intellectual Heritage: A Book of Sources.* Philadelphia: Temple University Press, 1996.

Assmann, Jan. *Moses the Egyptian: The Memory of Egypt in Western Monotheism.* Cambridge, Mass.: Harvard University Press, 1997.

Aubert, Jean-Jacques. "Du Noir en noir et blanc: eloge de la dispersion." *MH* 56 (1999): 159–82.

Bach, Alice. *Women, Seduction, and Betrayal in Biblical Narrative.* Cambridge: Cambridge University Press, 1997.

Bacon, Helen H. *Barbarians in Greek Tragedy.* New Haven: Yale University Press, 1961.

Bagnall, Roger S. *Egypt in Late Antiquity.* Princeton: Princeton University Press, 1993.

———. "Greeks and Egyptians: Ethnicity, Status, and Culture." Pages 21–27 in *Cleopatra's Egypt: The Age of the Ptolemies 305–30 BCE.* Brooklyn: Brooklyn Museum in association with P. von Zabern, 1988.

———. *Reading Papyri, Writing Ancient History.* London: Routledge, 1995.

———. "The Fayum and its People." Pages 17–20 in *Ancient Faces: Mummy Portraits from Roman Egypt.* Ed. Susan Walker and Morris Bierbrier. London: British Museum, 1997.

Bailey, Randall C. "Academic Biblical Interpretation among African Americans in the United States." Pages 696–711 in *African Americans and the Bible.* Ed. Vincent L. Wimbush. New York: Continuum, 2000.

———. "Beyond Identification: The Use of Africans in Old Testament Poetry and Narratives." Pages 165–84 in *Stony the Road We Trod.* Ed. Cain Hope Felder. Minneapolis: Fortress, 1991.

Bailey, Randall C., and Jacquelyn Grant, eds. *The Recovery of Black Presence: An Interdisciplinary Exploration. Essays in Honor of Charles B. Copher.* Nashville: Abingdon, 1995.

Ball, John. *Egypt in the Classical Geographers.* Cairo: Government Press, Bulaq, 1942.

Balsdon, J.P.V.D. *Romans and Aliens.* London: Duckworth, 1979.

Barnard, L.W. "The Shepherd of Hermas in Recent Study." *HeyJ* 9 (1968): 29–36.

Barth, Fredrik. "Ethnic and Group Boundaries." Pages 294–324 in *Theories of Ethnicity.* Ed. Werner Sollors. New York: New York University Press, 1996.

Bastide, Roger. "Color, Racism, and Christianity." Pages 34–49 in *Color and Race.* Ed. John Hope Franklin. Boston: Houghton Mifflin, 1968.

Bauer, Angela, "Bearing 'Whiteness': Race, Culture, and Biblical Interpretation." Paper presented at the annual meeting of the American Academy of Religion and Society of Biblical Literature. Nashville, November 20, 2000.

Bauer, Walter. *A Greek-English Lexicon of the New Testament and Other Early Christian Literature.* 2nd rev. ed. from the 5th German edition. Ed. F. Wilbur Gingrich and Frederick W. Danker. Chicago: University of Chicago Press, 1979.

———. *Orthodoxy and Heresy in Earliest Christianity.* Ed. and trans. Robert A. Kraft, Gerhard Krodel et al. Philadelphia: Fortress, 1971.

Baumann, Gerd. *The Multicultural Riddle: Rethinking National, Ethnic, and Religious Identities.* New York: Routledge, 1999.

Beal, Timothy K. *The Book of Hiding: Gender, Ethnicity, Annihilation, and Esther.* London: Routledge, 1997.

Beardsley, Grace H. *The Negro in Greek and Roman Civilization: A Study of the Ethiopian Type.* New York: Russell & Russell, 1967 (1929).

Bennett, Jr., Robert A. "Africa and the Biblical Period." *HTR* 64 (1971): 483–500.

———. "The Black Experience and the Bible." *ThTo* 27 (1971): 422–33.

Berkowitz, Luci, and K.A. Squitier. *Thesaurus Linguae Graecae: Canon of Greek Authors and Works.* 3rd ed. New York: Oxford University Press, 1990.

Berlinerblau, Jacques. *Heresy in the University: The Black Athena Controversy and the Responsibilities of American Intellectuals.* New Brunswick, N.J.: Rutgers University Press, 1999.

Bernal, Martin. *Black Athena: The Afroasiatic Roots of Classical Civilization.* 2 vols. New Brunswick, N.J.: Rutgers University Press, 1987–91.

———. *Black Athena: The Afroasiatic Roots of Classical Civilization.* Vol. 2: *The Archaeological and Documentary Evidence.* New Brunswick, N.J.: Rutgers University Press, 1991.

———. "The Afrocentric Interpretation of History: Bernal Replies to Lefkowitz." *Journal of Blacks in Higher Education* 11 (1996): 86–94.

———. "The Case for Massive Egyptian Influence in the Aegean." *Archaeology* (September–October 1992): 53–55, 82, 86.

Bernand, Étienne. *Inscriptions grecques d'Egypte et de Nubie au Musée du Louvre.* Paris: Centre National de la Recherche Scientifique, 1992.

———. *Inscriptions métriques de l'Égypte gréco-romaine.* Annales Littéraires de l'Université de Besançon vol. 98. Paris: Les Belles Lettres, 1969, no. 26.5–10.

Beyer, Hans-Veit. *Prosopographisches Lexikon der Palaiologenzeit 7.* Vienna: Verlag der Österreichischen Akademie der Wissenschaften, 1985.

Bianchi, Robert Steven. "Postdynastic Egypt." Pages 201–5 in *The Oxford Encyclopedia of Archaeology in the Near East.* Ed. Eric M. Meyers. Vol. 2. New York: Oxford University Press, 1997.

Bible and Culture Collective. "Feminist and Womanist Criticism." Pages 225–71 in *The Postmodern Bible.* New Haven: Yale University Press, 1995.

———. *The Postmodern Bible.* New Haven: Yale University Press, 1995.

Bilde, Per, Troels Engberg-Pedersen, Lise Hannestad, and Jan Zahle, eds. *Ethnicity in Hellenistic Egypt.* Aarhus: Aarhus University Press, 1992.

Binns, John. *Ascetics and Ambassadors of Christ: The Monasteries of Palestine 314–631.* New York: Oxford University Press, 1994.

Blount, Brian K. "A Social-Rhetorical Analysis of Simon of Cyrene: Mark 15:21 and Its Parallels." *Semeia* 64 (1993): 171–98.

——. *Cultural Interpretation: Reorienting New Testament Criticism.* Minneapolis: Fortress, 1995.

Boswell, John. *Christianity, Social Tolerance, and Homosexuality: Gay People in Western Europe from the Beginning of the Christian Era to the Fourteenth Century.* Chicago: University of Chicago Press, 1980.

Bourdieu, Pierre. *Language and Symbolic Power.* Trans. Gino Raymond and Matthew Adamson. Cambridge, Mass.: Harvard University Press, 1991.

Bourget, Pierre du. "La couleur noire de la peau du démon dans l'iconographie chrétienne a-t-elle une origine précise?" Pages 271–72 in *Actas del VIII Congreso Internacional de Arqueologia Cristiana – Barcelona 5–11 Octubre 1969.* Barcelona: Città del Vaticano, 1972.

Bovon, François, Ann Graham Brock, and Christopher R. Matthews, eds. *The Apocryphal Acts of the Apostles.* Cambridge, Mass.: Harvard University Press, 1999.

Bowersock, Glen W. *Fiction as History: Nero to Julian.* Berkeley: University of California Press, 1994.

——. "Rescuing the Greeks: A Classicist Defends the Traditional Version of Greek Cultural Achievement." Review of *Not Out of Africa,* by Mary R. Lefkowitz, and *Black Athena Revisited.* Ed. Mary R. Lefkowitz and Guy M. Rogers. *New York Times Book Review,* February 25, 1996, 6–7.

Bowman, Alan K. *Egypt after the Pharaohs: 332 BC – AD 642 from Alexander to the Arab Conquest.* Berkeley: University of California Press, 1989.

Brakke, David B. *Athanasius and the Politics of Asceticism.* Oxford: Clarendon, 1995. Repr. Baltimore: Johns Hopkins University Press, 1998.

——. "Ethiopian Demons: Male Sexuality, the Black-Skinned Other, and the Monastic Self." *Journal of the History of Sexuality* 10.3/4 (2001): 501–35.

Braxton, Bernard. *Women, Sex, and Race.* Washington, D.C.: Verta, 1973.

Bremmer, Jan N. "Aspects of the *Acts of Peter*: Women, Magic, Place and Date." Pages 1–20 in *The Apocryphal Acts of Peter: Magic, Miracles and Gnosticism.* Ed. J.N. Bremmer. Leuven: Peeters, 1998.

——., ed. *The Apocryphal Acts of Peter: Magic, Miracles and Gnosticism.* Leuven: Peeters, 1998.

Brenner, Athalya. *Colour Terms in the Old Testament.* JSOTSup 21. Sheffield: JSOT Press, 1982.

——. *The Intercourse of Knowledge: On Gendering Desire and "Sexuality" in the Hebrew Bible.* Biblical Interpretation Series 26. Leiden: E.J. Brill, 1997.

Brett, Mark G. "Interpreting Ethnicity: Method, Hermeneutics, Ethics." Pages 3–22 in *Ethnicity and the Bible.* Ed. Mark G. Brett. Leiden: E.J. Brill, 1996.

——., ed. *Ethnicity and the Bible.* Leiden: E.J. Brill, 1996.

Brock, Sebastian P., and Susan Ashbrook Harvey, eds. and trans. *Holy Women of the Syrian Orient.* Berkeley: University of California Press, 1987.

Brown, L.C. "Color in Northern Africa." Pages 186–204 in *Color and Race.* Ed. John Hope Franklin. Boston: Houghton Mifflin, 1968.

Brown, Peter. "From the Heavens to the Desert: Anthony and Pachomius." Pages 81–101 in *The Making of Late Antiquity.* Cambridge, Mass.: Harvard University Press, 1978.

——. *The Body and Society: Men, Women, and Sexual Renunciation in Early Christianity.* New York: Columbia University Press, 1988.

Brown, Peter. "The Rise and Function of the Holy Man in Late Antiquity." Pages

103–52 in *Society and the Holy in Late Antiquity*. Berkeley: University of California Press, 1982.

Brown, S. Kent. "The Egyptian." In *ABD* 2: 412–13.

Bruce, F.F. *The Acts of the Apostles: The Greek Text with Introduction and Commentary*. Grand Rapids: Eerdmans, 1984.

Budge, E.A. Wallis. *The Life of Antony* in *The Paradise of the Holy Fathers*. 2 vols. London: Chatto & Windus, 1907.

Buell, Denise Kimber. "Ethnicity and Religion in Mediterranean Antiquity and Beyond." *RelSRev* 26 (2000): 243–49.

——. *Making Christians: Clement of Alexandria and the Rhetoric of Legitimacy*. Princeton: Princeton University Press, 1999.

——. "Rethinking the Relevance of Race for Early Christianity." *HTR* 94, no. 1 (2001): 49–76.

Bultmann, Rudolf. *Theology of the New Testament*. 2 vols. Trans. K. Grobel. New York: Charles Scribner's Sons, 1955.

——. "Zur Geschichte der Lichtsymbolik im Altertum." *Phil* 97 (part 1/2, 1948): 1–36.

Bunbury, E.H. *A History of Ancient Geography Among the Greeks and Romans from the Earliest Ages Till the Fall of the Roman Empire*. 2 vols. New York: Dover, 1959 (1932).

Burrus, Virginia. "The Heretical Woman as Symbol in Alexander, Athanasius, Epiphanius, and Jerome." *HTR* 84 (1991): 229–48.

——. "Word and Flesh: The Bodies and Sexuality of Ascetic Women in Christian Antiquity." *JFSR* 10, no. 1 (1990): 27–51.

Burstein, Stanley M. *Graeco-Africana: Studies in the History of Greek Relations with Egypt and Nubia*. New Rochelle, N.Y.: A.D. Caratzas, 1995.

Burton-Christie, Douglas. *The Word in the Desert: Scripture and the Quest for Holiness in Early Christian Monasticism*. New York: Oxford University Press, 1993.

Bynum, Caroline Walker. *Jesus as Mother: Studies in the Spirituality of the High Middle Ages*. Berkeley: University of California Press, 1982.

—— et al. *Religion and Gender: Essays on the Complexity of Symbols*. Boston: Beacon, 1987.

Calderini, A. *Dizionario dei nomi geografici e topografici dell' Egitto Greco-Romano*. Cairo: Società reale di geografia d'Egitto, 1935– .

Calenko, Theodore, ed. *Egypt in Africa*. Indianapolis: Indiana University Press, 1997.

Cameron, Alan. "Black and White: A Note on Ancient Nicknames." *AJP* 110 (1998): 113–17.

Cameron, Averil. *Christianity and the Rhetoric of Empire: The Development of Christian Discourse*. Sather Classical Lectures 55. Berkeley: University of California Press, 1991.

——, ed. *History as Text: The Writing of Ancient History*. Chapel Hill: University of North Carolina Press, 1989.

——. *The Mediterranean World in Late Antiquity AD 395–600*. London: Routledge, 1993.

Campenhausen, H. von. *Formation of the Christian Bible*. Philadelphia: Fortress, 1972.

Carson, Anne. "Putting Her in Her Place: Women, Dirt, and Desire." Pages 135–70 in *Before Sexuality: The Construction of Erotic Experience in the Ancient Greek World*. Ed.

David M. Halperin, John J. Winkler, and Froma I. Zeitlin. Princeton: Princeton University Press, 1990.

Carson, Cottrel R. "'Do You Understand What You Are Reading?': A Reading of the Ethiopian Eunuch Story (Acts 8:26–40) from a Site of Cultural Marronage." Ph.D. diss., Union Theological Seminary, 1999.

Castelli, Elizabeth A., ed. *Women, Gender, Religion: A Reader.* New York: Palgrave, 2001.

———. "'I Will Make Mary Male': Pieties of the Body and Gender Transformation of Christian Women in Late Antiquity." Pages 29–49 in *Body Guards: The Cultural Politics of Gender Ambiguity.* Ed. Julia Epstein and Kristina Straub. New York: Routledge, 1991.

Chadwick, Henry. *Heresy and Orthodoxy in the Early Church.* Brookfield, Vt.: Gower, 1991.

Chitty, Derwas. *The Desert A City: An Introduction to the Study of Egyptian and Palestinian Monasticism Under the Christian Empire.* Oxford: Basil Blackwell, 1966.

Christides, V. "Ethnic Movements in Southern Egypt and Northern Sudan." *Listy Filologicke* 103 (1980): 129–43.

Christie-Murray, David. *A History of Heresy.* Oxford: Oxford University Press, 1990 (1976).

Clark, D.L. *Rhetoric in Greco-Roman Education.* New York: Columbia University Press, 1957.

Clark, Elizabeth A. "Holy Women, Holy Words: Early Christian Women, Social History, and the 'Linguistic Turn'." *JECS* 6, no. 3 (1998): 413–30.

———. "Ideology, History, and the Construction of 'Woman' in Late Ancient Christianity." *JECS* 2 (1994): 155–84.

———, trans. *Life of Melania the Younger.* New York: Edwin Mellen, 1984.

———. *Reading Renunciation: Asceticism and Scripture in Early Christianity.* Princeton: Princeton University Press, 1999.

———. "Sex, Shame, and Rhetoric: En-gendering Early Christian Ethics." *JAAR* 59 (1991): 221–45.

Clark, Gillian. "Women and Asceticism in Late Antiquity: The Refusal of Status and Gender." Pages 33–48 in *Asceticism.* Ed. Vincent L. Wimbush and Richard Valantasis. New York: Oxford University Press, 1995.

Clark, John Henrik. "Africa in the Ancient World." Pages 45–54 in *Kemet and the African Worldview: Research, Rescue and Restoration.* Ed. Maulana Karenga and Jacob H. Carruthers. Los Angeles: University of Sankore Press, 1986.

Clarke, M.L. *Rhetoric at Rome: A Historical Survey.* Rev. ed. Introduction by D.H. Berry. London: Routledge, 1996.

Classen, Constance. *The Color of Angels: Cosmology, Gender, and the Aesthetic Imagination.* London: Routledge, 1998.

Classen, Constance, David Howes, and Anthony Synnott. *Aroma: The Cultural History of Smell.* New York: Routledge, 1994.

Clifford, James, and George E. Marcus, eds. *Writing Culture: The Poetics and Politics of Ethnography.* Berkeley: University of California Press, 1986.

Clifton, Chas S. *Encyclopedia of Heresies and Heretics.* Santa Barbara, Calif.: ABC-CLIO, 1992.

Cochrane, Charles Norris. *Christianity and Classical Culture: A Study of Thought and Action from Augustus to Augustine.* London: Oxford University Press, 1957 (1944).

185

Cohen, Shaye J.D. "Ἰουδαῖος το γένος and Related Expressions in Josephus." Pages 23–38 in *Josephus and the History of the Greco-Roman Period: Essays in Memory of Morton Smith*. Ed. F. Parente and J. Sievers. Leiden: E.J. Brill, 1994.

——. *The Beginnings of Jewishness: Boundaries, Varieties, Uncertainties*. Berkeley: University of California Press, 1999.

Collins, Adela Yarbro. *Crisis and Catharsis: The Power of the Apocalypse*. Philadelphia: Westminster, 1984.

——. "Insiders and Outsiders in the Book of Revelation and Its Social Context." Pages 187–218 in *"To See Ourselves as Others See Us": Christians, Jews, "Others" in Late Antiquity*. Ed. Jacob Neusner and Ernest S. Frerichs. Chico, Calif.: Scholars Press, 1985.

——. "The Early Christian Apocalypses." *Semeia* 14 (1979): 61–121.

——. "Vilification and Self-Definition in the Book of Revelation." *HTR* 79 (1986): 308–20.

Collins, John J. *The Apocalyptic Imagination: An Introduction to the Jewish Matrix of Christianity*. New York: Crossroad, 1984.

Comaroff, John and Jean. *Ethnography and the Historical Imagination*. Boulder, Colo.: Westview, 1992.

Cone, James H., and Gayraud S. Wilmore, eds. *Black Theology: A Documentary History*. 2 vols. Maryknoll, N.Y.: Orbis, 1979–93.

Copher, Charles B. *Black Biblical Studies: An Anthology of Charles B. Copher*. Chicago: Black Light Fellowship, 1993.

——. "Egypt and Ethiopia in the Old Testament." *Journal of African Civilizations* 6, no. 2 (1984): 163–78.

——. "The Bible and the African Experience: The Biblical Period." *Journal of the Interdenominational Theological Center* 16, nos. 1 and 2 (1988–89): 32–50.

——. "Three Thousand Years of Biblical Interpretation with Reference to Black Peoples." *Journal of the Interdenominational Theological Center* 13 (1986): 225–46.

Courtès, Jean Marie. "The Theme of 'Ethiopia' and 'Ethiopians' in Patristic Literature." Pages 9–32 of vol. 2/1 in *The Image of the Black in Western Art*. 2 vols. Ed. Jean Devisse. New York: W. Morrow, 1979.

Cox, Patricia. *Biography in Late Antiquity: A Quest for the Holy Man*. Berkeley: University of California Press, 1983.

Cracco Ruggini, Lellia. "Il negro buono e il negro malvagio nel mondo classico." Pages 108–35 in *Conoscenze etniche e rapporti*. Ed. Marta Sordi. Vol. 6. Milan: Università Cattolica del Sacro Cuore, 1979.

——. "Leggenda e realtà degli Etiopi nella culturatardoimperiale." Pages 141–93 in *Atti del IV congresso internazionale di studi etiopici – 10–15 Aprile 1972*. Vol. 1. Rome: Accademia Nazionale dei Lincei, 1974.

Cross, F.L., and E.A. Livingstone, eds. "Apostolic Fathers." Pages 90–91 in *The Oxford Dictionary of the Christian Church*. 3rd ed. New York: Oxford University Press, 1997.

Dahl, Nils A. "Nations in the New Testament." Pages 54–68 in *New Testament Christianity for Africa and the World: Essays in Honor of Harry Sawyer*. Ed. Mark E. Glasswell and Edward Fasholé-Luke. London: SPCK, 1974.

Daley, Brian E. *The Hope of the Early Church: A Handbook of Patristic Eschatology*. Cambridge: Cambridge University Press, 1991.

Davis, Simon. *Race-Relations in Ancient Egypt: Greek, Egyptian, Hebrew, Roman.* London: Methuen, 1951.

Delia, Diana. *Alexandrian Citizenship during the Roman Principate.* Atlanta: Scholars Press, 1991.

Demicheli, Anna Maria. *Rapporti di pace e di guerra dell' Egitto romano con le popolazioni dei deserti africani.* Univ. di Genova, Fondazione Nobile Agostino Poggi 12. Milan: A. Giuffre, 1976.

Deonna, W. "ΕΥΩΔΙΑ: Croyances antiques et modernes: l'odeur suave des dieux et des élus." *Genava* 17 (1939): 167–263.

Desanges, Jehan. "The Iconography of the Black in Ancient North Africa." Pages 246–68, 308–12 in *Image of the Black in Western Art.* Vol. 1. Ed. Ladislas Bugner. New York: W. Morrow, 1976.

Detienne, Marcel. *The Gardens of Adonis: Spices in Greek Mythology.* Trans. Janet Lloyd. Hassocks, Sussex: Harvester, 1977.

Devine, A.M. "Blacks in Antiquity? (The Case of Apollonios ὁ μέλας)." *Ancient History Bulletin* 2, no. 1 (1988): 9.

Devisse, Jean. "Christians and Blacks." Pages 37–80 in *The Image of the Black in Western Art.* Vol. 2.1. From the Early Christian Era to the "Age of Discovery." Gen. ed. Jean Devisse. New York: W. Morrow, 1979.

DeVries, Carl E. "Egypt." Pages 293–98 in *NIDB.*

Dibelius, Martin. *Studies in the Acts of the Apostles.* Ed. Heinrich Greeven. London: SCM Press, 1956.

Dihle, A. *The Conception of India in Hellenistic and Roman Literature,* Proceedings of the Cambridge Philological Association, CXC 1964.

Diller, Aubrey. *Race Mixture Among the Greeks Before Alexander.* Urbana: University of Illinois Press, 1937.

Diop, Cheikh Anta. "Ancient Egypt Revisited." *Black Issues in Higher Education* 28 (1991): 12–16.

———. *Civilization or Barbarism: An Authentic Anthropology.* Trans. Y.M. Ngemi. Chicago: L. Hill, 1991 (1981).

———. "Origin of the Ancient Egyptians." *Journal of African Civilizations* 4, no. 2 (1982): 9–37.

———. *The African Origin of Civilization: Myth or Reality.* Trans. Mercer Cook. Chicago: L. Hill, 1974.

Dölger, Franz Joseph. "Der Kampf mit dem Ägypter in der Perpetua-Vision: Das Martyrium als Kampf mit dem Teufel." *Antike und Christentum* 3 (1932): 177–88.

———. *Die Sonne der Gerechtigkeit und der Schwarze: Eine religionsgeschichtliche Studie zum Taufgelobnis.* Liturgiewissenschaftliche Quellen und Forschungen 14. 2nd ed. Münster: Aschendorff, 1971.

Douglas, Kelly Brown. *Sexuality and the Black Church: A Womanist Perspective.* Maryknoll, N.Y.: Orbis, 1999.

Drake, St. Clair. *Black Folk Here and There: An Essay in History and Anthropology.* 2 vols. Los Angeles: Center for Afro-American Studies, University of California, 1987–90.

DuBois, W.E.B. *Souls of Black Folk.* New York: Signet Classics, 1969 (1903).

———. *The Negro.* London: Oxford University Press, 1970 (1915).

Dunston, Jr., Alfred G. *The Black Man in the Old Testament and its World.* Trenton, N.J.: Africa World, 1992.

Dyer, Jacob A. *The Ethiopian in the Bible.* New York: Vantage, 1974.

Dyson, Michael Eric. *Reflecting Black: African American Cultural Criticism.* Minneapolis: University of Minnesota Press, 1993.

Early, Gerald. "Black Like Them." Review of *The Future of the Race*, by Henry Louis Gates, Jr., and Cornel West. *New York Times Book Review* (April 21, 1996): 7, 9.

Edwards, Catharine. *The Politics of Immorality in Ancient Rome.* Cambridge: Cambridge University Press, 1993.

Ehrman, Bart. *The New Testament: A Historical Introduction to the Early Christian Writings.* 2nd ed. New York: Oxford University Press, 2000.

Elm, Susanna, *"Virgins of God": The Making of Asceticism in Late Antiquity.* New York: Oxford University Press, 1994.

Esler, Philip F. "Group Boundaries and Intergroup Conflict in Galatians: A New Reading of Galatians 5:13–6:10." Pages 215–40 in *Ethnicity and the Bible.* Ed. Mark G. Brett. Leiden: E.J. Brill, 1996.

Evans-Pritchard, E.E. *The Nuer: A Description of the Modes of Livelihood and Political Institutions of the Nilotic People.* Oxford: Clarendon, 1940.

Fantham, Elaine, Helene Peet Foley, Natalie Boymel Kampen, Sarah B. Pomeroy, and H.A. Shapiro. *Women in the Classical World: Image and Text.* New York: Oxford University Press, 1994.

Felder, Cain Hope. "Racial Motifs in the Biblical Narratives." Pages 37–48 in *Troubling Biblical Waters.* Maryknoll, N.Y.: Orbis, 1989.

—— ed. *Stony the Road We Trod: African American Biblical Interpretation.* Minneapolis: Fortress, 1991.

—— *Troubling Biblical Waters: Race, Class, and Family.* Maryknoll, N.Y.: Orbis, 1989.

Felton, D. *Haunted Greece and Rome: Ghost Stories from Classical Antiquity.* Austin: University of Texas Press, 1999.

Fernandez, James W. *Beyond Metaphor: The Theory of Tropes in Anthropology.* Stanford: Stanford University Press, 1991.

——. *Persuasions and Performances: The Play of Tropes in Culture.* Bloomington: Indiana University Press, 1986.

——. "Race Prejudice in the Ancient World." *Listener* 79 (1968): 146–47.

Flax, Jane. "Postmodernism and Gender Relations in Feminist Theory." *Signs* 12 (1986): 621–43.

Fletcher, Richard. *The Barbarian Conversion: From Paganism to Christianity.* Berkeley: University of California Press, 1997.

Foertmeyer, Victoria Ann. "Tourism in Graeco-Roman Egypt." Ph.D. diss., Princeton University, 1989.

Folliet, G. "Aux origines de l'ascétisme et du cénobitisme africain," *SA* 46 (1961): 25–44.

Foster, Herbert J. "The Ethnicity of the Ancient Egyptians." *Journal of Black Studies* 5, no. 2 (1974): 175–91.

Foucault, Michel. *The History of Sexuality: An Introduction.* 3 vols. Trans. Robert Hurley. New York: Vintage, 1978–86.

Fowden, Garth. *The Egyptian Hermes: A Historical Approach to the Late Pagan Mind.* Princeton: Princeton University Press, 1993 (1986).

Fox, Robin Lane. *Pagans and Christians.* New York: HarperCollins, 1986.

France, Peter. *The Rape of Egypt: How the Europeans Stripped Egypt of its Heritage.* London: Barrie & Jenkins, 1991.

Frankfurter, David. *Religion in Roman Egypt: Assimilation and Resistance*. Princeton: Princeton University Press, 1998.

Franklin, Eric. *Luke: Interpreter of Paul, Critic of Matthew*. JSNTSup 92. Sheffield: Sheffield Academic Press, 1994.

Franklin, John Hope, ed. *Color and Race*. Boston: Houghton Mifflin, 1968.

Freyne, Sean. "Vilifying the Other and Defining the Self: Matthew's and John's Anti-Jewish Polemic in Focus." Pages 117–43 in *To See Ourselves as Others See Us: Christians, Jews, "Others" in Late Antiquity*. Ed. Jacob Neusner and Ernest S. Frerichs. Chico, Calif.: Scholars Press, 1988.

Frost, Peter. "Attitudes toward Blacks in the Early Christian Era." *SecCent* 8, no. 1 (1991): 1–11.

Furman, James E. "Egypt in the Bible." *Coptic Church Review* 14 (1993): 11–17.

Gager, John. *The Origins of Anti-Semitism: Attitudes Toward Judaism in Pagan and Christian Antiquity*. New York: Oxford University Press, 1983.

Gangutia, Elvira, et al. *Diccionario Griego-Español*. Madrid: Consejo Superior de Investigaciones Científicas, 1980– .

Garnsey, Peter, Keith Hopkins, and C.R. Whittaker, eds. *Trade in the Ancient Economy*. Berkeley: University of California Press, 1983.

Garrison, Roman. *The Greco-Roman Context of Early Christian Literature*. JSNTSup 137. Sheffield: Sheffield Academic Press, 1997.

Gates, Jr., Henry Louis. *The Signifying Monkey: A Theory of Afro-American Literary Criticism*. New York: Oxford University Press, 1988.

———. "'What's in a Name?' Some Meanings of Blackness." Pages 131–51 in *Loose Canons: Notes on the Culture Wars*. New York: Oxford University Press, 1992.

———, ed. *"Race," Writing, and Difference*. Chicago: University of Chicago Press, 1986.

Gaventa, Beverly R. *From Darkness to Light: Aspects of Conversion in the New Testament*. Philadelphia: Fortress, 1986.

Geary, Patrick J. "Barbarians and Ethnicity." Pages 107–29 in *Late Antiquity: A Guide to the Postclassical World*. Ed. G.W. Bowersock, Peter Brown, and Oleg Grabar. Cambridge, Mass.: Harvard University Press, 1999.

Georgi, Dieter. "The Resurrection and the South," Lecture 12 of a course entitled "Cash and Creed in Early Christianity." Union Theological Seminary, spring 1997.

Gero, Stephen. "Parerga to 'The Book of Jannes and Jambres'." *JSP* 9 (October 1991): 67–85.

Gibbs, Nancy. "Death and Deceit." *Time Magazine* (November 14, 1994): 43–51.

Gier, Nicholas F. "The Color of Sin/The Color of Skin: Ancient Color Blindness and the Philosophical Origins of Modern Racism." *JRT* 46, no. 1 (1989–90): 42–52.

Glare, P.G.W. *Oxford Latin Dictionary*. New York: Oxford University Press, 1982.

Godelier, Maurice. "The Origins of Male Domination." *New Left Review* 127 (1981): 3–17.

Goehring, James E. "The World Engaged: The Social and Economic World of Early Egyptian Monasticism." Pages 134–44 in *Gnosticism and the Early Christian World: Essays in Honor of James M. Robinson*. Ed. James Goehring et al. Sonoma, Calif.: Polebridge, 1990.

———. "Through a Glass Darkly: Diverse Images of the APOTAKTIKOI(AI) of Early Egyptian Monasticism." *Semeia* 58 (1992): 25–45.

Gokey, F.X. *The Terminology for the Devil and Evil Spirits in the Apostolic Fathers.* Washington, D.C.: Catholic University of America Press, 1961.

Goudriaan, Koen. "Ethnical Strategies in Graeco-Roman Egypt." Pages 74–99 in *Ethnicity in Hellenistic Egypt.* Ed. P. Bilde, Troels Engberg-Pedersen, Lise Hannestad, and Jan Zahle. Aarhus: Aarhus University Press, 1992.

Grant, Robert M. *Early Christian Literature and the Classical Intellectual Tradition.* Ed. William R. Schoedel and Robert L. Wilken. Paris: Beauchesne, 1979.

———. *Heresy and Criticism: The Search for Authenticity in Early Christian Literature.* Louisville: Westminster/John Knox, 1993.

Gray, Herman. *Watching Race: Television and the Struggle for "Blackness".* Minneapolis: University of Minnesota Press, 1995.

Green, Henry A. "The Socio-Economic Background of Christianity in Egypt." Pages 100–113 in *Roots of Egyptian Christianity.* Ed. Birger A. Pearson and James E. Goehring. Philadelphia: Fortress, 1986.

Greene, Ellen. *The Erotics of Domination: Male Desire and the Mistress in Latin Love Poetry.* Baltimore: Johns Hopkins University Press, 1998.

Griffiths, J. Gwyn. "Was Damaris an Egyptian? (Acts17:34)." *BZ* 8 (1964): 293–95.

Grimal, Nicolas. *A History of Ancient Egypt.* Oxford: Basil Blackwell, 1992.

Haas, Christopher. *Alexandria in Late Antiquity: Topography and Social Conflict.* Baltimore: Johns Hopkins University Press, 1997.

Habermehl, Peter. *Perpetua und der Aegypter oder Bilder des Bösen im Frühen Afrikanischen Christentum: Ein Versuch zur "Passio Sanctarum Perpetuae et Felicitatis".* TUGAL 140. Berlin: Akademie, 1992.

Habinek, Thomas N. *The Politics of Latin Literature: Writing, Identity, and Empire in Ancient Rome.* Princeton: Princeton University Press, 1998.

Hadas, Moses. "Utopian Sources in Herodotus." *CP* 30 (1935): 113–21.

Haenchen, Ernst. *Acts of the Apostles: A Commentary.* Philadelphia: Westminster, 1971.

Haley, Shelley P. "Black Feminist Thought and Classics: Re-membering, Re-claiming, Re-empowering." Pages 23–43 in *Feminist Theory and the Classics.* Ed. Nancy Sorkin Rabinowitz and Amy Richlin. New York: Routledge, 1993.

Hall, Edith. *Inventing the Barbarian: Greek Self-Definition through Tragedy.* Oxford: Oxford University Press, 1989.

Hall, Jonathan M. *Ethnic Identity in Greek Antiquity.* Cambridge: Cambridge University Press, 1997.

Hall, Stuart. *Race: The Floating Signifier* [videorecording]. Produced, directed, and edited by Sut Jhally. Northampton, Mass.: Media Education Foundation, 1996.

———. *Representation: Cultural Representations and Signifying Practices.* London: Thousand Oaks, 1997.

Hamman, Adalbert. "The Turnabout of the Fourth Century: A Political, Geographical, Social, Ecclesiastical, and Doctrinal Framework of the Century." In *Patrology.* Vol. 4. Ed. Johannes Quasten, 1–32. Westminster, Md.: Christian Classics, 1994.

Hannaford, Ivan. *Race: The History of an Idea in the West.* Washington, D.C.: Woodrow Wilson Center, 1996.

Hanson, Paul D. *The Dawn of the Apocalyptic: The Historical and Sociological Roots of Jewish Apocalyptic Eschatology.* Philadelphia: Fortress, 1975.

Harnack, Adolf. "Excursus: Christians as a Third Race in the Judgment of their Opponents." Pages 336–52 in *The Expansion of Christianity in the First Three Centuries.* 2 vols. Trans and ed. J. Moffatt. New York: G.P. Putnam's Sons, 1904.

Harper, Phillip Brian. *Are We Not Men: Masculine Anxiety and the Problem of African-American Identity*. New York: Oxford University Press, 1996.

Harpham, Geoffrey Galt. *The Ascetic Imperative in Culture and Criticism*. Chicago: University of Chicago Press, 1987.

Harris, Joseph E., ed. *Africa and Africans as Seen by Classical Writers: The William Leo Hansberry African History Notebook*. Vol. 2. Washington, D.C.: Howard University Press, 1977.

Harris, Joseph E. *Africans and their History*. Rev. ed. New York: Penguin, 1987 (1972).

———., ed. *Pillars in Ethiopian History: The William Leo Hansberry African History Notebook*. Vol. 1. Washington, D.C.: Howard University Press, 1974.

Harris, W.V. *Ancient Literacy*. Cambridge, Mass.: Harvard University Press, 1989.

Hartog, François. *The Mirror of Herodotus: The Representation of the Other in the Writing of History*. Berkeley: University of California Press, 1988.

Harvey, John. *Men in Black*. Chicago: University of Chicago Press, 1995.

Harvey, Susan Ashbrook. "Olfactory Knowing: Signs of Smell in the *Vitae* of Simeon Stylites." Pages 23–34 in *After Bardaisan: Studies on Continuity and Change in Syriac Christianity in Honour of Professor Han J.W. Drijvers*. Ed. G.J. Reinink and A.C. Klugkist. Leuven: Peeters, 1999.

———. "St. Ephrem on the Scent of Salvation." *JTS* 49 (1998): 109–28.

Hawley, John Stratton, ed. *Saints and Virtues*. Berkeley: University of California Press, 1987.

Hays, J. Daniel. "The Cushites: A Black Nation in the Bible." *BSac* 153 (1996): 396–409.

Heeren, Arnold Hermann. *Politics, Intercourse, and Trade of the Carthaginians, Ethiopians, and Egyptians*. 4 vols. London: H.G. Bohn, 1846–57.

Heldman, Marilyn, et al. *African Zion: The Sacred Art of Ethiopia*. New Haven: Yale University Press, 1993.

Hendricks, Obery M. "A Discourse of Domination: A Socio-Rhetorical Study of the Use of *Ioudaios* in the Fourth Gospel." Ph.D. diss., Princeton University, 1995.

———. "Guerrilla Exegesis: A Post Modern Proposal for Insurgent African American Biblical Interpretation." *Journal of the Interdenominational Theological Seminary* 22, no. 1 (1994): 92–109.

Hermann, A. "Farbe." In *Reallexikon für Antike und Christentum* 7: 358–447. Ed. T. Klauser. Stuttgart, 1969.

Herzog II, William R. "The New Testament and the Question of Racial Injustice." *ABQ* 5 (1989): 12–32.

Hess, Richard S. "Egypt." In *ABD*, 2: 321.

Hill, Jonathan D., ed. *History, Power, and Identity: Ethnogenesis in the Americas, 1492–1992*. Iowa City: University of Iowa Press, 1996.

Hine, Darlene Clark. "In the Kingdom of Culture: Black Women and the Intersection of Race, Gender, and Class." Pages 337–51 in *Lure and Loathing: Twenty Black Intellectuals Address W.E.B. DuBois's Dilemma of the Double-Consciousness of African Americans*. Ed. Gerald Early. New York: Penguin, 1993.

Hintze, Fritz, ed. *Africa in Antiquity: The Arts of Ancient Nubia and the Sudan*. Vol. 1. New York: Brooklyn Museum, 1978.

Holmes, Michael, ed. *Apostolic Fathers*. Trans. J.B. Lightfoot and J.R. Harmer. 2nd ed. Grand Rapids: Baker, 1989.

Holmes, Urban T. "Taxonomy of Contemporary Spirituality." Pages 26–45 in *Christians at Prayer*. Ed. John Gallen. Notre Dame, Ind.: University of Notre Dame Press, 1977.

Hood, Robert E. *Begrimed and Black: Christian Traditions on Blacks and Blackness*. Minneapolis: Fortress, 1994.

hooks, bell. "Postmodern Blackness." Pages 23–31 in *Yearnings: Race, Gender, and Cultural Politics*. Boston: South End, 1990.

Hopkins, Keith. *Conquerors and Slaves*. Sociological Studies in Roman History 1. Cambridge: Cambridge University Press, 1978.

Horowitz, Donald L. *Ethnic Groups in Conflict*. Berkeley: University of California Press, 1985.

Hourihane, Colum, ed. *Virtue and Vice: The Personifications in the Index of Christian Art*. Princeton: Princeton University Press, 2000.

Huzar, Eleanor G. "Augustus, Heir of the Ptolemies." Pages 343–82 in *ANRW* 10.1. New York: W. DeGruyter, 1988.

Irwin, Eleanor. *Colour Terms in Greek Poetry*. Toronto: Hakkert, 1974.

Isichei, Elizabeth Allo. *Political Thinking and Social Experience: Some Christian Interpretations of the Roman Empire from Tertullian to Salvian*. Canterbury: University of Canterbury, 1964.

Iversen, Erik. "Egypt in Classical Antiquity: A Résumé." Pages 295–305 in *Hommages à Jean Leclant* 3: Études Isiaques Bd. 106/3. Ed. C. Berger et al. Cairo: IFAO, 1994.

Jackson, Alvin A. *Examining the Record: An Exegetical and Homiletical Study of Blacks in the Bible*. New York: P. Lang, 1994.

Jackson, John G. "Egypt and Christianity." *Journal of African Civilizations* 4, no. 2 (1982): 65–80.

———. *Ethiopia and the Origin of Civilization*. Baltimore: Black Classic, 1985 (1939).

Jaeger, Werner. *Early Christianity and Greek Paideia*. Cambridge, Mass.: Harvard University Press, 1961.

James, George G.M. *Stolen Legacy: Greek Philosophy is Stolen Egyptian Philosophy*. Trenton: Africa World, 1992 (1954).

Johnson, Janet, ed. *Life in a Multi-Cultural Society: Egypt from Cambyses to Constantine and Beyond*. SAOC 51. Chicago: Oriental Institute of the University of Chicago, 1992.

Johnson, Luke T. "The New Testament's Anti-Jewish Slander and the Conventions of Ancient Polemic." *JBL* 108, no. 3 (1989): 419–41.

Kakosy, L. "Nubien als mythisches Land im Altertum." Pages 3–10 in *Annales Universitatis Scientiarum Budapestinensis de Rolando Eötvös nominatae*. Sectio Historica 8. Budapest: Universitatis Scientiarum Budapestinensis, 1966.

Kelly, Henry Ansgar. "The Devil in the Desert." *CBQ* 26, no. 2 (1964): 190–220.

Kelly, J.N.D. *Jerome: His Life, Writings and Controversies*. Peabody, Mass.: Hendrickson, 1998 (1975).

Kennedy, George A. *A New History of Classical Rhetoric*. Princeton: Princeton University Press, 1994.

———. *Classical Rhetoric and its Christian and Secular Tradition from Ancient to Modern Times*. Chapel Hill: University of North Carolina Press, 1980.

———. *Greek Rhetoric under Christian Emperors*. Princeton: Princeton University Press, 1983.

——. *New Testament Interpretation Through Rhetorical Criticism*. Chapel Hill: University of North Carolina Press, 1984.

Kilpatrick, George D. "The Land of Egypt in the New Testament." *JTS* 17 (1966): 70.

Kirk, J. Andrew. "Race, Class, Caste and the Bible." *Them* 10, no. 2 (1985): 4–14.

Kirwan, L.P. "Rome Beyond the Southern Egyptian Frontier." *Geographical Journal* 123 (1957): 13–19.

Kitchen, K.A. "Egypt, Egyptian." *NIDNTT* 1: 530–32.

Kober, Alice Elizabeth. "The Use of Color Terms in the Greek Poets, including all the Poets from Homer to 146 BCE except the Epigrammatists." Ph.D. diss., Columbia University, 1932.

Koester, Helmut. "GNOMAI DIAPHOROI: The Origin and Nature of Diversification in the History of Early Christianity." *HTR* 58 (1965): 279–318.

——. *Introduction to the New Testament*. 2 vols. 2nd ed. New York: W. de Gruyter, 1995–2000 (1982).

Koster, Severin. *Die Invektive in der griechischen und römischen Literatur*. Beiträge zur Klassischen Philologie 99. Meisenheim am Glan: A. Hain, 1980.

Knust, Jennifer Wright. "God Has Abandoned Them to Their Lust: The Politics of Sexual Vice in Early Christian Discourse." Ph.D. diss., Columbia University, 2000.

Kraemer, Ross S. *Her Share of the Blessings: Women's Religions Among Pagans, Jews, and Christians in the Greco-Roman World*. New York: Oxford University Press, 1992.

——, ed. *Maenads, Martyrs, Matrons, Monastics: A Sourcebook on Women's Religions in the Greco-Roman World*. Philadelphia: Fortress, 1988.

Kraemer, Ross S., and Mary Rose D'Angelo, eds. *Women and Christian Origins*. New York: Oxford University Press, 1999.

Krawiec, Rebecca S. *Shenoute and the Women of the White Monastery*. New York: Oxford University Press, 2002.

Krupat, Arnold. *Ethnocriticism: Ethnography, History, Literature*. Berkeley: University of California Press, 1992.

Kuefler, Mathew. *The Manly Eunuch: Masculinity, Gender Ambiguity, and Christian Ideology in Late Antiquity*. Chicago: University of Chicago Press, 2001.

Ladner, Gerhart B. "On Roman Attitudes Toward Barbarians in Late Antiquity." *Viator* 7 (1976): 1–26.

Lampe, G.W.H. *A Patristic Greek Lexicon*. Oxford: Clarendon, 1961.

La Piana, George. "Foreign Groups in Rome during the First Centuries of the Empire." *HTR* 20 (1927): 183–403.

Lawrence, Jr., William Frank. "The History of the Interpretation of Acts 8:26–40 by the Church Fathers Prior to the Fall of Rome." Ph.D. diss., Union Theological Seminary, New York, 1984.

Leahy, Anthony. "Ethnic Diversity in Ancient Egypt." Pages 225–34 in *Civilizations of the Ancient Near East*. Vol. 1. Ed. Jack M. Sasson. New York: Scribner, 1995.

Leclant, Jean. "Egypt, Land of Africa, in the Greco-Roman World." Pages 269–85 in *The Image of the Black in Western Art*. Vol. 1. New York: W. Morrow, 1976.

Lefkowitz, Mary R. "Afrocentrists Wage War on Ancient Greeks." *Wall Street Journal* (April 7, 1993): A14.

——. *Not Out of Africa: How Afrocentrism Became an Excuse to Teach Myth and History*. New York: Basic, 1996.

——. "Not Out of Africa: The Origins of Greece and the Illusions of Afrocentrists." *New Republic* (February 10, 1992): 29–36.

Lefkowitz, Mary R., and Guy MacLean Rogers, eds. *Black Athena Revisited.* Chapel Hill: University of North Carolina Press, 1996.

Lentz, John Clayton. *Luke's Portrait of Paul.* Cambridge: Cambridge University Press, 1993.

Lesky, Albin. "Aithiopika." *Hermes* 87 (1957): 27–38.

Levine, Amy-Jill, ed. *"Women Like This": New Perspectives on Jewish Women in the Greco-Roman World.* Atlanta: Scholars Press, 1991.

Levine, Molly Myerowitz. "The Use and Abuse of Black Athena." *AHR* 97 (1992): 440–60.

Lewis, Bernard. *Race and Color in Islam.* New York: Harper & Row, 1971.

Lewis, Naphtali. *Life in Egypt Under Roman Rule.* Oxford: Clarendon, 1983.

Liddell, H.G., and R. Scott. *A Greek-English Lexicon.* Oxford: Clarendon, 1968.

Liebeschuetz, J.H.W.G. *Barbarians and Bishops: Army, Church, and State in the Age of Arcadius and Chrysostom.* Oxford: Clarendon, 1990.

Lincoln, Bruce. *Discourse and the Construction of Society: Comparative Studies of Myth, Ritual, and Classification.* New York: Oxford University Press, 1989.

List, Johann. *Das Antoniusleben des hl. Athanasius des Grossen: eine literarhistorische Studie zu den Anfängen der byzantinischen Hagiographie.* Athens: P.D. Sakellarios, 1931.

Locher, Josef. *Topographie und Geschichte der Region am Ersten Nilkatarakt in Griechisch-Romischer Zeit.* APF 5. Stuttgart: B.G. Teubner, 1999.

Long, Charles H. *Significations: Signs, Symbols, and Images in the Interpretation of Religion.* Philadelphia: Fortress, 1986.

Long, Jacqueline. *Claudian's In Eutropium: Or, How, When, and Why to Slander a Eunuch.* Chapel Hill: University of North Carolina Press, 1996.

Long, Timothy. *Barbarians in Greek Comedy.* Carbondale: Southern Illinois University Press, 1986.

Lonis, Raoul. "Les trois approches de l'Ethiopien par l'opinion gréco-romaine." *Ktema* 6 (1981): 69–87.

Lüdemann, Gerd. *Heretics: The Other Side of Early Christianity.* Trans. John Bowden. Louisville: Westminster/John Knox, 1996.

MacDonald, Margaret Y. *Early Christian Women and Pagan Opinion: The Power of the Hysterical Woman.* Cambridge: Cambridge University Press, 1996.

Mack, Burton L. *Rhetoric and the New Testament.* Minneapolis: Fortress, 1989.

——. *Who Wrote the New Testament? The Making of the Christian Myth.* San Francisco: HarperCollins, 1995.

MacMullen, Ramsay. *Christianizing the Roman Empire (AD 100–400).* New Haven: Yale University Press, 1984.

——. *Enemies of the Roman Order: Treason, Unrest, and Alienation in the Empire.* London: Routledge, 1992 (1966).

——. *Roman Social Relations: 50 BC to AD 284.* New Haven: Yale University Press, 1974.

Malherbe, Abraham J., ed. *Moral Exhortation: A Greco-Roman Sourcebook.* Philadelphia: Westminster, 1986.

Malti-Douglas, Fedwa. *Woman's Body, Woman's Word: Gender and Discourse in Arabo-Islamic Writing.* Princeton: Princeton University Press, 1991.

Mann, Michael. *The Sources of Social Power: A History of Power from the Beginning to AD 1760*. Vol. 1. Cambridge: Cambridge University Press, 1986.

Marable, Manning. *Beyond Black and White: Transforming African-American Politics*. New York: Verso, 1995.

——. *Dispatches from the Ebony Tower: Intellectuals Confront the African-American Experience*. New York: Columbia University Press, 2000.

Markus, Robert. *The End of Ancient Christianity*. Cambridge: Cambridge University Press, 1990.

Marshall, I. Howard. *The Acts of the Apostles*. Grand Rapids: Eerdmans, 1983.

Martin, Clarice J. "A Chamberlain's Journey and the Challenge of Interpretation for Liberation." *Semeia* 47 (1989): 105–35.

——. "The Acts of the Apostles." Pages 763–99 in *Searching the Scriptures*. Vol. 2. Ed. Elisabeth Schüssler Fiorenza. New York: Crossroad, 1994.

——. "The Function of Acts 8:26–40 within the Narrative Structure of the Book of Acts: The Significance of the Eunuch's Provenance for Acts 1:8c." Ph.D. diss., Duke University, 1985.

——. "Womanist Biblical Interpretation." Pages 655–58 in *Dictionary of Biblical Interpretation*. Vol. 2. Ed. John H. Hayes. Nashville: Abingdon, 1999.

——. "Womanist Interpretations of the New Testament: The Quest for Holistic and Inclusive Translation and Interpretation." *JFSR* 6, no. 2 (1990): 41–61.

——. "The Rhetorical Function of Commercial Language in Paul's Letter to Philemon (verse 18)." Pages 321–37 in *Persuasive Artistry: Studies in New Testament Rhetoric in Honor of George A. Kennedy*. Ed. Duane F. Watson. Sheffield: Sheffield University Press, 1991.

Mason, Philip. *Patterns of Dominance*. London: Oxford University Press, 1970.

Mayerson, Philip. "Anti-Black Sentiment in the *Vitae Patrum*." *HTR* 71 (1978): 304–11.

McCasland, S. Vernon. "The Black One." Pages 77–80 in *Early Christian Origins*. Ed Allen Wikgren. Chicago: Quadrangle, 1961.

McCray, Walter M. *The Black Presence in the Bible*. Chicago: Black Light Fellowship, 1990.

McGowan, Andrew. "'A Third Race' or Not: The Rhetoric of Ethnic Self-Definition in the Christian Apologists." Paper delivered at the North American Patristic Society Annual Meeting. Chicago, May 26, 2001.

Meeks, Wayne. "The Social Functions of Apocalyptic Language in Pauline Christianity." Pages 687–705 in *Apocalypticism in the Mediterranean World and the Near East*. Proceedings of the International Colloquium on Apocalypticism – Uppsala, August 12–17, 1979. Ed. David Hellholm. Tübingen: J.C.B. Mohr, 1983.

Miles, Margaret R. *Carnal Knowing: Female Nakedness and Religious Meaning in the Christian West*. Boston: Beacon, 1989.

Modrzejewski, Joseph Mélèze. *The Jews of Egypt: From Rameses II to Emperor Hadrian*. Princeton: Princeton University Press, 1997.

Momigliano, Arnaldo. *Alien Wisdom: The Limits of Hellenization*. Cambridge: Cambridge University Press, 1975.

——. "The Rhetoric of History and the History of Rhetoric: On Hayden White's Tropes." Pages 259–68 in *Comparative Criticism: A Year Book*. Vol. 3. Ed. E.S. Shaffer. Cambridge: Cambridge University Press, 1981.

Montet, Pierre. *Egypt and the Bible.* Trans. Leslie R. Keylock. Philadelphia: Fortress, 1968.

Montserrat, Dominic. *Akhenaten: History, Fantasy, and Ancient Egypt.* London: Routledge, 2000.

———. *Sex and Society in Graeco-Roman Egypt.* London: Kegan Paul, 1996.

Morrison, Toni. *Playing in the Dark: Whiteness and the Literary Imagination.* Cambridge, Mass.: Harvard University Press, 1992.

Mouw, Richard J. "The Bible in Twentieth-Century Protestantism: A Preliminary Taxonomy." Pages 139–62 in *The Bible in America: Essays in Cultural History.* Ed. Nathan O. Hatch and Mark A. Noll. New York: Oxford University Press, 1982.

Morland, Kjell. *The Rhetoric of Curse in Galatians: Paul Confronts Another Gospel.* Emory Studies in Early Christianity 5. Atlanta: Scholars Press, 1995.

Mullen, Jr., E. Theodore. *Ethnic Myths and Pentateuchal Foundations: A New Approach to the Formation of the Pentateuch.* SBLSymS. Atlanta: Scholars Press, 1997.

Müller, K.E. *Geschichte der antiken Ethnographie und ethnologischen Theoriebildung von den Anfängen bis auf die byzantinischen Historiographen 2.* Wiesbaden: F. Steiner, 1980.

Murphy, Francis Xavier. *Politics and the Early Christian.* New York: Desclée, 1967.

———, ed. *A Monument to Saint Jerome: Essays on Some Aspects of His Life, Works and Influence.* New York: Sheed & Ward, 1952.

———. *Rufinus of Aquileia (345–411): His Life and Works.* Washington, D.C.: Catholic University of America Press, 1945.

Murphy-O'Connor, Jerome. *Paul the Letter-Writer: His World, His Options, His Skills.* Collegeville: Liturgical Press, 1995.

Mveng, Engelbert, ed. *Les sources grecques de l'histoire negro-africaine: depuis Homère jusqu'à Strabon.* Paris: Présence Africaine, 1972.

Nadeau, J.Y. "Ethiopians Again and Again." *Mnemosyne* 30 (1977): 75–78.

———. "Ethiopians." *CQ* 20, no. 2 (1970): 339–49.

Neusner, Jacob, and Ernest S. Frerichs, eds. *"To See Ourselves as Others See Us": Christians, Jews, "Others" in Late Antiquity.* Chico, Calif.: Scholars Press, 1985.

Nicolet, Claude. *Space, Geography, and Politics in the Early Roman Empire.* Ann Arbor: University of Michigan Press, 1991.

Nissinen, Martti. *Homoeroticism in the Biblical World: A Historical Perspective.* Minneapolis: Fortress, 1998.

O'Connor, David. *Ancient Nubia: Egypt's Rival in Africa.* Philadelphia: University Museum of Archaeology and Anthropology, 1993.

O'Leary, DeLacy. *The Saints of Egypt.* London: SPCK; New York: Macmillan, 1937.

Olster, David M. "Classical Ethnography and Early Christianity." Pages 9–31 in *The Formulation of Christianity by Conflict Through the Ages.* Ed. Katherine B. Free. Lewiston: Edwin Mellen, 1995.

O'Malley, T.P. *Tertullian and the Bible: Language – Imagery – Exegesis.* Utrecht: Dekker & Van de Vegt, N.V. Nijmegen, 1967.

Opelt, Ilona. *Die Polemik in der christlichen lateinischen Literatur von Tertullian bis Augustin.* Heidelberg: C. Winter – Universitätsverlag, 1980.

Oréal, Elsa. "'Noir parfait': un jeu de mot de l'égyptien au grec." *REG* 111 (1998): 551–65.

Osiek, Carolyn. "Apostolic Fathers." Pages 503–24 in *The Early Christian World.* Vol. 1. Ed. P. Esler. London: Routledge, 2000.

———. *Rich and Poor in the Shepherd of Hermas: An Exegetical-Social Investigation*. CBQMS 15. Washington, D.C.: The Catholic Biblical Association of America, 1983.

———. *Shepherd of Hermas: A Commentary*. Hermeneia Series. Minneapolis: Fortress, 1999.

———. "The Genre and Function of the Shepherd of Hermas." *Semeia* 36 (1986): 113–21.

———. "The Second Century through the Eyes of Hermas: Continuity and Change." *BTB* 20 (1990): 116–22.

———. "The Shepherd of Hermas: An Early Tale that Almost Made It into the New Testament." *BRev* 10 (1994): 48–54.

Otabil, Mensa. *Beyond the Rivers of Ethiopia: A Biblical Revelation of God's Purpose for the Black Race*. Accra, Ghana: Altar International, 1992.

Page, Hugh Rowland. "Ethnological Criticism: An Apologia and Application." Pages 84–107 in *Exploring New Paradigms in Biblical and Cognate Studies*. Macon: Mellen Biblical Press, 1996.

Pagels, Elaine. *The Origin of Satan*. New York: Random House, 1995.

Paget, James Carelton. *The Epistle of Barnabas: Outlook and Background*. Tübingen: J.C.B. Mohr, 1994.

Palanque, Jean-Remy. "St. Jerome and the Barbarians." Pages 173–99 in *A Monument to Saint Jerome: Essays on Some Aspects of His Life, Works and Influence*. Ed. Francis X. Murphy. New York: Sheed & Ward, 1952.

Pérez, Emma. "Sexuality and Discourse: Notes From a Chicana Survivor." Pages 159–84 in *Chicana Lesbians: The Girls Our Mothers Warned Us About*. Ed. Carla Trujillo. Berkeley: Third Women, 1991.

———. *The Decolonial Imaginary: Writing Chicanas into History*. Bloomington: Indiana University Press, 1999.

Perkins, Judith. *The Suffering Self: Pain and Narrative Representation in the Early Christian Era*. London: Routledge, 1995.

Pernveden, L. *The Concept of the Church in the Shepherd of Hermas*. Studia Theologica Lundensia 27. Lund: Gleerup, 1966.

Peskowitz, Miriam B. *Spinning Fantasies: Rabbis, Gender, and History*. Berkeley: University of California Press, 1997.

Petersen, Norman R. *The Gospel of John and the Sociology of Light: Language and Characterization in the Fourth Gospel*. Valley Forge, Pa.: Trinity Press International, 1993.

Pohl, Walter, and Helmut Reimitz, eds. *Strategies of Distinction: The Construction of Ethnic Communities, 300–800*. Leiden: E.J. Brill, 1998.

Pomeroy, Sarah B. *Goddesses, Whores, Wives, and Slaves: Women in Classical Antiquity*. New York: Schocken, 1975.

———. *Women in Hellenistic Egypt: From Alexander to Cleopatra*. Detroit: Wayne State University Press, 1990.

Quasten, Johannes. *Patrology*. 4 vols. Westminster, Md.: Christian Classics, 1951–86.

Rajak, Tessa. "The Location of Cultures in Second Temple Palestine: The Evidence of Josephus." Pages 1–14 in *The Book of Acts in Its Palestinian Setting*. Ed. Richard Bauckham. Grand Rapids: Eerdmans, 1995.

Rathbone, Dominic W. "The Ancient Economy and Graeco-Roman Egypt." Pages 159–76 in *Egitto e Storia Antica Dall'Ellenismo All'età Araba: Bilancio di un Confronto*. Ed. Lucia Criscuolo and Giovanni Geraci. Bologna: Clueb, 1989.

Redding, Ann Holmes. "Together, Not Equal: The Rhetoric of Unity and Headship in the Letter to the Ephesians." Ph.D. diss., Union Theological Seminary, 1999.

Reiling, J. *Hermas and Christian Prophecy: A Study of the Eleventh Mandate*. NovTSup 37. Leiden: E.J. Brill, 1973.

Reitzenstein, Richard. *Poimandres: Studien zur griechischägyptischen und früchristlichen Literatur*. Leipzig: Teubner, 1904.

Reynolds, Edwin Earl. "The Sodom/Egypt/Babylon Motif in the Book of Revelation." Ph.D. diss., Andrews University, 1994.

Riall, Robert. "Athanasius Bishop of Alexandria: The Politics of Spirituality." Ph.D. diss., University of Cincinnati, 1987.

Rickman, G.E. "The Grain Trade under the Roman Empire." In *The Seaborne Commerce of Ancient Rome*. MAAR 36. Ed. J.H. D'Arms and E.C. Kopff. Rome: American Academy in Rome, 1980.

Rives, James B., trans. and ed. *Germania*. New York: Oxford University Press, 1999.

Robbins, Gay. *Women in Ancient Egypt*. Cambridge, Mass.: Harvard University Press, 1993.

Robbins, Vernon K. *The Tapestry of Early Christian Discourse: Rhetoric, Society and Ideology*. London: Routledge, 1996.

Robinson, James M., and Helmut Koester. *Trajectories Through Early Christianity*. Philadelphia: Fortress, 1971.

Robinson, Thomas A. *The Bauer Thesis Examined: The Geography of Heresy in the Early Christian Church*. Lewiston: Edwin Mellen, 1988.

Romm, James S. *The Edges of the Earth in Ancient Thought: Geography, Exploration, and Fiction*. Princeton: Princeton University Press, 1992.

Roth, Ann Macy. "Building Bridges to Afrocentrism: A Letter to my Egyptological Colleagues: Part 1." *American Research Center in Egypt Newsletter* 167 (1995): 1, 14–17.

———. "Building Bridges to Afrocentrism: A Letter to my Egyptological Colleagues: Part 2." *American Research Center in Egypt Newsletter* 168 (1995): 1, 12–15.

———. Review of *Not Out of Africa*, by Mary R. Lefkowitz and *Black Athena Revisited*. Ed. Mary R. Lefkowitz and Guy M. Rogers. *AHR* 102 (1997): 493–95.

Rousselle, Aline. *Porneia: On Desire and the Body in Antiquity*. Trans. Felicia Pheasant. Cambridge and Oxford: Blackwell, 1988.

Rowe, Christopher. "Conceptions of Colour and Colour Symbolism in the Ancient World." Pages 327–64 in *Die Welt der Farben le Monde des Couleurs*. Ed. A. Portmann and R. Ritsema. Leiden: E.J. Brill, 1974.

Rowlandson, Jane, ed. *Women and Society in Greek and Roman Egypt: A Sourcebook*. Cambridge: Cambridge University Press, 1998.

Rubenson, Samuel. "Christian Asceticism and the Emergence of the Monastic Tradition." Pages 49–57 in *Asceticism*. Ed. Vincent L. Wimbush and Richard Valantasis. New York: Oxford University Press, 1995.

Ruether, Rosemary Radford. *Faith and Fratricide: The Theological Roots of Anti-Semitism*. New York: Seabury, 1974.

Russell, Jeffrey Burton. *Satan: The Early Christian Tradition*. Ithaca: Cornell University Press, 1981.

———. *The Devil: Perceptions of Evil from Antiquity to Primitive Christianity*. Ithaca: Cornell University Press, 1977.

——. *The Prince of Darkness: Radical Evil and the Power of Good in History.* Ithaca: Cornell University Press, 1988.

Russell, Norman. *The Lives of the Desert Fathers.* Oxford: Mowbray, 1980.

Saddington, D.B. "Race Relations in the Early Roman Empire." Pages 112–37 in *ANRW* 2.3. Ed. H. Temporini and W. Haase. Berlin: W. de Gruyter, 1975.

Said, Edward. "An Ideology of Difference." Pages 38–58 in *"Race," Writing, and Difference.* Ed. Henry Louis Gates, Jr. Chicago: University of Chicago Press, 1986.

——. *Orientalism.* New York: Vintage, 1979.

Salisbury, Joyce E. *Perpetua's Passion: The Death and Memory of a Young Roman Woman.* New York: Routledge, 1997.

Sangren, P. Steven. "Rhetoric and the Authority of Ethnography: 'Postmodernism' and the Social Reproduction of Texts." *Current Anthropology* 29 (1988): 405–23.

Satlow, Michael L. *Tasting the Dish: Rabbinic Rhetorics of Sexuality.* BJS 303. Atlanta: Scholars Press, 1995.

Schäfer, Peter. *Judeophobia: Attitudes Toward the Jews in the Ancient World.* Cambridge, Mass.: Harvard University Press, 1997.

Schüssler Fiorenza, Elisabeth. "The Rhetoricity of Historical Knowledge: Pauline Discourse and its Contextualizations." Pages 443–69 in *Religious Propaganda and Missionary Competition in the New Testament World: Essays Honoring Dieter Georgi.* Ed. Lukas Bormann et al. Leiden: E.J. Brill, 1994.

——. *In Memory of Her: A Feminist Theological Reconstruction of Christian Origins.* New York: Crossroad, 1983.

——, ed. *Searching The Scriptures.* 2 vols. New York: Crossroad, 1993–94.

Scott, Joan Wallach. *Gender and the Politics of History.* Rev. ed. New York: Columbia University Press, 1999.

——. "Gender: A Useful Category of Historical Analysis," *AHR* 91, no. 5 (1986): 1053–75. Pages 152–80 (repr.) in *Feminism and History.* Ed. Joan Wallach Scott. Oxford: Oxford University Press, 1996.

Scourfield, J.H.D. *Consoling Heliodorus: A Commentary on Jerome, Letter 60.* New York: Oxford University Press, 1993.

Scroggs, Robin. *The New Testament and Homosexuality: Contextual Background for Contemporary Debate.* Philadelphia: Fortress, 1983.

Segovia, Fernando. *Reading from this Place: Social Location and Biblical Interpretation in the United States.* 2 vols. Ed. Fernando F. Segovia and Mary Ann Tolbert. Minneapolis: Fortress, 1995.

——. "Racial and Ethnic Minorities in Biblical Studies." Pages 469–92 in *Ethnicity and the Bible.* Ed. Mark G. Brett. Leiden: E.J. Brill, 1996.

Sertima, Ivan van. *Egypt: Child of Africa.* New Brunswick, N.J.: Transaction, 1994.

——., ed. *Black Women in Antiquity.* New Brunswick, N.J.: Transaction, 1989.

Setzer, Claudia. *Jewish Responses to Early Christians: History and Polemics 30–150 CE.* Minneapolis: Fortress, 1994.

Sheppard, Phillis. "Fleshing the Theory: A Critical Analysis of Theories of the Body in Light of African American Women's Experiences." Ph.D. diss., Chicago Theological Seminary, 1997.

Sheridan, Daniel P. "Discerning Difference: A Taxonomy of Culture, Spirituality, and Religion." *JR* 66 (1986): 37–45.

Sherwin-White, A.N. *Racial Prejudice in Imperial Rome.* Cambridge: Cambridge University Press, 1967.

Sider, Robert Dick. *Ancient Rhetoric and the Art of Tertullian*. New York: Oxford University Press, 1971.

Sigrist, Christian, and Rainer Neu. *Ethnologische Texte zum Alten Testament*. Vol. 1. Neukirchen-Vluyn: Neukirchener Verlag, 1989.

Simonetti, Manlio. *Biblical Interpretation in the Early Church: An Historical Introduction to Patristic Exegesis*. Trans. John A. Hughes. Edinburgh: T&T Clark, 1994.

Smith, Abraham. "'Do You Understand What You are Reading?': A Literary Critical Reading of the Ethiopian (Kushite) Episode (Acts 8:26–40)." *Journal of the Interdenominational Theological Center* 22, no. 1 (1994): 48–70.

Smith, Jonathan Z. "What a Difference a Difference Makes." Pages 3–48 in *"To See Ourselves as Others See Us": Christians, Jews, "Others" in Late Antiquity*. Ed. J. Neusner and E.S. Frerichs. Chico, Calif.: Scholars Press, 1985.

Smith, Morton. "Book Review of *Blacks in Antiquity*." *AHR* 76 (1971): 139–40.

Snowden, Jr., Frank M. *Before Color Prejudice: The Ancient View of Blacks*. Cambridge, Mass.: Harvard University Press, 1983.

———. "Bernal's 'Blacks' and the Afrocentrists." Pages 112–28 in *Black Athena Revisited*. Ed. Mary R. Lefkowitz and Guy MacLean Rogers. Chapel Hill: University of North Carolina Press, 1996.

———. *Blacks in Antiquity: Ethiopians in the Greco-Roman Experience*. Cambridge, Mass.: Harvard University Press, 1970.

———. "Ethiopians and the Graeco-Roman World." Pages 11–36 in *The African Diaspora: Interpretive Essays*. Ed. Martin L. Kilson and Robert I. Rotberg. Cambridge, Mass.: Harvard University Press, 1976.

———. "Iconographical Evidence on the Black Populations in Greco-Roman Antiquity." Pages 133–245, 298–307 in *From the Pharaohs to the Fall of the Roman Empire*. Vol. 1 of *Image of the Black in Western Art*. Ed. Ladislas Bugner. New York: W. Morrow, 1976.

Sollors, Werner. "Ethnicity." Pages 288–305 in *Critical Terms for Literary Study*. Ed. Frank Lentricchia and Thomas McLaughlin. Chicago: University of Chicago Press, 1990.

———, ed. *The Invention of Ethnicity*. New York: Oxford University Press, 1989.

———, ed. *Theories of Ethnicity: A Classical Reader*. New York: New York University Press, 1996.

Sordi, Marta, ed. *Conoscenze etniche e rapporti di convivenza nell' antichita autori vari*. Vol. 6. Contributi dell' Instituto di storia antica. Milan: Vita e Pensiero, 1979.

Sorenson, John. *Imagining Ethiopia: Struggles for History and Identity in the Horn of Africa*. New Brunswick, N.J.: Rutgers University Press, 1993.

Sparks, Kenton L. *Ethnicity and Identity in Ancient Israel: Prolegomena to the Study of Ethnic Sentiments and Their Expression in the Hebrew Bible*. Winona Lake, Ind.: Eisenbrauns, 1999.

Spencer, F. Scott. "The Ethiopian Eunuch and His Bible: A Social-Science Analysis." *BTB* 22, no. 4 (1992): 155–65.

Stegemann, Wolfgang. "Anti-Semitic and Racist Prejudices in Titus 1:10–16." Pages 271–94 in *Ethnicity and the Bible*. Ed. Mark Brett. Leiden: E.J. Brill, 1996.

Steidle, P. Basilius. "Der 'schwarze kleine Knabe' in der alten Mönchserzählung." *Benediktinische Monatschrift* 34 (1958): 339–50.

Sterling, Gregory E. *Historiography and Self-Definition: Josephos, Luke-Acts and Apologetic Historiography*. Leiden: E.J. Brill, 1992.

Stewart, Columba. *Cassian the Monk.* New York: Oxford University Press, 1998.

Thesaurus Linguae Graecae. CD-ROM. Data Bank, Version D. University of California at Irvine.

Thomas, Latta R. *Biblical Faith and the Black American.* Valley Forge, Pa.: Judson, 1976.

Thomas, Richard F. *Lands and Peoples in Roman Poetry: The Ethnographic Tradition.* Cambridge Philological Society Suppl. 7. Cambridge: Cambridge University Press, 1982.

Thompson, E.A. *Romans and Barbarians: The Decline of the Western Empire.* Madison: University of Wisconsin Press, 1982.

Thompson, Lloyd A. *Romans and Blacks.* Norman: University of Oklahoma Press, 1989.

Tilley, Maureen A. *The Bible in Christian North Africa: The Donatist World.* Minneapolis: Fortress, 1997.

Török, László. *Late Antique Nubia: History and Archaeology of the Southern Neighbor of Egypt in the 4th–6th c. AD.* Antaeus 16. Budapest: Archaeological Institute of the Hungarian Academy of Sciences, 1988.

———. *The Kingdom of Kush: Handbook of the Napatan-Meriotic Civilization.* New York: E.J. Brill, 1997.

Torres, Arlene, and Norman E. Whitten, Jr., eds. *Blackness in Latin America and the Caribbean: Social Dynamics and Cultural Transformation.* 2 vols. Bloomington: Indiana University Press, 1998.

Trible, Phyllis. *God and the Rhetoric of Sexuality.* Philadelphia: Fortress, 1978.

———. *Texts of Terror: Literary-Feminist Readings of Biblical Narratives.* Philadelphia: Fortress, 1984.

Ullendorff, Edward. "Candace (Acts VIII.27) and the Queen of Sheba." *NTS* 2 (1955–56): 53–56.

———. *Ethiopia and the Bible.* London: Oxford University Press, 1968.

———. *The Ethiopians: An Introduction to the Country and People.* Oxford: Oxford University Press, 1973.

Updegraff, Robert T., and L. Török. "The Blemmyes I: The Rise of the Blemmyes and the Roman Withdrawal from Nubia under Diocletian." Pages 44–106 in *ANRW* 10.1. New York: W. DeGruyter, 1988.

Vaage, Leif, and Vincent L. Wimbush, eds. *Asceticism and the New Testament.* New York: Routledge, 1999.

Valantasis, Richard J., ed. "Constructions of Power in Asceticism." *JAAR* 63, no. 4 (1995): 775–821.

———. "Demons and the Perfecting of the Monk's Body: Monastic Anthropology, Daemonology, and Asceticism." *Semeia* 58 (1992): 47–79.

Vööbus, Arthur. *A History of Asceticism in the Syrian Orient.* CSCO 184, Subsidia 14. Louvain: CSCO, 1958.

Wallace, S.L. *Taxation in Egypt from Augustus to Diocletian.* Princeton University Studies in Papyrology 2. Princeton: Princeton University Press, 1938.

Walters, James C. *Ethnic Issues in Paul's Letter to the Romans: Changing Self-Definitions in Earliest Roman Christianity.* Valley Forge, Pa.: Trinity Press International, 1993.

Wan, Sze-Kar. "Collection for the Saints as Anticolonial Act: Implications of Paul's Ethnic Reconstruction." Pages 191–215 in *Paul and Politics.* Ed. Richard A. Horsley. Harrisburg, Pa.: Trinity Press International, 2000.

Ward, Benedicta, trans. *Harlots of the Desert: A Study of Repentance in Early Monastic Sources*. Kalamazoo, Mich.: Cistercian, 1987.

———. *The Lives of the Desert Fathers: The Historia Monachorum in Aegypto*. Intro. Benedicta Ward. Trans. Norman Russell. Kalamazoo, Mich.: Cistercian, 1981.

———. *The Sayings of the Desert Fathers: The Alphabetical Collection*. Kalamazoo, Mich.: Cistercian, 1984 (1975).

———. *The Wisdom of the Desert Fathers: Apophthegmata Patrum – The Anonymous Series*. Fairacres, Oxford: SLG, 1975.

Ware, Kallistos. "The Way of the Ascetics: Negative or Affirmative?" Pages 3–15 in *Asceticism*. Ed. Vincent L. Wimbush and Richard Valantasis. New York: Oxford University Press, 1995.

Warmington, B.H. "Book Review of *Blacks in Antiquity*." *African Historical Studies* 4, no. 2 (1971): 383–86.

Waszink, J.H. "Some Observations on the Appreciation of the 'Philosophy of the Barbarians' in Early Christian Literature." Pages 41–56 in *Mélanges Christine Mohrmann*. Utrecht, Anvers: Spectrum, 1963.

Weems, Renita J. *Battered Love: Marriage, Sex, and Violence in the Hebrew Prophets*. Minneapolis: Fortress, 1995.

———. *Just a Sister Away: A Womanist Vision of Women's Relationships in the Bible*. San Diego: LuraMedia, 1988.

———. "Reading Her Way through the Struggle: African American Women and the Bible." Pages 57–77 in *Stony the Road We Trod: African American Biblical Interpretation*. Ed. Cain Hope Felder. Minneapolis: Fortress, 1991.

———. "Song of Songs." Pages 361–434 in *NIB*. Vol. 5. Nashville: Abingdon, 1997.

———. "The Hebrew Women Are Not Like the Egyptian Women: The Ideology of Race, Gender and Sexual Reproduction in Exodus 1." *Semeia* 59 (1992): 25–34.

Weever, Jacqueline de. *Sheba's Daughters: Whitening and Demonizing the Saracen Woman in Medieval French Literature*. New York: Garland, 1998.

White, Hayden. *Tropics of Discourse: Essays in Cultural Criticism*. Baltimore: Johns Hopkins University Press, 1978.

White, John C. "The Interaction of Language and World in the 'Shepherd of Hermas'." Ph.D. diss., Temple University, 1973.

Wicker, Kathleen O. "Ethiopian Moses (Collected Sources)." Pages 329–48 in *Ascetic Behavior in Greco-Roman Antiquity: A Sourcebook*. Ed. Vincent L. Wimbush. Minneapolis: Fortress, 1990.

Wilken, Robert L. *John Chrysostom and the Jews: Rhetoric and Reality in the Late 4th Century*. Berkeley: University of California Press, 1983.

———. *The Christians as the Romans Saw Them*. New Haven: Yale University Press, 1984.

Williams, Gareth D. *Banished Voices: Readings in Ovid's Exile Poetry*. Cambridge: Cambridge University Press, 1994.

Wilson, John A. *The Culture of Ancient Egypt*. Chicago: University of Chicago Press, 1951.

Wimbush, Vincent L. "Ascetic Behavior and Color-ful Language: Stories about Ethiopian Moses." *Semeia* 58 (1992): 81–92.

———. "Contemptus Mundi: The Social Power of an Ancient Rhetorics and World-view." *USQR* 47 (1993): 1–13.

———. "Introduction: Reading Darkness, Reading Scriptures." Pages 1–43 in *African*

Americans and the Bible: Sacred Texts and Social Textures. Ed. Vincent L. Wimbush. New York: Continuum, 2000.

———. "'. . . Not of This World . . .': Early Christianities as Rhetorical and Social Formation." Pages 23–36 in *Reimagining Christian Origins: A Colloquium Honoring Burton L. Mack.* Ed. Elizabeth A. Castelli and Hal Taussig. Valley Forge, Pa.: Trinity Press International, 1996.

———. "The Ecclesiastical Context of the New Testament." Pages 43–55 in *NIB.* Vol. 8. Nashville: Abingdon, 1994.

———, ed. *Ascetic Behavior in Greco-Roman Antiquity: A Sourcebook.* Minneapolis: Fortress, 1990.

Windisch, Hans. "βάρβαρος." *TDNT* 1: 546–53.

Winter, Bruce W., and Andrew D. Clarke, eds. *The Book of Acts in its Ancient Literary Setting.* Grand Rapids: Eerdmans, 1993.

Wolfram, Herwig. *The Roman Empire and Its Germanic Peoples.* Trans. Thomas Dunlap. Berkeley: University of California Press, 1997.

Wordelman, Amy L. "The Gods Have Come Down: Images of Historical Lycaonia and the Literary Construction of Acts 14." Ph.D. diss., Princeton University, 1994.

Yinger, J.M. "Ethnicity." *Annual Review of Sociology* 11 (1985): 151–80.

Young, Iris Marion. *Justice and the Politics of Difference.* Princeton: Princeton University Press, 1990.

Zayed, A.H. "Egypt's Relations with the Rest of Africa." Pages 136–52 in *Ancient Civilizations of Africa* 2. Ed. G. Mokhtar. Berkeley: University of California Press, 1981.

INDEX OF BIBLICAL AND OTHER ANCIENT SOURCES

SUBJECT INDEX

Leclant, Jean 144 n.7
Lefkowitz, Mary R. 133 n.27,
134 n.29
Lefkowitz, Mary R. and Rogers, Guy
Maclean 133 n.27
Lentz, John Clayton 151 n.140
Lesky, Albin 145 n.20
Letter to Diognetus 152 n.17
leukos, see whiteness
Levine, Amy-Jill 141–2 n.51
Lewis, Naphtali 162 n.44
light and darkness, symbolism of 23,
50, 62–3, 116, 123
Lightfoot, J.B. and Harmer, J.R.
156 n.107
Lincoln, Bruce 29
List, Johann 163–4 n.70
Locher, Josef 163 n.63
Long, Charles H. 127, 141 n.48,
174 nn.13–15
Long, Jacqueline 131 n.7, 159 n.3,
171 n.67
Long, Timothy 132 n.14
Lonis, Raoul 143–4 n.1

McCasland, S. Vernon 130 n.2,
153 n.37
McCray, Walter M. 135–6 n.43
McGowan, Andrew 141 n.35
Mack, Burton 138–9 n.3, 138 n.68,
149 n.93
Malherbe, Abraham J. 153 n.40
Manichaeism, and blackness 46, 105
Mann, Michael 125–6, 174 n.8
Marcionites 105
Marshall, I. Howard 170 n.42
Martin, Clarice J.:
"A Chamberlain's Journey" 109,
110, 135 n.42, 169 nn.27, 35,
170 nn.41, 43–4
"The Function of Acts 8:26–40"
110, 135 n.42, 169 n.29
"Womanist Biblical Interpretation"
143 nn.69–74
and womanist interpretation 25–7,
127–8
"Womanist Interpretations of the
New Testament" 138 n.66,

141–2 n.51, 143 nn.66–8,
174 nn.15–16
Mas'udi, Abu 'l-Hasan 148 n.78
Mayerson, Philip 134–5 n.35, 159 n.1,
163 n.65, 165 nn.99–100,
173 nn.112,116
and Ethiopian Moses 115–16,
173 n.110
Meeks, Wayne A. 154 n.53
Melania the Younger 6, 46, 104,
106–8
melas, see Black One, the; Blacks/
blackness
Meyer, Robert 164 nn.77–8, 167 n.149
Miles, Margaret R. 150 n.113
misogyny, in monastic literature 94–5
Modrzejewski, Joseph Mélèze 155 n.68,
170 n.53
Momigliano, Aernaldo 130–1 n.3
monastic literature, Egyptian 10, 11
and aesthetic values 50, 95–6, 98,
125, 128
and Alexandrian influence 79, 81
and color symbolism 85–9, 95
and definition of boundaries 25, 95,
99–100, 104–21
Ethiopians and Blacks in 77–80,
85–8, 91–103, 123, 125
and hagiography 81–2, 85–93,
115–20
and personification of demons 45,
46, 77, 80, 87–8, 91–3, 101
and sexuality as threat 46–7, 77–80,
84, 85–93, 94–102, 125
and women 94–5
Ethiopian 6, 10, 24–5, 47, 78,
95–102, 128
monasticism:
and Arianism 86
in late Antique Egypt 80–2
and politico-economic situation
81–2, 93–4, 102–3
spread 80, 160 n.18
types 80–1
Monophysitism 108
Montet, Pierre 133 n.27
morality:
and color symbolism 35, 36–7